More praise for *Wal-Smart*

"Wal-Mart is the case study but *Wal-Smart* is the answer key!"

—Chris Fisher, partner, Ducker Worldwide

"It is a rare chef who will pass along his favorite recipe complete— with all ingredients and preparation instructions. Bill Marquard is such a chef. His book *Wal-Smart* is a complete and useful recipe for success."

—Leo J. Shapiro Ph.D., founder, Leo J. Shapiro & Associates

"Creating an environment for optimum performance is not an option in today's global business climate. *Wal-Smart* shows us the way. An insightful, MUST read!"

—Spencer A. Tillman, author, *Scoring in the Red Zone*, CBS Sports analyst and businessman

"The times keep changin' and the giants keep growin'. Bill tells us like it is if we intend to grow and prosper in today's megacompetitive environment. Read it or weep!"

—Norm Miller, chairman, Interstate Batteries

"*Wal-Smart* is *the* business strategy book for the 21st century. It is essential reading for any leader facing the daunting challenges of this global economy. Marquard brilliantly distills the essence of what makes Wal-Mart so successful, and then prescribes twelve critical strategic choices that will make leaders in any organization and in any industry wildly successful."

—Mark Hansen, former president and chief executive officer, SAM'S CLUB

"Compelling insights powerfully expressed: Marquard's clear distillation of the Wal-Mart magic—drawn from his work with both the largest company in the history of the planet and with many of its competitors and victims—offers the best guide yet for any business facing the daunting challenge of a dominant competitor."

—Hank Meijer, cochairman, Meijer, Inc.

"This book is *not* just about how to compete as a retailer, but how to win in any competitive business environment. Many executives seek to lead 'Strong-Process Organizations' like Wal-Mart. As an insider, Bill Marquard does an excellent job revealing strategies to make this a reality."

—Corey A. Griffin, chief executive officer,
The Boston Company Asset Management, LLC

"*Wal-Smart* reminds me why I have hired and worked with Bill over many years. He and his book are focused on the right business DNA."

—James B. Adamson, former chairman and
chief executive officer, Kmart

"Wal-Mart certainly is one of the outstanding corporate success stories, sneaking up on the world scene as one of the most influential and dominating global players. Marquard helped lead Wal-Mart in its first strategic planning in the 1990s and helps us to understand how this all happened. It seems it was not by luck but by diligent planning and strategic positioning. A key insight is to 'Find the AND': doing two different things that other companies think of as alternatives. The book is full of deep insights from Wal-Mart that will help any company rethink how it can approach and dominate its market."

—Jeffrey K. Liker, Ph.D., author, The Toyota Way

WAL ☀ SMART

Be Wal-Smart!

Bill Marquard

WAL✷SMART

What It Really Takes to Profit in a Wal-Mart World

William H. Marquard

with

Bill Birchard

McGraw-Hill

New York   Chicago   San Francisco   Lisbon   London   Madrid
Mexico City   Milan   New Delhi   San Juan   Seoul
Singapore   Sydney   Toronto

The McGraw·Hill Companies

1 2 3 4 5 6 7 8 9 0 DOC/DOC 0 9 8 7 6

ISBN-13: 978-0-07-147516-7
ISBN-10: 0-07-147516-8

Wal-Smart is in no way authorized by, endorsed by, a trademark of, or affiliated
with Wal-Mart Stores, Inc., or its subsidiaries or its affiliates. All references to
Wal-Mart and other trademarked properties are used in accordance with the
Fair Use Doctrine and are not meant to imply that this book is a Wal-Mart
product for advertising or other commercial purposes.

McGraw-Hill books are available at special quantity discounts to use as
premiums and sales promotions, or for use in corporate training programs. For
more information, please write to the Director of Special Sales, Professional
Publishing, McGraw-Hill, Two Penn Plaza, New York, NY 10121-2298.
Or contact your local bookstore.

Library of Congress Cataloging-in-Publication Data

Marquard, William.
   Wal-smart / by William Marquard.
     p.cm.
   Includes bibliographical references and index.
   ISBN 0-07-147516-8 (alk. paper)
   1. Wal-Mart (Firm)–Management. 2. Discount houses (Retail trade)–
United States–Management. I. Title.

   HF5429.215.U6 M37 2007
   658.8'79–dc22   2006022753

To my wonderful wife, Leslie,
my life partner and best friend
and
to my sons, Christopher and Patrick,
whom I am more proud of than you will ever know.
I love you always and always,
More and more,
Forever and ever,
No matter what ...
And God loves you even more!

Contents

CONTENTS

When you have to make a choice and don't make it, that is in itself a choice.

—William James

To see what is right and not do it is want of courage.

—Confucius

I know all the things you do, that you are neither hot nor cold. I wish you were one or the other! ... you are like lukewarm water.

—Revelation 3:15–16a

Introduction
Choose or Lose

For Fred Meijer, the day of reckoning came in August 2003. He could no longer avoid making a choice. Wal-Mart stores had wandered into his life, first like a curious visitor and then like a vengeful rival. This Midwestern businessman could no longer ignore the resulting upheaval. With his work and life threatened, he had to ask himself, "How do I win in a world dominated by Wal-Mart?"

Meijer, who founded and built a chain of over 170 supercenters that bear his name, sought answers as he gathered 70 of his top executives in Grand Rapids, Michigan. He was hosting a three-day strategy session that I helped to choreograph as part of a strategy consulting team. Meijer reminded the executives that Wal-Mart had just opened its fourteenth supercenter in Meijer's home state. Several Meijer stores—combination grocery and discount superstores—had slipped from money makers to money losers under pressure from the goliath retailer. There was reason to believe that by 2008, Meijer would confront Wal-Mart head to head in most of its upper Midwest locations.

Meijer, the company's chairman emeritus, recounted an old story to set the tone for this critical meeting. "Two friends were being

1

chased through the forest by a bear," he said. "The first suddenly skidded to a stop. His chest heaved for air as he sat on a rock and frantically laced on some running shoes. In disbelief, the second friend gasped, 'You're crazy. You'll never be able to outrun that bear.' The first friend replied, 'I don't have to outrun the bear. I only have to outrun you!'"

The story drew cautious chuckles from Meijer executives, but everyone knew how serious the boss was. The question that hung in the air was simple: How was the Meijer chain going to survive and thrive in the shadow of the bear that is Wal-Mart? As the company's leader, Meijer had already pondered the options himself, and he understood one thing clearly: If the company didn't make some key choices—and quickly—it was going to get eaten for lunch.

Meijer wondered: Should the company sharpen its skills and become a direct competitor with Wal-Mart? Should it retreat and join the roster of companies vanquished by Wal-Mart? Should it reduce its costs radically while maintaining a unique standing in the eyes of its customers?

How Fred Meijer responded to this competitive threat illustrates the primary message of *Wal-Smart:* We all must make smart choices—intentionally and explicitly—to profit in a global marketplace that is dominated not only by Wal-Mart but also by many giants of industry.

The message in short is: *Choose or lose.*

Choosing is an imperative for every one of us, regardless of whether Wal-Mart affects us directly or not. Today, Wal-Mart is the prime example of the corporate goliath. As a colossus of unprecedented scale, it represents the awesome power of industry to change our lives and change our relationships with all those around us. This is why leaders of all organizations—public and private, manufacturing and service, local and international, large and small—must respond to the challenges posed by Wal-Mart and other dominant players. *Wal-Smart* equips leaders, managers, and anyone in the business community with the essential strategies that really work to survive and thrive in this brave, new Wal-Mart world.

The first half of *Wal-Smart* helps us to understand how we ended up in a Wal-Mart world by exploring the elements of Wal-Mart's success that few people see. Outside observers often cite Wal-Mart's visible competitive advantages, such as its efficient logistics system, low cost structure, and everyday-low-price perception, as the reasons for its success. But it is what's behind the scenes that really makes the difference in creating and sustaining these visible advantages.

Wal-Smart reveals that Wal-Mart's economic engine, or "productivity loop," underpins its operational genius. Several subtle but powerful management disciplines sustain its strong-process architecture. Critical elements of its hidden management "DNA" ultimately generate its visible competitive advantages.

The second half of *Wal-Smart* answers our most gut-wrenching question as business leaders: Now that we're enmeshed in the Wal-Mart world, what are we going to do about it? Part II prescribes the compelling strategies to make smart choices in every aspect of our business: as competitors, suppliers, employers, and community members. Each of the four chapters describes stories of triumph—and stories of defeat—as it distills the critical "choose or lose" strategic choices we all must make to either triumph in the shadow of industry giants ... or become the giant ourselves.

WHY THIS BOOK?

Wal-Smart is not a book about Wal-Mart. It is a book about what it really takes to profit in a Wal-Mart world: how to examine our options, how to choose the right ones, and how to win a second chance to succeed. Of course, the Wal-Mart world has changed the traditional rules of the economic game. But there is significant potential for all of us to raise our quality of economic life while Wal-Mart continues to flex its economic muscle.

There are generally four types of books on Wal-Mart. There is the economic analysis: "Wal-Mart is big. It poses a problem." There is the insider account: "Here's what Wal-Mart did. Copy it exactly, and you'll succeed." There is the self-help book: "Follow this checklist of ideas, and you can hold on against Wal-Mart." And there is the activist treatise: "Wal-Mart is the evil empire. Here is how to defeat it at all costs."

This book is different. Unlike previous authors on the subject, I have a unique perspective on Wal-Mart. As a consulting partner at Ernst & Young, I designed Wal-Mart's first-ever strategic planning process and ran it for three and a half years in the late 1990s. In the years since, I have been competing against that strategy, both as a Fortune 200 corporate executive and as a strategy consultant. As an outsider with the rare chance to get inside the head of the bear, I understand what makes Wal-Mart what it is. My firsthand experiences—both triumphs and scars—enable me to prescribe winning strategies for business leaders who are required to wear multiple hats, acting as competitors, suppliers, employers, and community members, in the world created by Wal-Mart and other industry giants.

HOW ARE YOU AFFECTED BY THE GIANT?

Futurists used to describe chaos theory as the effect that a butterfly flapping its wings in Brazil would have on U.S. weather patterns. When a decision made by Wal-Mart executives in Arkansas to grow organic cotton in a Turkish field affects the economy of a small town in Mexico, the future is already here. Like it or not, we are living in a Wal-Mart world.

Whether it's Wal-Mart or any other industry giant, dominant players force changes in our lives. Those changes demand a string of unfamiliar, anxiety-provoking decisions. And in the current climate, we can be sure that that string of decisions will present circumstances where black-and-white principles from the past don't apply. Wal-Mart and, by extension, its counterparts in other industries have grown so big and powerful that they force us to constantly redefine our strategies as business leaders.

Supercenters such as Meijer have not been the only ones on the receiving end of Wal-Mart's power. Other retailers shaken by Wal-Mart include convenience stores, grocers, tire centers, toy stores, bookstores, hair salons, and more. Wal-Mart also rattles the lives and relationships of suppliers, manufacturers, employees, communities, and even countries. Consider that in 2002, Wal-Mart bought 14 percent of the $1.9 billion in clothing shipped to the United States from Bangladesh. It even hosts high-level envoys from Bangladesh, who travel to Arkansas to build relationships with the retailer. Wal-Mart alone accounts for 10 percent of the U.S. trade deficit with China.

Many groups have felt the impact of Wal-Mart's competitive mission:

- *Convenience stores.* Once feeding on the heavy traffic flowing to the giant retailer, they have felt the sting of the more than 1,500 Wal-Mart stores that have installed gas pumps since 1996. Convenience stores now suffer from the thinnest margins on gas in decades.
- *Grocers.* Since 1988, when Wal-Mart entered the grocery business by opening its first supercenter, 13,500 U.S. supermarkets have closed. Research suggests that Wal-Mart alone has been a major catalyst in the closing or bankruptcy of 27 supermarket chains.
- *Financial services.* Although Wal-Mart's banking application to the FDIC claimed that it only intended to process its own credit- and debit-card payments, banks still suspect that it covets

their turf. Surveys show that most bank customers have little desire to put all their money in one institution, giving Wal-Mart an enticing opportunity to capture its shoppers' assets.

- *Wholesalers.* Perhaps the hardest hit among the constituencies affected by Wal-Mart have been the middlemen: product wholesalers. Fifty percent of Wal-Mart's $18 billion of annual imports from China are already sourced directly through the company's global procurement function. In the United States and across the world, wholesalers have consolidated or gone out of business.
- *Manufacturers.* Wal-Mart has forced manufacturers to negotiate deals based on net cost alone. Whereas many manufacturers cut deals with such industry enticements as upfront fees to display products, promotional allowances, and offers of "freebees" such as Superbowl tickets, Wal-Mart cuts deals based only on the bottom dollar. Wal-Mart even specifies operating and shipping practices that some manufacturers must follow.
- *Employees.* Wal-Mart's concentration of low-paying, entry-level retail jobs has shifted the wage structure in many markets. It has in the meantime weakened the power of unions and forced factory jobs overseas. While Wal-Mart creates more than 100,000 new jobs every year, it often forces competitors to slash just about as many.
- *Unions.* Like few other companies, Wal-Mart has compromised the clout of unions. When workers in Jonquière, Quebec, voted to unionize, Wal-Mart shut the store down. Union grocery-worker wages are often at least 30 percent more than nonunion wages, making Wal-Mart the single greatest threat to grocery-worker wage scales.
- *Communities.* Wal-Mart's expansion plans have fueled age-old debates about preserving local character and supporting local businesses in the face of large-scale development. More than

220 Wal-Mart sites have been blocked by local communities, from Inglewood, California, to Greenfield, Massachusetts.

Of course, Wal-Mart is not alone among big companies in throwing its weight around. There are others who dominate our lives—FedEx, Cisco Systems, Microsoft, Disney, and The Coca-Cola Company, to name a few. And there are emerging stars that will dominate our future, such as online music store iTunes and DVD-rental firm Netflix. (In a story of the tables turned, Wal-Mart actually signed a deal in 2005 to cede its DVD rental business to Netflix in return for Netflix sending customers to Wal-Mart to buy DVDs.)

Fred Meijer was one of the leaders affected by an industry giant, and he made smart choices to succeed. He didn't cower from choosing a new course in the face of industry domination. He and his top managers chose—and delivered—over $400 million in annual cost savings since that August 2003 meeting. Fred Meijer positioned his namesake company to outrun competitors, even if he couldn't outrun the bear.

WHAT DOES IT MEAN TO CHOOSE OR LOSE?

If a dominant player has hurt our business, and if our traditional ways of working and living don't fit, we have to change our approach. We have to make smart choices, or we will lose. And with a giant of industry breathing hard behind our backs—a giant driven by a take-no-prisoners competitive streak—we can't dither.

Choose or lose urges us to make explicit, intentional choices—and execute them consistently—to significantly increase our chances of success. Choose or lose does not imply that we have to change course. Sticking with the status quo is itself a choice, as long as we choose it explicitly and intentionally. The alternative—not making a choice—invites outsiders and outside circumstances to shape our future. The plaque my parents gave me early in my business career warns of this danger: "Stress is when you let your environment manage you."

I took those words to heart when I was executive vice president of Fleming Companies, the country's largest consumer goods wholesaler. We were the largest supplier to Kmart, shipping Heinz ketchup, Bounty towels, California lettuce, Purina Dog Chow, and a host of other products amounting to 17 percent of the discounter's annual revenue. Kmart was Fleming's biggest customer, with $3 billion of annual shipments, and I was the executive responsible for the Kmart relationship.

On Friday afternoon, January 18, 2002, I wrestled with the most critical choose-or-lose crisis of my career. I had learned that Kmart, which had enjoyed an investment-grade credit rating when we started supplying them a year earlier, was likely to file for bankruptcy the following week. Kmart normally paid Fleming's invoices every Friday by wire transfer. On this day, the cash was five hours late to our bank, and the wires closed in a half hour. My phone rang incessantly with calls from Kmart executives, Fleming's chairman, bankers, Fleming's treasurer, Kmart's bankruptcy lender, and Fleming warehouses. The choice before me was colossal: Do I cut off shipments to our biggest customer, the sixth largest retailer in America?

If I chose to halt shipments, Kmart's shelves would go barren over the weekend, precipitating a bankruptcy for which Fleming inevitably would be blamed. If I let the trucks go, Fleming would ship $25 million of product for which we might never get paid. If I made *no* choice and ignored the situation entirely, Fleming most certainly would have lost.

Ultimately, I did choose. I sent word to all Fleming warehouses to halt shipments and turn back the trucks in transit. Choosing swiftly and decisively paid big dividends. Kmart did file for bankruptcy, and Fleming saved the $25 million of product. By stopping shipments, we were able to negotiate a $75 million payment from Kmart via the bankruptcy court in return for agreeing to resume shipments. If I hadn't recognized that I had to choose quickly, Fleming was guaranteed to lose.

President John F. Kennedy summed it up well: "There are costs and risks to a program of action. But they are far less than the long-range risks and costs of comfortable inaction."

To be sure, the choose-or-lose principle has limits. We can and sometimes will choose and still lose. Recall a couple of the more muddleheaded comments in business history. Famed actor Charlie Chaplin once dismissed the burgeoning film industry: "Movies are a fad. Audiences really want to see live actors on a stage." A Decca Recording executive turned down the Beatles in 1962 with the comment, "We don't like their sound, and guitar music is on the way out."

Just because we have made choices doesn't mean that we will absolutely win. But doing so dramatically increases the chances of our success.

Choose or lose is a pretty easy principle to understand, but executing it is not so easy. The first step in choosing is deciding *what not to do*. The second step is making explicit, well-reasoned decisions about *what to do*. To ensure the success of our decisions, the last step is to *choose with intentionality*.

CHOOSING WHAT NOT TO DO

Strategy is the elimination of options. That's right, the first step in making a choice is choosing *what not to do*. The failure of many corporate strategies can be traced to having too many priorities and therefore too broad a focus. Organizations with strategies of this type tend to wander aimlessly, offering something for everyone, but standing for nothing to anyone.

Soon after Chuck Conaway took over as chairman and CEO of Kmart in 2000, he began promoting over 60 different initiatives to improve Kmart's operations. Banners proclaimed Conaway's "Playing to Win" effort in the hallways at Kmart's headquarters. The initiatives ranged from inventory-reduction programs to new logistics configurations to updated warehouse management systems. Kmart's corporate staff was constantly confused by the voluminous and ever-shifting priorities, which contributed to Kmart's bankruptcy in 2002.

By contrast, my sole objective in the first year of Wal-Mart's strategic planning process was to help management decide the five most important things each Wal-Mart business unit needed to get right that year. For Wal-Mart's discount stores, improving in-stock conditions was one of the five priorities. At SAM'S CLUB, determining the optimal mix of customers, business versus consumer, was paramount.

One of Wal-Mart's senior leaders reduced the strategies to five simple sound bites to communicate the priorities to all Wal-Mart discount stores: Stock it. Price it right. Show the value. Take the money. Teach them.

As I led the planning process over the next three years, Wal-Mart executives said "no" to one opportunity after another. Company leaders came to strategic planning sessions with hundreds of great ideas. Yet they disciplined themselves to focus on the five most important ones, and they agreed to devote the necessary resources and people to execute those strategies. By saying "no" and focusing on the "Top Five," they drove up Wal-Mart's stock price by over 600 percent during the time I worked with them.

How do we as business leaders know that we have effectively eliminated options? We stress-test our strategies with rigorous cross-examination. If we can't say "no" to many enticing opportunities, our strategies may not be narrow enough to be useful.

CHOOSING WHAT TO DO

The second imperative of choosing is selecting good alternatives, that is, choosing *what to do*. How do we generate a few good choices, and how do we select the right one?

As the planning process evolved in subsequent years at Wal-Mart, we gathered more facts and research to give us the information we needed to make more rigorous, explicit choices. We made a choice to compete with "category killers" such as Toys "R" Us by stocking the 20 percent of the toys that sold 80 percent of the volume. The result? Wal-Mart's toy industry market share in the United States exceeded the share of Toys "R" Us within two years. We also made the choice to sharpen the grocery strategy, making explicit, specific choices on branding, location, operations, and micromerchandising. The result? Wal-Mart's market share in groceries vaulted from third in 1998 to first by 2000.

CHOOSING WITH INTENTIONALITY

The third imperative of choosing is to *choose with intentionality*. Merely selecting one from an array of options will not ensure results; we must choose in a way that makes our choices happen.

Intentionality is the gut-level desire that enables all of us to overcome the inevitable roadblocks and disappointments that accompany any change process. Intentionality is the commitment to carry on despite the short-term cost. Without it, nothing much changes.

Managers may make a choice to go in a new direction, but their people often revert to old ways. Behavior change is difficult. It is a commonly held belief that people have to repeat a behavior up to 30 times for it to become a habit. Choosing a new direction in an organization requires change at an organizational level. What makes change harder is that the organization is composed of hundreds—often thousands—of employees whose individual behaviors need to change repeatedly for the corporate change to take effect.

One of the pleasures of leading strategic planning for Wal-Mart was that once the organization chose a direction, people would walk through walls to reach the goal because we had built intentionality into the choices. Building intentionality begins with involving the people who must execute the new direction. It includes addressing the fears of those affected. It requires setting honest expectations and fairly assessing the difficulty of roadblocks. And it demands unyielding accountability.

WHAT ABOUT EXECUTION?

Ultimately, execution is what delivers results. Missing any of the three steps in making smart choices can lead to a disaster in execution:

- When leaders fail to choose *what not to do,* the organization loses *resources.* The excessive choices dilute the pool of people and money needed to attack the highest-value strategies. Employees in these organizations often complain of having too few resources to "accomplish everything on my plate." As we all know, the organization cannot sustainably deliver everything for everyone.
- When leaders fail to explicitly choose *what to do,* the organization loses *focus.* Without clearly defined priority initiatives, managers devote time and effort to their pet projects. Employees often refer to these constantly shifting priorities as the "flavor of the month."
- When leaders fail to choose with *intentionality,* the organization loses *energy.* The emotional commitment that is so essential to overcome the inevitable roadblocks in any change effort quickly dissipates. Change then stagnates. Entrenched employees often wait out the frequent but ineffectual change efforts by adopting a "this, too, shall pass" philosophy.

When all is said and done, making smart choices in a world of dominant players demands all three steps—deciding what not to do, deciding what to do, and deciding to do it with intentionality.

ROAD-TESTED CHOICES

I have been applying the choose-or-lose approach to strategy for most of my career as a consultant and executive. In 1996, I began working on strategy at Wal-Mart with John Menzer (who was then Wal-Mart's CFO). Until then, Sam Walton had been Wal-Mart's strategy. Wal-Mart's sophistication evolved into annual strategic planning for its discount store, supercenter, specialty, and SAM'S CLUB units. I also led strategy development for specific areas such as tires, food, and merchandising processes.

In 1999, I became executive vice president of new business development and chief knowledge officer for Fleming, a $16 billion retailer and wholesaler. At its height, Fleming supplied consumable products (e.g., meat, produce, deli products, groceries, and health/beauty aids) to over 50,000 customer locations. Its customers included independent grocery stores, convenience-store chains, grocery chains such as Albertsons, and supercenters such as Target. Fleming even supplied Wal-Mart stores in Hawaii, where the retailer did not have its own food distribution center. I witnessed firsthand retailers who were thriving—and failing—in the wake of Wal-Mart.

At Fleming, I also started a new concept of limited-assortment stores called yes!Less which featured private-label food and general merchandise. The yes!Less chain was designed to compete against dollar-store companies such as Dollar General, Family Dollar, Aldi, and Save-A-Lot, a market niche in which Wal-Mart had decided not to open stores. It was intended to be a safe haven for Fleming's independent grocery customers, who could migrate to a yes!Less franchise when the grocery competition from Wal-Mart became too intense.

In early 2001, Kmart became Fleming's biggest customer. Fleming and Kmart formed a supply alliance whereby Fleming served Kmart's 2,200 stores, so I had the chance to witness (from the inside) Kmart's failed attempt to compete head to head with Wal-Mart, which I cover more in Chapter 6. I left Fleming six months before Kmart's bankruptcy dragged Fleming into its own Chapter 11 bankruptcy filing. I therefore have the benefit of a perspective gained both on the field and in the front row of the stands for two companies who lost to the dominant retailer of our time.

Since then, I have advised companies such as Meijer on how to compete effectively against the bear by reducing their cost structure, improving product flow, and clarifying their brand position. In my current role, I serve as a strategist and thinking partner for CEOs in a variety of industries. As a thinking partner, I help senior executives examine and work through their most difficult strategic and operational problems. Since I have worked with over 100 companies in over 25 industries during my career—with clients ranging from Walt Disney World, to McDonald's, to the Brick Industry Association, to the Department of Homeland Security—I have found that the best answers to strategic problems often come from outside an executive's industry.

The lessons in *Wal-Smart* thus come from my broad experience across company and industry borders. Organizations that are directly involved with Wal-Mart or far removed can benefit from the same approach to choosing strategy outlined in the pages ahead. Meijer did, and now the chain of supercenters operates with hundreds of millions of dollars of savings while serving its customers better than ever. If you work in an industry with a dominant player or you want to become the dominant player yourself, being "Wal-Smart" is critical to your success.

PART I

HOW DID WE END UP IN THE WAL-MART WORLD?

Chapter 1

How the Super-Retailer Defines Our World

New Economy, New Challenges

In 2004, Michael Marx, director of a coalition of 54 environmental and social advocacy groups, gathered his leaders to plot their next move. Marx's Portland, Oregon–based Business Ethics Network, counting Friends of the Earth, Oxfam, and Greenpeace among its members, had supported many successful single-issue corporate campaigns. It had fought to stop overfishing, sweatshop labor, genetically engineered foods, and other perceived ills of big companies.

Now the group was about to instigate a sea change. It wanted to move away from narrow special-interest initiatives and attack a single, powerful corporation whose work cut across the spectrum of issues activists decry. The group wanted to go after a big fish, a very big fish. "How about a campaign against Wal-Mart?" asked Marx, kicking off the discussion.

"Think about it," he said. "In many cases, it is the biggest or one of the biggest buyers and sellers of food, fish, clothes, diamonds, gold, cosmetics, prescription drugs, and chemicals." In Marx's mind, Wal-Mart could be turned into a lightning rod for outrage over labor rights, human rights, women's issues, urban sprawl, energy consumption, small-town decline, you name it.

"A small movement by Wal-Mart would have huge ripple effects," remarked another activist at the meeting.

In a world still raw from globalization protests in cities from Seattle to Genoa, Marx assembled a coalition of labor unions, human rights groups, environmental groups, socially responsible investors, and others to prod the premier symbol of global capitalism to rethink its practices. After meetings with Wal-Mart CEO Lee Scott, the threat of a unified campaign effort by these organizations helped produce several concessions. Among the first were commitments to use less packaging and biodegradable materials, to decrease energy consumption significantly in stores and in the truck fleet, and to require environmental certification for products ranging from jewelry to seafood.

Marx's work to put together the Wal-Mart campaign marked a milestone for business. Business was no longer facing a ragtag collection of vocal social, environmental, and community advocates working in isolation. It was facing a new kind of coalition. Thanks to the catalyzing effect of Wal-Mart, business was witnessing the birth of a new progressive social movement. It is a force Wal-Mart has begun to reckon with and a force that all business now faces.

But that's getting ahead of the story. The response of Marx and his compatriots reflected something else as well: the pervasiveness of the single most dominant company in the world. Wal-Mart has spread its operations so broadly that even activists recognize that when the retailer tinkers with the fine points of its operations, it can shake the economy as a whole. The activists recognize that just one company can reset the agenda for how business operates.

We have all become actors in a drama staged by Wal-Mart—whether intentionally, accidentally, or serendipitously. In the United States, nearly 1 of every 100 workers works at Wal-Mart. Almost 9 out of 10 Americans shop at Wal-Mart. Globally, Wal-Mart already runs stores in countries where 33.9 percent of the world's population lives—countries that generate 55.0 percent of the world's gross domestic product (GDP). In Mexico, Wal-Mart is the number one retailer. In December 2005 alone, it added 50,000 people to its work rolls when it bought 545 new stores in Japan and South America. In one way or another, people the world over are all players in the Wal-Mart economy.

The Wal-Mart economy?

Think about it. Wal-Mart's revenues of $312 billion exceed the GDP of all but 21 nations, including Argentina, Saudi Arabia, and Indonesia. Like Standard Oil in the 1900s, U.S. Steel in the 1920s, General Motors in the 1950s, and IBM in the 1980s, Wal-Mart is the dominant company of our era.

Even if Wal-Mart were to disappear tomorrow, it would leave such an imprint that the Wal-Mart economy would remain. The speed, the behaviors, the expectations, and the standards of excellence—all the success factors related to Wal-Mart—would persist to challenge business people in the same way as the goliath retailer does today. Wal-Mart has defined the global economy, what I call the "Wal-Mart world." Its reach goes well beyond its own supply chain, beyond its customer base, and beyond its geographic boundaries.

Why has Wal-Mart had the power to effect this transformation? What is it about the company that has enabled it to define the world in its own image? First of all, it is ubiquitous. Second, it has single-handedly pioneered new rules that annul the conventions of the old economy. Third, its "customer is us." And last, its momentum can't slow quickly. Wal-Mart not only dominates our era; it will shape the era to come. To make smart choices in this economy, we need to understand it from the inside out.

THE UBIQUITOUS CORPORATION

Wal-Mart's economic size and pervasiveness give it unparalleled power to shape our work and private lives. A few more numbers further demonstrate just how much. In one year alone, Wal-Mart sells more than $1,000 worth of merchandise for every man, woman, and child in the United States. It does more business than its next four competitors combined, Home Depot, Kroger, Target, and Sears, scooping up roughly 10 cents of every retail dollar spent in the United States.

Wal-Mart competes in four main formats, and together they blanket the landscape. Discount stores offer general merchandise and limited food. Supercenters offer a wide assortment of general merchandise and a full-line supermarket. SAM'S CLUB warehouse stores serve small businesses—restaurants, contractors, convenience stores, child-care centers, church groups, and small offices—as well as a vast consumer base. Neighborhood Markets offer a full-line supermarket and some general merchandise.

Fed by sales from each format, Wal-Mart's share of the entire global economy approaches 1 percent. Its share of the U.S. economy has grown to 2.5 percent. This is not the biggest ever, but it is fast closing in on the record. U.S. Steel had a 3.1 percent share of the U.S. economy in 1917, and GM's share was 2.4 percent in 1955. For comparison, Sears Roebuck's share in 1983 was 1.0 percent, and IBM's share in 1990 was 1.1 percent.

Wal-Mart has 3,900 stores in the United States, at least 4 in every state and 415 in the "Republic" of Texas. Counting units in Argentina, Brazil, Canada, China, Costa Rica, El Salvador, Guatemala, Honduras, Japan, Mexico, Nicaragua, Puerto Rico, and the United Kingdom (and excluding the over 100 stores in Germany and South Korea it sold in 2006), it has 6,600 stores. Each month the company spends well over $1 billion for land and buildings.

The number of people who depend on Wal-Mart is staggering. It buys from 61,000 suppliers in 70 countries, spending $240 billion a year. It serves 176 million shoppers globally each week. It employs 1.8 million "associates." It became the biggest employer in the world in 1999 (when it employed 1,140,000). It has more people in uniform than the U.S. Army.

Wal-Mart's influence extends directly to the 35 million people who work in the retail, manufacturing, and wholesaling businesses Wal-Mart affects. Six million more work in industries threatened by its expansion—the travel, financial, and insurance industries.

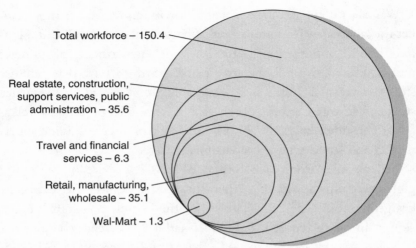

Total workforce – 150.4

Real estate, construction, support services, public administration – 35.6

Travel and financial services – 6.3

Retail, manufacturing, wholesale – 35.1

Wal-Mart – 1.3

Figure 1-1 Wal-Mart Sphere of Influence: U.S. Jobs by Industry, 2006 (millions)

Thirty-six million people work in industries that serve Wal-Mart such as real estate, construction, utilities, waste management, and health care. All told, Wal-Mart directly affects roughly half the U.S. workforce of 150 million and varying percentages elsewhere in the world (see Figure 1-1).

Wal-Mart runs stores in most counties in the United States and in thousands of communities worldwide. It even touches the lives of those millions of citizens who believe that they have nothing to do with Wal-Mart. It affects tax bills, rents, welfare spending, traffic patterns, and the environment. Indeed, the company's tentacles extend into almost everyone's life and into every corner of the global economy. By virtue of scale and scope alone, Wal-Mart has written a new playbook for this economy.

DEFYING CONVENTION

Wal-Mart's pervasiveness, however, is only one reason it has redefined the world around us. The second is that it has defied tradition, intuition, and convention to develop new laws of production, distribution, and merchandising. It has challenged norms and upset existing rules of thumb. It has pioneered new assumptions in business. Consider five of the most important.

1. You *Can* Squeeze Costs Out of a Low-Growth Commodity Business

Conventional wisdom used to dictate that any company selling commodity products in a market with low overall growth rates didn't have much room for cost cutting, much less growth. The major costs had been cut by industry leaders years ago. The only cost-cutting opportunities remaining were marginal.

But Wal-Mart has squeezed more than a little blood out of the retail cost turnip. A few numbers once again make this point. Wal-Mart's reported selling, general, and administrative expenses (SG&A) as a percentage of sales are bare bones: 18.2 percent, much lower than the 20 percent or more at competitors Sears (21.9 percent), Target (22.7 percent), and Home Depot (20.2 percent). Its total distribution costs run just 3 percent of sales, 25 percent lower than the 4 to 5.5 percent of sales at competitors.

2. Candy Bars and Barbie Dolls Have Lots in Common

When I became chief knowledge officer at Fleming, it seemed like we had more data than most competitors, but we had very little knowledge. Data are the residue from tracking every company transaction. Knowledge is the capability to summarize, analyze, and mine that data for strategic decisions. Data are the raw material; knowledge is the finished product.

Wal-Mart has raised data accumulation and knowledge generation to a science. Its data center tracks an unrivaled 680 million stock-keeping units (SKUs) weekly (SKUs are individual items; a 14-ounce plastic bottle and a 20-ounce easy squeeze bottle of Heinz ketchup are separate SKUs). Its information warehouse holds 570 terabytes of data, more than all the fixed pages on the Internet. The Federal Reserve even tracks the impact of tax policy on spending by consulting Wal-Mart sales data.

By mining those data, Wal-Mart is able to track a host of consumer buying patterns. One year it discovered that about 25 percent of the people pushing shopping carts containing a Barbie doll also bought one of three types of candy. Wal-Mart responded by building secondary displays of those three candy products in the toy department next to the Barbie dolls.

3. Posted Speed Limits Are Made for Breaking

Most industries abide by established "speed limits"—limits that innovative companies then have broken. Executives assumed that packages could not be delivered the next day—until FedEx CEO Frederick Smith proved them wrong. Banking could only be done during bankers' hours—until John Reed at Citicorp championed automatic teller machines (ATMs) and online banking. Airplanes couldn't be turned around at the gate in 20 minutes—until Herb Kelleher at Southwest Airlines demonstrated otherwise. Researching facts for books such as this took months—until Sergey Brin and Larry Page at Google unlocked a new online information universe.

Wal-Mart has been a key instigator and exemplar in this need for speed. It moves product through its pipeline with such astonishing swiftness that its inventory turnover exceeds nine turns per year, the equivalent of emptying its shelves completely every 40 days. It has shortened its product-introduction pipeline to such an extent that it aims to capture 100 percent of the first two weeks of sales of any new product and 70 percent of the first four weeks—that is, selling tons of new product before other retailers have any to sell at all. In a recent test with a new Gillette razor, Wal-Mart gained 11 extra days of sales using radio frequency identification (RFID) technology.

4. Vendors Are Allies, Not Enemies

The customer-supplier relationship used to be a zero-sum game. If the vendor won the extra dollar in a negotiation, the buyer lost a dollar. Starting in 1987, however, Wal-Mart led the way in building vendor partnerships, initiating the practice with Procter & Gamble. By working with suppliers, Wal-Mart continuously removes costs from its supply chain, from product manufacturing to shipping to in-store merchandising. Wal-Mart helped to define the win-win deal.

Suppliers today work with Wal-Mart to devise new products and, through connections to Wal-Mart's "Retail Link" system, manage replenishment. Selected suppliers even manage Wal-Mart's entire range of in-store product categories—such as hair care or mailing supplies or hardware. Using their product expertise, supplier "category advisors" choose and organize the product mix to make Wal-Mart's merchandising more successful.

Many suppliers work so closely with Wal-Mart that the line between vendor and customer appears almost indistinguishable. General Electric manages Wal-Mart's inventory of GE light bulbs inside Wal-Mart warehouses. This saves GE (and Wal-Mart) the cost of stocking duplicate inventory. Along with GE, over 1,200 suppliers now staff offices near Wal-Mart's headquarters in Bentonville. The traffic to and from this rural part of Arkansas runs so heavy that the Northwest Arkansas airport handles 1.2 million passengers annually.

5. A Falling Tide Lifts All Boats

Setting prices was once a cagey game to see what the market would bear. One player would watch another increase prices and observe who else would follow. If the prices stuck, they became the new standard. When one company raised productivity, it often pocketed the savings and didn't affect other companies. Some industries, such as airlines and oil, still act this way. Yet Wal-Mart continuously lowers costs and lowers prices, and other companies often have to follow the pricing tide as it drops—which lifts the purchasing power of consumers.

Consumers can attest to Wal-Mart's efficiency just by comparing prices. A study released in 2005 by Emek Basker of the University of Missouri tracked prices over 20 years, 1982 to 2002. Basker found that when Wal-Mart enters a market, it lowers average prices in that market from 1.5 percent to 3 percent in the short run to four times that much in the long run. In cities with Wal-Mart stores, she found that select drugstore items such as deodorant, feminine hygiene items, and detergent averaged 15 percent less than in cities that do not have a Wal-Mart.

People recently have called Wal-Mart many pejoratives: "Beast from Bentonville," "Evil Empire," "Godzilla-Mart." But the people using the pejoratives are not complaining about Wal-Mart prices. In fact, many activists are careful not to suggest that Wal-Mart change in a way that suddenly would hike the cost of shopping for some of the neediest people in society. Blue-chip economics consulting firm Global Insight calculated (in a study paid for by Wal-Mart) just how much Wal-Mart's continuous lowering of prices since 1985 has saved the consumer. The average American household saves $2,329 per year. Real disposable household income is 0.9 percent greater than it would be without Wal-Mart.

Economists widely note the "Wal-Mart effect," the now-common term for price declines and efficiency increases resulting from Wal-Mart's well-oiled operation (and now the name of the best-selling book by Charles Fishman). The McKinsey Global Institute concluded in 2002 that retail productivity growth in the United States at the end of the last century jumped from 2 percent (1987–1995) to 6.3 percent (1995–1999). *Half* of this increase in retail productivity growth could be traced, directly or indirectly, to Wal-Mart.

Year in and year out, as Wal-Mart continuously improves the way it runs, it spurs similar improvements in the retail sector as a whole—and then, in domino fashion, in a host of other sectors. Few managers don't look to Wal-Mart for secrets to managing more cost-effectively. The vice chairman of Target once remarked that his company was the "world's premier student of Wal-Mart." By virtue of the way Wal-Mart can rewrite the rules of business, it defines a new world of commerce.

THE CUSTOMER IS US

A third reason why Wal-Mart defines our world is that it simply has so many customers. Or to put it another way, it enjoys the support of tens of millions of people who vote with their wallets—and who vote often. In effect, the Wal-Mart economy has emerged mainly because "the customer is us."

The customer is the shopper who likes low prices; who likes a broad assortment with plenty of stock under one roof; who likes a choice of entry-, middle-, and high-quality-level products. The customer is our mother, our brother, our neighbor, ourselves—in fact, just about everybody at least some of the time.

I once asked a Wal-Mart marketing executive who Wal-Mart's target customer was. His answer: "Everyone in America shops at Wal-Mart." While this is a slight exaggeration, it's not far from the truth.

Although fewer people shop at Wal-Mart in many countries outside North America, surveys show that Wal-Mart attracts plenty of interest internationally. Analysts at market research firm Retail Forward found that in countries Wal-Mart has already entered, shoppers are itching to get into the store. Eighty-three percent of Brazilians and 80 percent of Chinese say that they would shop at Wal-Mart if one opened nearby. Even in many countries without any Wal-Marts at all, interest is often keen. Seventy-three percent of Malaysians and 55 percent of Russians say that they would shop at Wal-Mart if one opened nearby.

Studies even show that people who dislike Wal-Mart shop at the store. A study of Oklahoma City shoppers by Leo J. Shapiro & Associates partly explains Wal-Mart's incredible drawing power. The study divided people in the market into four Wal-Mart shopping groups: champions (29 percent of the population, generally younger people who like one-stop shopping), enthusiasts (27 percent, who consider Wal-Mart a "trusted advocate"), rejecters (29 percent, who consider Wal-Mart inconvenient), and conflicted (15 percent, who both love and hate the retailer). Even the rejecters, mainly from double-income households with no kids, spent $39 per month at Wal-Mart supercenters. The conflicted, mainly upscale families who look down on Wal-Mart's social impacts, spent a monthly average of $289 at Wal-Mart supercenters.

The key reason these last two groups still shopped at Wal-Mart is because there are so many stores in Oklahoma City (25 in 2006), including all four formats. But it's also because Wal-Mart delivers the two top things surveys show Wal-Mart customers consider "extremely important": competitive prices and in-stock products.

Elsewhere, where Wal-Mart stores populate less of the landscape than in Oklahoma City, Wal-Mart obviously pockets a smaller share of consumers' wallets. Still, shopping behavior mimics the Oklahoma City pattern. Ninety-three percent of households in the United States include someone who shops at Wal-Mart at least once a year. We know from anecdotal reports that even union workers, who rail at Wal-Mart's antiunion stance, still shop at the company's stores to make their paychecks go farther.

Wal-Mart executives admit that the majority of their customers are "opening price point" shoppers who are looking for the entry-level product, such as a store-brand cola or a bare-bones DVD player. The average Wal-Mart customer earns between $40,000 to $45,000, consistent with the $44,000 median United States household income. Modest-income customers tend to go first for the product at the lowest price, lest they have to sacrifice other purchases by having spent too much of their paycheck.

This explains why 86 percent of Americans with household incomes of less than $25,000 have shopped Wal-Mart or Wal-Mart supercenters in the last six months. It also explains why Wal-Mart notched a 10 percentage point gain in the number of shoppers earning less than $25,000 who say they shopped more at Wal-Mart or Wal-Mart supercenters in the previous year. It notched no gain at all among shoppers with household incomes over $100,000.

Still, high-income shoppers do file regularly through the aisles of the giant retailer. Seventy-three percent of families with household incomes over $100,000 do so. And Wal-Mart recently has dedicated itself to broadening its customer base. It is targeting higher-income shoppers and stocking higher-margin products in its clothing, home fashion, and electronics lines. It recently started buying advertising in *Vogue* magazine, a first for the budget-minded retailer.

Wal-Mart's move to go upscale could lead to even greater power to shape commerce of the future. Some detractors say that Wal-Mart "monopolizes" retail trade. It certainly dominates the trade, and it is the support of all of us—from all of our money-laden votes—that has given Wal-Mart a mandate to shape the world of business.

MORE POWERFUL THAN A LOCOMOTIVE

A fourth and final reason that Wal-Mart sets the agenda—and will continue to set the agenda—is that it has momentum. Like a freight train rushing forward, it has huge mass and velocity. It takes a long time to stop a moving train, even after the brakes are applied. As large as Wal-Mart's mass is today, Wal-Mart executives note that the company has only a 3 percent share of the global retail market. This leaves a juicy 97 percent from which to take a bite. The company's 10 percent share in the United States leaves an appetizing 90 percent open for dining.

So what is its velocity? Around the time Lee Scott took the helm of Wal-Mart in 1999, he remarked to me that if Wal-Mart maintained a 15 percent annual growth rate, it would be a $750 billion company by the time he retired. "What does that look like?" he wondered aloud.

The company has continued to grow apace, although its domestic sales growth has slowed. In 2005, Scott said that Wal-Mart could be three or four times bigger in the United States alone. Its U.S. real estate committee has already approved 1,500 stores for future growth, although the company announced in late 2006 it would pare its growth plans moderately. In just one month in 2006, it opened 51 supercenters and 18 SAM'S CLUBS.

And Wal-Mart's ambitions span the globe. Its international sales of $63 billion exceed the total sales of Target, its arch competitor. Analysts at Retail Forward count Spain, France, and Russia as likely new markets in the next five years. In 2006, it opened an office in

India to ready itself to expand in a country almost as populous as China. If it were to carve out the same market share in India as in the United States, it would ring up sales in just that country of roughly $25 billion.

Wal-Mart's annual growth rate of 10 to 15 percent is deceptive. When it had $10 billion in sales, its growth didn't mean much to the world economy—just $1.5 billion in GDP. But when it has $312 billion in sales, that means $47 billion in growth. Retail Forward projects that, by 2010, it will ring up more than $500 billion in sales. By 2015, at 15 percent growth, it could bring in a mind-bending $1 trillion, more than twice the budget of the U.S. Defense Department.

Revenue alone tells only part of the growth story. Wal-Mart has entered and probably will continue to enter new segments of the retail market. In the early 1990s, it was a novice upstart in the grocery sector. Today, it owns roughly 10 to 15 percent of the $775 billion market (depending on what you count as groceries). In the Dallas area, it owns over 28.5 percent, far exceeding second-place supermarket giant Kroger's 15.5 percent.

That Wal-Mart can grow so much every year in both local and national markets stems from its strategy to both grow globally and saturate locally. Sam Walton called it "spreading out, then filling in."

Wal-Mart's Oklahoma City expansion is a good example of the saturation strategy. In 1997, Wal-Mart had just three stores in Oklahoma City, two supercenters and one discount store. It then filled in not just geographically but also with its four formats. By 2002, it ran 10 supercenters, 6 discount stores, 7 neighborhood markets, and 4 SAM'S CLUBS. The supercenters are spaced five miles apart, the Neighborhood Markets two.

Oklahoma City is a microcosm of Wal-Mart's potential presence across America—and an example of how quickly it can "fill in." Even if Wal-Mart doesn't run many stores in your neighborhood, in just several years it can saturate the market. Translate Oklahoma

City to markets across the entire globe, and it's easy to see why Wal-Mart executives think that Wal-Mart can get so much bigger.

YES, EVEN GIANTS CAN FALL

You may be wondering about the rough patch Wal-Mart has hit in recent years. Who hasn't read about its travails in daily reports about wages, health care, sales growth, community resistance, and bankruptcies of venerable family businesses? This raises a few questions: Will Wal-Mart stumble or fall? If so, what would bring it down? And how would Wal-Mart's decline affect the challenges posed by the Wal-Mart economy?

Internally, Wal-Mart could get bogged down with its growing operations. Systems may not handle the growth. Layers of management could slow communication and execution. As Sam Walton wrote in his autobiography in 1992, "The folks who come after me are eventually going to have to face up to this question. Even by thinking small, can a $100 billion retailer really function as efficiently and productively as it should?"

Wal-Mart's employees meanwhile have turned the screws on the company. Along with demands for higher wages, Wal-Mart faces thousands of lawsuits. These are typical of those faced by many big companies. But the company also faces or has faced a number of troublesome class-action suits. These suits have alleged that Wal-Mart forced employees to work off the clock, failed to pay overtime, and discriminated against women when it comes to promotions, pay, training, and job assignments. The class-action suit by women was filed with 1.6 million plaintiffs. Such lawsuits not only could cost Wal-Mart plenty of money, but they also could demotivate its workers and alienate customers.

When it comes to other operational roadblocks, any number could crop up. Wal-Mart is already beset with challenges finding new store sites. In the future, its real estate specialists are sure to have increasing trouble finding big parcels of land in crowded markets, and urban parcels are especially expensive. Retail marketing maven Leo Shapiro notes that ultimately Wal-Mart will run into the fruit-fly growth problem. If you put fruit flies in a jar, they will grow at an exponential rate until they run out of food or space. Wal-Mart may run out of space.

As for external threats, the retail climate shifts constantly, and Wal-Mart faces many worthy competitors. Deep-discount retailers' prices are lower. Target's profitability is greater. Costco's inventory turnover is higher. Each will fight to gain an advantage as consumer markets evolve, whether from changing buying behaviors, tastes, affluence, or other factors. History shows that when new models of business emerge, established giants often don't recognize them—or can't change—until it's too late.

Such complacency often occurs because the giant moves gradually from a growth cycle into what Shapiro calls the "hubris cycle." Executives don't see their faults. They become embattled. They even become angry. "Those whom the gods would destroy they first make mad," says Shapiro. Resentment and the swagger from success blind executives to making the changes necessary to compete in the changing world around them.

Community activists also could put a drag on Wal-Mart's growth. They have fought the company with increasing vigor for over 10 years. Communities have blocked scores of Wal-Marts through zoning, ordinances, and permit denial. Typical of the maneuvers by local politicians are those taken in Turlock, California, where the city council passed an ordinance banning retailers larger than 100,000 square feet. Wal-Mart planned to build a 226,000-square-foot store, and it sued Turlock to overturn the restriction. A federal appeals court has since ruled that the city of Turlock may ban big-box stores such as Wal-Mart.

The activists arrayed against Wal-Mart have mobilized to attack the retailer on a range of social issues. Two high-profile organizations are Wal-Mart Watch and WakeUpWalMart.com. Many also have attracted foundation funding to support their cause, and the outpouring of press coverage has blackened Wal-Mart's reputation. Even *Advertising Age* opined, "Wal-Mart has a brain. It needs a heart."

The result is that Wal-Mart's reputation is under strain, although the public appears schizophrenic about how it feels. Surveys show that people love the company and people hate the company. A recent American Demographics Perception Study showed that Wal-Mart is both one of the most trusted and one of the least trusted companies in America. Surveys showed that 5.6 percent of people called it the most trustworthy, tied with General Electric and ahead of Microsoft. Meanwhile 7.3 percent called it the least trustworthy, better off than Enron, worse than Ford.

Will all these threats facing Wal-Mart knock the goliath off balance? Will Wal-Mart run out of space? Will it succumb to hubris? Competitors certainly hope so.

The answers to these questions for us as business leaders are irrelevant. Even if the Wal-Mart world isn't ruled by Wal-Mart, the economy it has shaped will prevail. Wal-Mart has embedded a host of new norms and standards into the conduct of business. The economy will plunge ahead in the same fashion whether led by Target, Home Depot, the €75 billion Carrefour chain of France, or a company in another industry entirely. The competition today is not just Wal-Mart; it is the economy Wal-Mart has defined.

NEW ECONOMY, NEW CHALLENGES

The upshot is that the Wal-Mart economy almost certainly will continue to play a preeminent role in shaping our economic future. Our roles as business leaders haven't changed: We still have to craft strategies as competitors, suppliers, employers, and community members. But the Wal-Mart world has defined new challenges we have to master in each of these roles like never before.

Challenges As Competitors

- *Price is the ticket to the dance.* Low prices no longer provide a competitive advantage—they are a given. Customers can switch their business to competitors almost effortlessly if the price isn't right—for everything from car insurance to package delivery services. Expect the focus on pricing to intensify.
- *Competitive advantages are now built on "when" not "what."* In building competitive advantages in the past, business people debated "what" to do to get a long-term leg up on competition. In the Wal-Mart world, today's competitive advantage is tomorrow's "me too" because competitors can adopt your uniqueness rapidly. *Sustainable* competitive advantage no longer derives from a set of static, long-term differentiators. It is instead a continuous series of new advantages that, taken together, enable you to stay 6 to 12 months ahead of the next guy. Therefore, how quickly you develop and deploy new advantages and how quickly you copy the competition—the "when"—make competitive advantage sustainable.
- *The battle is for trips, not loyalty.* Grocers, car dealers, and even defense contractors once nurtured "one and only" relationships. In the Wal-Mart world, the battle is fought not over loyalty but over every shopping trip, every purchase decision, every time a customer wants to buy. Consider that the average customer buys grocery items four times a week, and even loyal Wal-Mart supercenter customers visit the store just four times a month. Winners in the Wal-Mart world will succeed by capturing an "unfair share" of individual customer choices.

- *Customers are smarter than we admit.* Remember the theory of efficient markets? Famed economist Eugene Fama posited that you can't beat the stock market over time because prices reflect all relevant information. Markets for goods of all kinds have become just as efficient. With the help of sites such as Nextag, Bizrate, and B2B exchanges, customers use real-time pricing and product information to strike deals on everything from raw materials to floor-cleaning services.

  In the Wal-Mart economy, we face the challenge of doing business in a world of immediate and transparent information on quality, service, and especially pricing. Even shoppers for next-day delivery of caskets can cut prices by 50 percent with a few mouse clicks.

- *Industry boundaries provide no shelter.* Boundaries between industries once provided barriers to market entry. We could enjoy a safe haven from outside aggressors by hiding in the computer industry or the grocery industry. In the Wal-Mart world, companies are crashing tradition. Apple's iTunes propelled the computer industry onto the recording industry's turf. Cellphones are becoming personal digital assistants (PDAs), PDAs are becoming cellphones, and they are both becoming handheld gaming devices.

  Where will the blurring of traditional channels and markets end? It won't. Wal-Mart's ambition illustrates the point. During one executive committee meeting at Wal-Mart, executives were celebrating what was then a 7 percent share of the total U.S. retail market. Mark Hansen, the CEO of SAM'S CLUB, remarked that he was more concerned about the 93 percent customer rejection rate that the share implied.

In sum, as competitors in the Wal-Mart economy, we face a host of new challenges: Low prices are a given; competitive advantages have a waning half-life; the emerging battle is over "share of trips," not loyalty; customers often know more than we do, or at least more than we ever give them credit for; and we can't duck behind industry boundaries for safety.

Challenges As Suppliers

- *End-to-end supply costs rank first.* Forget price increases. Vendor profit today comes from rooting out inefficiencies in processes. In the early 1990s, Ford embarked on a 2/2/3 program, which required suppliers to cut product and/or related supply chain costs by 2 percent in the first year, 2 percent in the second, and 3 percent in the third. Ford's approach presaged practices championed by Wal-Mart, which presses suppliers to minimize total delivered costs. All suppliers face this challenge today.
- *No way but the global way.* In today's market, sellers and buyers often sit on opposite sides of the international dateline. Smart manufacturers are configuring their supply chains to minimize costs by maximizing supply opportunities around the world. Yesterday's management mantra was, "Think locally, act globally." Today, it's "Deliver locally, supply globally."
- *Make them need you more than you need them.* In the Wal-Mart world, the bargaining power of dominant players usually tips in favor of buyers. Our challenge as suppliers is to make dominant buyers need us more in order to pull the scales back toward us. Some suppliers focus on building brand value. In a market of millions of SKUs and store-label products, middling brands fade. Vendors have placed bets on the big brands, such as Crest and Pampers, yet retain entry-level-priced products that form the foundation of the price-driven market.
- *Data flow creates cash flow.* Suppliers who have not electronically linked to companies both upstream and downstream in the supply chain are way behind. The challenge is to enhance those links continuously. Wal-Mart connects suppliers to its point-of-sale

data, updated several times a day, which allows suppliers to adjust distribution, manufacturing, and marketing. Wal-Mart is now synchronizing product data such as packaging dimensions, color, and weight, working with 800 suppliers, 2,000 product categories, and 60,000 unique items.

Gone is the day when the supplier had the power in the market. With the balance of power on the customer's side, suppliers must respond by reducing total delivered costs, creating a flexible network for global supply, focusing on advantages such as strong brands to shift bargaining power back in their favor, and linking electronically to make better, faster, and more profitable decisions. As suppliers in the Wal-Mart economy, these are the challenges we have to overcome to gain competitive advantage.

Challenges As Employers

- *Global markets recalibrate wages.* Entry of Wal-Mart or other dominant employers amplifies pressures to either shrink domestic wages or shift labor-intensive jobs to lower-wage countries. Wage levels once sheltered from competition by trade barriers are either proving their value or, in the global marketplace, falling. Unions will continue to delay but not stem the trend. And don't think just unskilled jobs are in play. Consider that doctors now are performing remote surgery on patients continents away.
- *Entitlements clash with reality.* Across the globe, workers are striking to protect benefits to which they feel "entitled" yet which conflict with present economic reality. Grocery workers in California struck to preserve benefit packages valued at roughly $3 per hour more than those at Wal-Mart. British workers struck to protest raising the age at which workers earned full retirement benefits. French workers marched to denounce a new law that allowed

companies to terminate employees for substandard performance. The burden is falling on the shoulders of corporate executives to reset worker expectations and negotiate a new equilibrium.

Conservative columnist Pat Buchanan may be right when he observes: "Except for those who can stay in the hunt in the Global Economy, the peoples of all Western nations will have to give up dreams of the good life and compete with the hungry young of the Second and Third Worlds."

- *It's not your father's workforce anymore.* Remember GM's ad campaign, "It's not your father's Oldsmobile"? Well, Oldsmobile is gone—and so is our fathers' workforce. Pay, power, and prestige used to drive the upwardly mobile worker of yesterday, as did loyalty to employers. Today's workers are motivated by flexible work schedules, copious free time to invest in nonwork interests, a work environment that fits their values, and a sense of serving a higher calling. The biggest challenge may be to provide ever higher pay along with these motivational carrots to the heterogeneous workforce typical in companies today. One size doesn't fit all.
- *Brains have feet.* For years we have been warned of the effect on health care, financial services, and retirement communities as baby boomers cross the retirement threshold. Overlooked until recently is the pending brain drain as experienced business leaders take their accumulated knowledge and business experience with them to the golf course. Prudent boards and executive teams are recognizing the negative effect of losing this brain trust. They are scrambling to offer incentives and unique retirement arrangements to maintain the human knowledge base until it can either be transferred to the next generation or becomes irrelevant.

As employers in the new economy, we are riding out a perfect storm. Globalization has upended traditional employee expectations of wages and work conditions. Job and culture change have reshaped the values motivating today's workforce. Companies are scrambling to retain the boomer generation's intellectual capital in the face of retirements tantamount to a mass walkout. In the Wal-Mart economy, the human resource challenge ranks among the most difficult.

Challenges As Community Members

- *Local communities are savvy and tough.* The perception of corporate wrongs has stirred a sleeping constituency—the citizens and community officials in municipalities around the world. The citizenry recognizes that corporations often take a pound of community flesh, and local officials now want a platter of critical economic benefits, infrastructure improvements, and job opportunities in return. As business leaders, we have to step outside the corporate fence to handle entirely new issues as community members.

  As a sign of the unforgiving business climate, one study of big-box stores by the San Diego Community and Economic Development Department complained of the zero-sum game of retailers slicing up the city's economic pie. "The City of San Diego," wrote the report authors, "has nothing to gain financially from the establishment of supercenters in San Diego County."

- *The activist agenda demands an answer.* As activist Marx showed at the beginning of this chapter, campaigns against companies will no longer stick to single issues. Wal-Mart has registered on the political Richter scale across the issues landscape. It is the icon of virtually everything people don't like about large corporations. Not just environmental issues, as at Exxon. Not just sweatshop issues, once the bane at Nike. Not just diversity issues, which smeared reputations at Texaco. Wal-Mart, justifiably or not, gets attacked on all counts—and its experience reflects a challenge all leaders are facing. Even if we disagree with the agendas of social issues advocates, we simply have to address the issues they raise.

- *Sustainability is the byword.* Companies invest billions of dollars annually in civic, social, and environmental causes. But the focus on annual philanthropic set-asides has come up short. Yesterday's "triple bottom line" mantra—measuring annual performance according to profit, social responsibility, and environmental responsibility—has evolved. The challenge today is to focus on sustainability. Corporations must focus more explicitly on making a noticeable, sustainable difference in their local, national, and global community.

  One example is Switzerland-based Novartis. Partnering with groups such as the World Health Organization, the global pharma-ceutical giant has tackled malaria in such developing countries as Angola, Ethiopia, and Nigeria, where the disease is endemic. Since 2001, Novartis has produced and sold 20 million Coartem brand treatment courses at or below cost. The drug has a para-sitological cure rate of 99 percent.

- *Who's in charge here?* The line of responsibility between the public and private sectors is blurring. The state of Maryland, in passing a law mandating health care benefits for specific classes of employers, explicitly set corporate health care spending levels (although the law was later overturned in court as unconstitu-tional). An entire private-sector disaster-relief industry is spring-ing up to fill a gap in government capabilities by displacing the public sector. Employment rights advocates railing against "sub-standard" wages are bypassing government to take their case directly to companies. The government is doing business, busi-nesses are doing government, and social issues advocates are doing both. The challenge in the Wal-Mart world is to pinpoint the boundaries—if any—between sectors of the economy.

41

Today, companies are running headlong into a clash between the principles of the free market, the aspirations of a free society, the agendas of special interests, and the oversight of government. This clash is a feature of the new Wal-Mart economy, and it requires us as business leaders to respond seriously to even perceived inequities. As government, business, and nongovernmental organizations shift seats under the pressure of global influence, executives need to figure out where they, and their companies, will come down on a range of tough issues.

WAL-MART OR NOT

Wal-Mart has unrivaled power today to set new standards across global markets. This is why Marx wanted CEO Scott to consider a range of reforms—everything from new benchmarks for wage rates in America and factory conditions in China to the safety of factory-farmed salmon and the fuel efficiency of trucks. He is even pushing Wal-Mart to get Procter & Gamble to reformulate cosmetics to do away with alleged endocrine disrupters—and figures Wal-Mart has the power to initiate change within the entire cosmetics industry.

But people like Marx recognize that not just Wal-Mart but all big businesses competing on Wal-Mart's terms perpetuate the Wal-Mart economy. This economy has become omnipresent, nearly inescapable. It mirrors Wal-Mart but also transcends it. It demands that we heed new rules of business, such as cutting costs when at first it feels like we are cutting at the core of our business. It requires that we rise to new challenges, such as making deals with advocates of various social issues when we would rather marginalize them and wall them out.

We all have to learn to live and work in the Wal-Mart economy. We all have to figure out how to master these new challenges. This is not an option. It is simply a fact of life. In the next few chapters we'll examine the hidden secrets of Wal-Mart's success that have spawned the challenges of this economy. Then in Part II of *Wal-Smart*, armed with our insider understanding, we'll find out how to make the smart choices to survive—and thrive.

Chapter 2

Joy on a Treadmill

The Loop that Changes Everything

or almost three decades, Jack Kahl was the chief executive of Manco, Inc., an Avon, Ohio, marketer of Duck brand duct tape, Duck brand mailing and shipping supplies, and other consumer products. From the time Kahl started doing business with Wal-Mart in 1976, he took his cue from Sam Walton and campaigned to cut costs relentlessly. He ratcheted down overhead expenses as a percentage of sales by 42 percent from the 1970s to today.

The lower expenses enabled Kahl to become more competitive and to increase profitability. In turn, Wal-Mart passed through some of those savings to customers. In 1997, Kahl created a 66-yard roll of duct tape in place of the normal 60-yard roll to serve a special Wal-Mart promotion called the VPI, or Volume-Producing Item. The rolls usually retailed for $3.97, but Wal-Mart rolled back the price to $3.50. Unit sales more than doubled—and the sales held up even after the promotion. Kahl won a permanent market-share increase and repeated the promotion in 2002 with similarly successful results.

The story of Manco illustrates the key engine underlying Wal-Mart's growth and thus the key engine behind the Wal-Mart economy: the productivity loop. The loop is an endless cycle: Reduce costs, invest savings in lower prices, use lower prices to boost sales, and generate higher profits to invest in reducing costs further. It is a guiding light for employees across Wal-Mart—and now among employees elsewhere. Anyone in a company can initiate a change to drive the loop. When they finish, they start again. At Wal-Mart, people have been at it for decades.

In the world of management writing, observers frequently maintain that the first place to look for Wal-Mart's enduring success and awesome marketplace power is in the mastery of distribution. Or in buyer power. Or in information systems.

They are wrong.

The first place to look is to the company's disciplined adherence to the productivity loop.

Suppliers such as Kahl can attest. In 1976, when Manco began shipping to Wal-Mart, it was a small $4 million-a-year company. By the time Kahl sold the business to The Henkel Group 22 years later, his dogged adherence to the productivity loop had grown the business by almost 20 percent per year to $180 million.

Asked how important the loop has been to serving Wal-Mart over the years, Jack Kahl doesn't hesitate: "On a scale of one to ten, it is an eleven."

Any company that hopes to profit in the Wal-Mart economy must grasp the ageless formula of the loop. It then must either copy its genius or consciously choose a profit-making concept of equal power. As a legacy of Kahl's zeal, the company still posts a diagram of the loop on the wall at its Avon headquarters. With the help of the loop, the company aims to hit an ambitious target: boosting sales at twice the rate of costs.

LOOP AND LOOP AGAIN

Where did the loop come from? It emerged largely as a reflection of Sam Walton's obsessive drive to pinch pennies. Walton didn't start out with an equation. By hook or crook, he sought to chop costs from retail sales. Trimming pennies was ingrained in his personality, and so it is today in the character of the company.

Walton loved a good retail deal as much as he loved building his business. A story from Wal-Mart lore has it that Walton once decided to make MoonPie brand snacks a special item. He went with his buyer to the manufacturer and jawboned unit costs down to 12.5 cents each. He then could sell the pies, a gooey southern marshmallow treat, for 20 cents instead of 23 cents each, or five for a dollar. In one week, he sold $100,000 worth—500,000 pies—at a tidy $37,500 gross profit. The story says a lot about Walton the merchandiser, but what's telling is that it begins with cutting costs, as do many Wal-Mart stories.

In some ways, the loop (see Figure 2-1) is even simpler than it appears. Only the first two parts are inputs. The second two are outputs. Wal-Mart does the first two, customers respond by doing the rest. Wal-Mart intentionally cuts its costs and consciously invests the savings in lower prices. Customers respond to lower prices by buying more, boosting Wal-Mart sales volume, and contributing to Wal-Mart's profit.

To make the loop easier to understand, let's do the math with a hypothetical example. Assume that Wal-Mart sells a bottle of Widget Shampoo for $0.99 per bottle and that the bottle costs

Figure 2-1 Wal-Mart's Engine: The Productivity Loop

Table 2-1 Profit Around the Loop

			Per Unit			
	Price	Cost	Gross Profit	Gross Margin	Units Sold	Total Gross Profit
Start	$0.99	$0.75	$0.24	24.2%	1,000	$240
Lap 1	$0.94	$0.73	$0.21	22.3%	1,400	$294
Lap 2	$0.88	$0.71	$0.17	19.3%	2,000	$340

Wal-Mart $0.75 to buy and deliver to stores. Wal-Mart's gross profit, the difference between what the bottle costs and sells for, is $0.24 per unit. Its gross margin, the ratio of gross profit to selling price, is 24.2 percent. If we assume that Wal-Mart sells 1,000 bottles of shampoo per week in a single store, the company makes $240 of total gross profit per store (see Table 2-1).

Now assume that Wal-Mart takes a lap around the productivity loop. It reduces the cost of a bottle of Widget Shampoo by 2 cents, to $0.73, by negotiating a lower price from the vendor. It then lowers the price in the store to $0.94, drawing attention to this bargain with a "shelf talker" sign. By undercutting competing retailers' prices, it sells more, increasing unit sales to 1,400 a week. The result: higher gross profit, $294, even though it makes 3 cents per unit less than before.

And this is just one round of the productivity loop. Wal-Mart next invests some of the increased profits in, say, technology to better manage its truck fleet. The fleet management system allows multipoint routing so that a truck emptied at a Wal-Mart store goes first to the Widget Shampoo Company five miles away. There it picks up a trailer load of shampoo before returning to a Wal-Mart distribution center. Such "backhauling" and other transportation efficiencies drop shampoo costs another 2 cents per bottle to $0.71.

Wal-Mart boldly announces a price rollback to $0.88, another 6-cents-per-bottle reduction. Customers respond, and weekly sales jump to 2,000 for the store. This second lap around the productivity loop is even more profitable than the first. Total gross profit rises to $340.

The $100 profit increase may not seem like much. However, as Wal-Mart multiplies the profit increase by 6,600 stores over 52 weeks per year, it increases profit by *$34 million annually on this one product*. Extend the profit on this single item to tens of thousands in a given store, reinvest some of the profits in more cost-saving initiatives, and Wal-Mart becomes a company with $11 billion in annual earnings.

These two laps produce some interesting paradoxes: decreasing costs *but* decreasing prices even more. Decreasing gross margin percentage and gross profit per unit, *but* increasing total gross profit. Note that Wal-Mart was willing to accept a lower gross margin percentage per unit (from 24.2 to 19.3 percent) to earn higher total dollars of profit ($240 to $340) when sales increased. Reduce costs ... reduce prices ... increase sales ... increase profits. That's the magic.

Wal-Mart has consistently executed the first two phases of the loop for years. As a result, the last two phases of the loop have delivered for the company. Wal-Mart sales have grown at a compound annual growth rate of over 21 percent over the last 20 years, and profits have grown at a compound rate of over 20 percent.

ALL FOR LOW PRICES ALWAYS

At first glance, the productivity loop could sound like nothing more than a simple way to describe the math behind Wal-Mart's novel approach to money making. But the loop has much greater power. It captures the essence of Wal-Mart's merchandising strategy—everyday low pricing (EDLP). EDLP is the goal of the second phase of the productivity loop, lowering prices, and sets Wal-Mart up to power the third phase, increasing sales. EDLP is Wal-Mart's customer value proposition—the core merchandising concept that wins over shoppers—and the productivity loop delivers it.

In its pure form, EDLP is a strategy that prices most of the products in a store at the lowest price of retailers in the market. For many years, this is just what Sam Walton did. He spurned sales, promotions, coupons, and loyalty cards. He dispensed with suppliers' payments for shelf space, displays, and other deal money. Walton didn't ask manufacturers to "pay to play," that is, pay extra fees or give discounts to obtain space on his shelves. He dedicated his life to—and built the Wal-Mart brand on—stocking shelves with what customers wanted at the lowest gimmick-free prices.

Wal-Mart's EDLP practice evolved with the times, and it came to mean lowering the customer's total cost of shopping as opposed to offering the lowest cost on every item. Today, therefore, Wal-Mart strives to offer the lowest total cost for a basket of goods. It develops and maintains its price image by ensuring that it has the lowest prices in the market for thousands of high-visibility items such as toothpaste and batteries—and by continuously driving down the prices of all items in the store.

Wal-Mart also reduces its customers' indirect cost of shopping not only by avoiding higher travel costs with its "one stop" approach but also by constantly upgrading replenishment systems to avoid out-of-stock items. Duct tape is a good example of the kind of product Wal-Mart wants to keep constantly in stock. Duct tape is such a key retail product that when Sam Walton struck his first deal with Kahl, he asked the tape marketer to promise him that Manco would never let Wal-Mart go out of stock on the professional grade duct tape that was the essence of the rural farmer's life. To Walton, duct tape was the "bailing wire of the twentieth century." Along with a handful of other items, duct tape showcased the store's price and quality standards. To keep his promise, Kahl ever after kept a small buffer inventory of tape to supply all of his retail customers with enough product to handle rush orders stemming from emergencies such as hurricanes.

Wal-Mart actually deviates from pure EDLP. It uses two forms of promotion. One is the *rollback* in which stores temporarily (and sometimes permanently) cut a product's price. Wal-Mart also features *special buys*, in which it cuts prices to create excitement or to clear out stock.

But Wal-Mart still follows the concept behind early EDLP thinking: Build a relationship of such trust with customers that they always expect to find items priced lower than at competitors' stores. Wal-Mart has spent decades making good on this promise. Its pricing stays focused on the EDLP commitment, and it advertises as much. The upshot is that the consistent approach and consistent message have trained consumers around the world in a new way to shop.

The advantages of EDLP extend to more than costs. Consumers no longer have to spend Wednesdays and Sundays scanning advertising circulars and clipping coupons to find good deals. They no longer have to spend time driving from store to store to compare prices. This is probably why, in a survey by market research firm Retail Forward, shoppers choose EDLP as the prime reason to shop supercenters for groceries.

EDLP also saves retailers money and headaches. They prepare fewer ads, spend less on labor to change prices on store shelves, spend less money and time on displays to call shoppers' attention to deals, spend less time on stock-outs, and spend less time entering and changing pricing data in company computers. This is no small thing when an average supercenter has over 100,000 different products.

Wal-Mart hardly ranks as the only champion of EDLP. National and international retailers such as Costco, Trader Joe's, Aldi, and others rank high as well. Shoppers at Trader Joe's are educated about EDLP via in-store signage and Web site messaging such as "We don't try to bait you in with sales...we offer the best prices we can every day," "We manage all of our costs very carefully so we can pass our savings on to you," and "We don't borrow money. We pay in cash, and on time, so our suppliers like to do business with us."

To be sure, EDLP has its risks. It elicits little excitement, surprise, or sense of urgency on the part of shoppers—indeed, it can be boring. If the price will be the same next week anyway, why buy today? This is why Wal-Mart still offers rollbacks (which are often four-week long sales) and special buys—because consumers haven't yet, and never will, prefer shopping EDLP exclusively.

This is also why, in contrast to using EDLP, other retailers use high-low pricing, often called *hi-lo*. Hi-lo retailers generate store traffic with appetizing promotions, great deals, and sales. Hi-lo retailers run frequent ads and print coupons. They trumpet prices of individual items and often appeal to shoppers by offering more targeted assortments, exclusive products, convenient locations, or better service. Among hi-lo retailers are Kmart, Albertsons, Target (to some extent), and J.C. Penney.

Hi-lo retailing is a fixture of retail culture, and many shoppers throng to stores that offer it. More than two-thirds of people look at flyers or ads for discounts either "often" or "extremely often" before they buy, according to a GartnerG2 study. For products costing over $50, three-quarters of people often delay buying until a sale. Safeway chief executive Steven Burd noted that in some food categories, as much as 95 percent of sales are driven by promotion.

Promotions are a big deal to many shoppers and certainly won't go away. Studies show that customers drawn to promotions not only enjoy shopping but also gain a sense of achievement by buying items on special. Although hi-lo pricing may provide retailers with skimpy or no profit on promoted items, it drives traffic for sales of everything else. And *cross-selling,* as it is called, whether in EDLP or hi-lo stores, boosts sales sharply.

Yet the hi-lo sector has shrunk steadily with the emergence of the Wal-Mart economy. One form or another of EDLP has proven its appeal. The success of Wal-Mart, Trader Joe's, and other stores is testimony to the success of EDLP with consumers. In surveys, consumers themselves say that they prefer EDLP. In the GartnerG2 study, 78 percent of consumers claimed that they prefer the EDLP format, whether in grocery or in general merchandise.

Over 30 years ago, Wal-Mart made a choice to teach customers about EDLP, and the company is now reaping the benefits of that choice. The cost savings internally can be much larger than you might think. Consider a 200-store chain operating with the hi-lo method that puts 3,000 items on sale each week. It has to generate over $250,000 of additional weekly sales just to pay the incremental labor cost to make those price changes.

Wal-Mart also saves money in the supply chain by using EDLP. Instead of sending roller-coaster waves of orders to manufacturers to respond to the binge/purge cycle of hi-lo sales, it can send a steady flow. The predictability allows vendors to run plants at higher utilization rates, increasing efficiency and lowering unit costs. It also cuts down the need for warehouse and back-room inventory space.

Local geography once protected stores from struggling with the EDLP versus hi-lo decision. Mom-and-pop storekeepers could keep prices high locally, knowing that customers would not take the time or spend the money to travel out of town. In the Wal-Mart world, however, the effects of EDLP have come to almost every corner of America and increasingly to every market on earth.

Research in Europe, Canada, and the United States shows that the entry of Wal-Mart either establishes or increases the preeminence of EDLP as a consumer buying preference. In Canada, Wal-Mart's entry prompted customers to reorder their priorities so that low prices rose to the top of consumer preferences ahead of assortment, convenience, product quality, and other attributes. In the United Kingdom, where low prices already ranked as a high preference at the time of Wal-Mart's entry, Wal-Mart reinforced that preference.

The evidence across hundreds of retail markets worldwide is that the economy has been transformed with the EDLP promise, and commerce will never be the same.

A DURABLE FITNESS PLAN

The productivity loop is akin to an economic fitness plan. Like all fitness plans, it only works when practiced over the long term. Some companies make the mistake of staying with the plan for one or two loops. Wal-Mart just keeps on with the program, proving that joy in competition is staying on the treadmill.

You might be thinking, "Wait a minute, Wal-Mart is an 800-pound gorilla. Its size helps it extract good deals from suppliers, and that's what allows it to practice EDLP."

But that's not the point. Wal-Mart's success hinges not on size— A&P once was huge, too—but on faithful adherence to the productivity loop. The loop explains why Wal-Mart can offer deals others can hardly believe. It also explains why Wal-Mart can enter new markets and drive costs down so quickly, introducing the cost-cutting loop in markets where it never before existed.

The boldness of the productivity loop runs counter to the thinking in many businesses. Many companies are struggling with rising costs, so they seek to raise prices whenever they can—airlines being the perennial example. This puts them in the position of running the productivity loop backwards. As profits fall, they raise prices, reduce volume, raise costs, and decrease profits. This is called variously a *doom loop* or *death spiral*. If a business can't halt the spiral, it files for bankruptcy or sells itself in a fire sale.

When Jim Adamson became chief executive at Burger King, he noted how executives were trying to raise prices to make up profit shortfalls caused by a drop in customer counts in the chain's restaurants. Adamson joked with his team that if they kept up that practice, the chain eventually would sell Whopper sandwiches for $1 million each—and as long as they could find one customer per store, they would make their sales goals. Such is the fate of running the productivity loop backwards.

The loop addresses every component of a product's cost, including packaging and transportation. It even focuses on adjusting the mix of product attributes to deliver greater value for the dollar. One Wal-Mart apparel executive responsible for a $35 billion clothing budget gives her suppliers a "plus one" mandate: Every year, she says, the supplier must either reduce the price or raise the quality one notch.

Wal-Mart does not run the productivity loop solely at the expense of suppliers. It runs on the productivity treadmill itself as hard as anyone, eager to cut its own fat. This means cutting costs for shipping, communication, warehousing, handling, distribution, stocking, merchandising, labor scheduling, serving customers, and more. The trick is continuing to find ways to trim costs year after year.

The focus on cutting costs can operate in very unexpected ways. Jack Kahl likes to tell a story about the early years at Manco. At the time, Kahl fielded complaints from customers in retail stores who couldn't separate rolls of his industrial-grade duct tape. The rolls stuck together. Although Manco had shipped them separated by wafers to prevent sticking, store staff discarded the wafers to make tidy stacks on shelves. Adhesive then oozed from the tape. One roll bonded to another. Five, six, or seven rolls would become one.

Kahl went into stores to talk with staff about the problem. Retail clerks pried with screwdrivers to break the tape apart. They whacked with hammers. They heated the rolls in the microwave to soften the adhesive. Nothing worked very well. Kahl was so unhappy with the spectacle that he decided to urge his Wal-Mart buyer to pay a couple of cents more for the cost to shrink wrap each roll and prevent the bonding.

Kahl met with resistance when he suggested a price increase to Wal-Mart's buyer. On his next visit to Wal-Mart's home office, however, Kahl walked into the buyer's office with a stack of five duct tape rolls all stuck together. Brandishing a sales receipt, he told the buyer he had just bought all five in the nearby Rogers, Arkansas, store for $2.97, the cost of *one* roll. Because they were stuck together, the cashier had mistakenly rung up the entire stack for the price of a single item. Kahl's point to the buyer was clear: Wal-Mart's total duct tape costs were soaring because of "shrink" from such unwitting five-for-one sales.

After letting his message sink in, Kahl revealed that he had actually asked the cashier to correct the mistake. When Kahl pitched the shrink-wrap idea again, the response from the buyer was swift: Absolutely! The buyer could now see easily that small increases in expenses to shrink wrap the product actually lowered the total cost of the product.

After so many years of making itself more efficient, what more can Wal-Mart do? As it turns out, people can come up with initiatives for costs savings almost endlessly. One big effort underway now at Wal-Mart is adopting electronic product codes (EPCs) as part of Wal-Mart's migration from bar codes to radio frequency identification (RFID) tags. A study to analyze out-of-stock merchandise at 12 Wal-Mart stores with and 12 without the new technology revealed a 16 percent reduction in out-of-stocks with RFID, a tripling in the replenishment rate over stores with traditional bar codes, and a reduction in manual orders by 10 percent.

As mentioned in Chapter 1, Wal-Mart is synchronizing product data worldwide. Historically, data such as package dimensions, color, and weight were not standardized globally among suppliers and retailers for easy logging on computers. Setting up new product data in Wal-Mart's computer used to take four days. With the new data already logged in a standard format, it now only takes four hours.

Such innovative measures save many thousands of dollars—and all because of the productivity loop. As a fitness plan, the loop continues to deliver not just incremental benefits but breakthrough gains. Day in and day out, Wal-Mart shows that companies ignore the loop at their own peril.

A MODEL FOR EVERYONE

As you may have started to notice, the beauty of Wal-Mart's focus on EDLP and its use of the productivity loop is that the concepts are so easy to understand. EDLP and the loop are simple for executives to communicate and easy for clerks to embrace. If a Wal-Mart employee wonders how to boost the fortunes of the company, he or she knows the answer is to cut costs somewhere in the supply chain between vendor and customer.

Employees who want to drive the productivity loop can take a penny out of labor costs by using RFID to restock with fewer store staff. Or take a penny out of data processing by entering data with fewer clerks. Or take a penny out of landfill costs by recycling more packaging. They know the message is always the same: A penny saved is a penny earned, both for the customer and for shareholders. As employees churn through the productivity loop multiple times and sales volumes increase with each turn, a single penny saved becomes multiple pennies earned.

Many businesses err by not being explicit about their economic formula or, more simply, by not defining how they really make money. They don't lay out clearly for employees the value they provide to customers. They don't highlight the levers to pull for making the company deliver that value more effectively day to day. They use a model for creating profit that is so tangled that only a handful of financial analysts understand it.

A good example is Fleming, where I worked from 1999 to 2002. As a wholesale supplier to many grocery, general merchandise, and convenience stores, Fleming and its customers swam in a soup of retail price complexity. The complexity stemmed from the plethora of promotional money—slotting fees, joint advertising money, and promotional allowances—that vendors offered to drive the hi-lo pricing format followed by most of Fleming's retail customers.

In some customer contracts, called *sell plans,* Fleming sold product to retailers for a stated list price. In other sell plans, it sold the product at Fleming's cost minus certain vendor rebates plus a variety of activity-based costs. Fleming also provided a smorgasbord of additional services to retailers, including the preparation of weekly ads, retail technology support, financing for leases, and store improvements.

Delivering to as many as 50,000 stores, from as many as 50 distribution centers, under multiple sell plans, few people at Fleming could understand the economic formula that actually generated profit. A math Ph.D. was on staff full time to manage the sell plans, but he could not make up for the confusion among the rank and file.

The sell plans simply were too complex for the organization to understand. The mistakes, paperwork, and costs of the sell plans contributed to Fleming's collapse.

Fleming mirrors the complexity at many companies with complicated business models, pricing plans, and cost structures. When employees throughout an organization can't explain how the business makes money—and describe the part they each play—their bosses cannot expect great bottom-line results. Wal-Mart made explicit choices about its economic model, the productivity loop, and communicated those choices frequently throughout the company.

Approaches other than Wal-Mart's certainly succeed, as stores such as Target attest. But companies still have to compete in an economy that favors what Wal-Mart has: a simple economic approach solidly aligned with its EDLP customer value proposition. Business leaders hoping to compete in the Wal-Mart world have to choose a similarly simple approach to guide their own economic success—or risk losing in the Wal-Mart economy.

For Jack Kahl, the simple choice of the productivity loop produced enviable results. With such thrift, Manco's sales grew at over 22 percent annually over the 27 years he owned the firm. The company is now the retail market share leader for all duct tape in the United States. And Kahl doesn't mind telling you the secret: He rode laps of the productivity loop the whole way.

Chapter 3

Gold Star Management

The Secret Behind Strong Processes

hil Jackson is one of the most successful coaches in the history of the National Basketball Association (NBA). He earned nine NBA championships as a head coach, six with the Chicago Bulls and three with the Los Angeles Lakers. One of the keys of his success was the *triangle offense*. The triangle was unique because rather than calling on players to run set plays, it trained them to capitalize on whatever weakness the defense exhibited. In the triangle, someone always was open on the court—you just didn't know who or where he would be.

As Bulls guard B. J. Armstrong observed, "In the system, *anyone* can shoot, *anyone* can score, *anyone* can make the pass. The system responds to whoever is open."

Jackson discovered that the key to running the triangle offense successfully was training every member of the team to respond instinctively to the flow of his teammates and the flow of the game. As Jackson writes in his book, *Sacred Hoops*, "The secret is not thinking. That doesn't mean being stupid; it means quieting the endless jabbering of thoughts so that your body can do instinctively what it's been trained to do without the mind getting in the way."

The triangle offense represents a process that everyone on the team followed. But the process explained only half of what made the team a success. The success also depended on such factors as practice, discipline, accountability, and an attitude to put team results ahead of personal glory. The process provided the structure for success. The management of the players, working within that structure, delivered the results.

So it is with Wal-Mart. Wal-Mart has many terrific processes—for global procurement, for inventory control, and for store construction, to name a few. Thanks to innumerable articles on Wal-Mart, everyone has heard plenty about how those strong processes, turbocharged with leading-edge technology, position Wal-Mart for winning. But what has led Wal-Mart to its world championship in business is not the set of processes alone: It has been making explicit choices about the managerial practices sustaining them.

As business leaders in the Wal-Mart economy, we have to grasp an important distinction — the difference between what I call *strong-process organizations* (SPOs) and *weak-process organizations* (WPOs). Over the years I have observed that most organizations fall into one of these two camps. On the surface, the executives at both often believe they are SPOs. They profess to having well-defined processes and the latest hardware and software to make them run at world-class speed. Only the real SPOs, however, deliver world-class results—because they run with the repetitive behaviors, good training, consistent reinforcement, and accountability that sustain success. Wal-Mart is clearly one of the organizations that fits the pattern of an SPO.

How do you know if you're a strong-process organization? One signal is whether you can execute new initiatives at the speed and precision of Wal-Mart. Sam Walton's "Gold Star Test" is a great illustration. Walton demanded execution so swift and certain that if he asked at 9 a.m. to have every store put a gold star in the upper corner of its front door by 5 p.m., stores nationwide would display that star. To this day, Wal-Mart is known for gold-star execution.

SPOs have strong-process discipline to ensure that their processes are adhered to throughout the organization. Changes to the processes are disseminated through the process design itself.

Because the organization supports employees so well, average people can achieve above-average results.

By contrast, most companies are WPOs. Their executives fail to realize superior results because managers launch ad hoc processes, usually related to "the way we've always done it." Employees have little discipline in following the official processes anyway, and managers regularly call "audibles" to patch up snafus. Perhaps most telling, WPOs require talented "stars" planted around the organization in key positions to muscle results over the goal line.

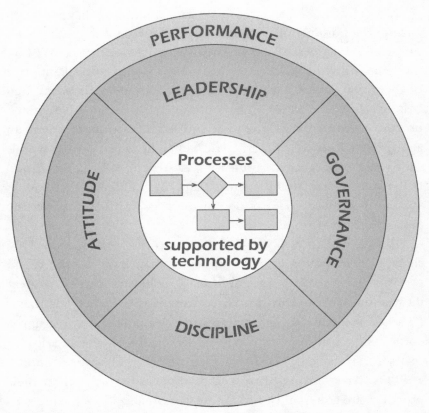

Figure 3-1 Gold Star Secret: The Strong-Process Organization

Make no mistake, well-defined processes, supported by technology, are central—without them, your company is by definition a WPO. What really sets Wal-Mart and other strong-process organizations apart are the choices their executives make when it comes to four key managerial factors: exerting the proper *leadership*, implementing clear *governance* practices, applying the right *discipline*, and championing the right *attitudes*. Only then do they create the environment for *performance* that typifies the strong-process organization (see Figure 3-1).

For business leaders who aspire to succeed in the Wal-Mart economy, these factors can distinguish between success and failure. Perhaps 10 percent of all companies practice strong-process management, but 90 percent of best-in-class companies do. Of course, the best-in-class companies will continue to survive and thrive in the world of Wal-Mart. But executives in other companies can vastly improve their odds of success by recognizing the fundamental divide between the SPO and the WPO. They then must make the conscious choices to bridge the gap.

LEADERSHIP

Wal-Mart's approach to leadership typifies the strong-process organization (see "The Leadership Difference" box). The most prominent

THE LEADERSHIP DIFFERENCE	
Strong-Process Organization	**Weak-Process Organization**
• Leaders are embedded throughout the business	• Leaders are distant from the front lines
• Leaders work themselves out of a job	• Leaders entrench themselves for job security
• Promotions are results-based	• Promotions are tenure-based
• Communications are frequent and comprehensive	• Communications are sporadic and disconnected

feature is that leaders are embedded throughout the business. This is especially apparent at Wal-Mart's famous Saturday morning meeting, a two-and-a-half-hour weekly assembly of 600 or more people. Headquarters staff and executives streaming in from the field meet at 7 a.m. in the home-office auditorium. Wal-Mart senior management opens the gathering, but everyone raises problems and helps to devise solutions on the spot.

Wal-Mart and other SPO leaders don't sit in their headquarters. They visit plants, stores, customers, and employees frequently and intentionally. They realize that keeping a finger on the pulse of the business is essential to understanding trends, opportunities, successes, and problems—and making sure that everyone knows what they're supposed to be doing. They don't hunker down "inside the bubble" like the leaders of WPOs, who, in contrast, hide behind overstuffed appointment calendars, protective administrative assistants, and closed doors.

Wal-Mart regional vice presidents spend the majority of their time in stores—Wal-Mart's and competitors'. District managers spend virtually all their time in the stores. Buyers, who have never performed their duties solely from their modest cubicles in Bentonville, visit the departments in stores for which they buy regularly. The buyers quickly learn about their successes and duds. People call it "eating what you cook."

Other well-known strong-process firms systematically embed leaders on the front lines. At McDonald's, new corporate office staff must work in a McDonald's restaurant for one week as part of orientation. Once a year, McDonald's corporate office executives are encouraged to work in restaurants to celebrate Founder's Day. Walt Disney World executives often staff the resort's parks and hotels during peak seasons. They do this not only to stay close to the customer but also to provide a vacation for full-time employees (whom Disney calls "cast members").

At one of Wal-Mart's WPO competitors that I visited, management stays ensconced on executive row and seldom ventures through the halls of the corporate office. Most meetings take place in the executives' conference rooms—not on the floors where merchandising, operations, marketing, and real estate planning actually happen.

One of the major auto makers is the archetype of a WPO. It is a badge of honor in the organization to be more overbooked for meetings than someone else. Executives openly stand in the hallways negotiating over their PDAs, marking their territory based on whose meeting they will attend and which meeting will limp along without them—while the processes continue to languish.

The leaders of SPOs have a singular goal: to work themselves out of a job. By training, growing, mentoring, and developing their teams, executives at Wal-Mart groom successors to take over their responsibilities. They free themselves up to do bigger and better things for the company. By contrast, managers in WPOs entrench themselves to enhance job security, ensuring that no one else can displace them. Correspondingly, SPOs reward and promote based on results, WPOs based on tenure.

Finally, Wal-Mart leaders are particularly good at communication, a skill honed to a high art in SPOs. The Saturday morning meeting is a nexus of Wal-Mart's communications network. Employees assemble from operations, human resources, logistics, finance, and merchandising. The meeting attendees address big issues and small. They rapidly disseminate the same information in the same way, reinforcing the process culture, and rededicating the company to accountability and execution. Management training at the Walton Institute further reinforces the key company communication messages.

Leaders of SPOs make sure that communication is frequent, targeted, and comprehensive. They realize that for processes to take root and changes to take place, employees need to be kept informed. I often remind CEOs how important it is, in cementing change throughout a big organization, to repeat a consistent message. I suggest a hyperbolic rule of thumb I call the *geometric rule of communication:* For every organizational level that a message travels beyond the CEO, the frequency of the communication needs to double.

For example, assume that a CEO issues a mandate to reduce inventory by 20 percent. If there are five levels in the organization, he or she needs to repeat the message at least 32 times (two to the fifth power) to truly reach the front lines. It needs to be repeated at plant tours, company-wide meetings, and employee training courses. A related rule of thumb: When the direct reports of an SPO leader are sick of hearing the same speech and when they practically can recite it verbatim, the leader is probably beginning to communicate enough to reach those in the field closest to the customer.

In a WPO, communication tends to be sporadic and disconnected. Frontline staff members often are unable to articulate company direction, purpose, and programs because they only hear about them indirectly. Employees frequently fill in communication gaps with rumors. In the absence of a clearly stated company line, managers foment the uncertainty by siding with the staff grapevine. Poor communication such as this often emerges as the most obvious symptom of a WPO. It is a tip-off that the company falls short of what's needed to compete in the Wal-Mart world.

GOVERNANCE

A second way in which Wal-Mart sustains an SPO is through process governance (see "The Governance Difference" box). Good governance of processes starts with clearly defined, stable goals—goals not only for the business as a whole but also for individual processes. Wal-Mart's productivity loop provides a clearly defined cost-cutting/profit-boosting goal for the business, and its repetition and longevity give it great power to create superior results. At the

THE GOVERNANCE DIFFERENCE

Strong-Process Organization	Weak-Process Organization
• Goals are clearly defined and stable	• Goals are vaguely defined and/or constantly shifting
• Guardrails guide local and global decision making	• Parameters and responsibility for decision making are unclear
• Processes are embedded in company	• Processes are embedded in people
• There is a process for changing processes	• Gatekeepers protect the status quo and control critical resources

process level, Wal-Mart sets goals related to inventory, in-stock position, labor hours, on-time deliveries, and a host of other factors.

One of Wal-Mart's clear and stable goals that illustrates its sophistication as an SPO is to reduce inventory while simultaneously increasing in-stock levels on the shelf. At first, these may seem like mutually exclusive objectives. If the company has more inventory, it should be in-stock more, shouldn't it? But this is not what Wal-Mart has found. Like many SPOs, it manages to achieve seemingly contradictory goals to improve performance in counterintuitive ways.

In this case, a recent global study supports Wal-Mart's view. The study found an *inverse* correlation between inventory levels and in-stock conditions: The higher the inventory level, the worse is the in-stock condition. This could be a sign of poor inventory management. Or it could be the unintended consequence of too much slow-moving inventory clogging the back room and getting in the way of employees trying to stock shelves with more popular items.

Wal-Mart cascades goals into the processes at each level of the organization. In the inventory management system at store level, for example, one goal is for the inventory count in Wal-Mart's perpetual inventory system to equal the number of units in the store. If the computer says that the store has 30 bottles of Heinz cocktail sauce, employees want to be sure that their store has 30 bottles. If the count is wrong, they follow a process to amend it.

The value to an SPO of diligently following processes becomes eminently clear in the case of amending inventory numbers. Accurate inventory counts support the company-wide forecasting process, which predicts product demand based on seasonal factors, historical buying patterns, planned price changes, and other variables. In turn, the forecasting process keeps Wal-Mart's replenishment process from buying too much—or too little—inventory. The frontline inventory process ties back to the corporate-wide inventory and in-stock goals.

In a WPO, purposes and goals often are vaguely defined, and priorities are shifting constantly. People linger around the network print stations of the WPO (the water cooler of the twenty-first century) bemoaning the inability of the company to stay any course long enough to make a difference. More than a few companies could use the sort of clearly defined goals expressed by the head of one corporate aviation department. "We have a very singular purpose," he told me. "Landings equal takeoffs."

A second element of process governance at which Wal-Mart excels is defining the guardrails within which employees operate for local and global decision making. Wal-Mart store managers have the authority to lower prices on any item below the prescribed national level to meet local market conditions. They cannot, however, increase prices above the prescribed national level. Wal-Mart shifts the responsibility for guardrails to the appropriate level as needed. Its international executives have leeway to set their own country-specific guardrails as long as they operate within expected sales and profit levels.

Employees in SPOs such as Wal-Mart know what decisions they can make and what decisions require approval. In a WPO, parameters and responsibilities for decision making are unclear. The authority for decision making is held tightly by a few key managers, who are often far removed from the action. Within the ranks, people push a lot of paper and make few decisions. In a WPO, decision authority equals power; in an SPO, it equals results.

Another distinguishing characteristic of process governance in Wal-Mart is that processes are embedded in the fabric of the company: Procedures are codified to help managers act, monitor, and reward results regardless of which employee occupies the seat. In a WPO, processes are embedded in people. When the people change jobs or leave, the process knowledge goes with them. The next employee has to learn the ropes—or make up a whole new process.

I once advised the lenders of a financially distressed manufacturer trying to execute a turnaround. The chief financial officer manually prepared daily cash-flow forecasts for the lenders and for management to monitor the firm's precarious cash position. Every time I probed about the assumptions underlying the current forecast, the CFO produced another "revised" forecast with different information. The cash forecast became a constantly moving target. The fact was that there was no cash forecasting process in place. The CFO had positioned himself to be indispensable to the company—and to the lenders—because he *was* the process.

The last distinguishing characteristic of strong-process governance that Wal-Mart exhibits is that it has a process to change a process. If workers in a distribution center want to load pallets in a different way, they refrain from any change until they fill out a "process change request." The process change request form describes the current process, the proposed one, the suggested results, and a pilot procedure to test the change. A regional vice president has to sign it, and internal auditors check for compliance. Notes on infractions go to senior management.

Wal-Mart executives don't want to slow innovation with a lot of red tape, but they do want to ensure that all changes cut costs and drive the productivity loop. If a change that increased costs were to creep into the system, the money lost would multiply fast. A change increasing labor in a store by just 1 hour a week, multiplied by 6,600 stores, multiplied by 52 weeks, multiplied by $10 per labor hour would exceed $3 million.

This perhaps explains why Wal-Mart has a process to train new workers in the process to change a process!

Like other SPOs, Wal-Mart designates specific managers throughout the company to champion and monitor changes. These sponsors cascade changes through the organization and ensure the continued integrity of the company's architecture of processes. In a WPO, executives can change processes only through brute force. The organization is filled with gatekeepers of the status quo who make themselves indispensable by controlling critical resources.

DISCIPLINE

A third way Wal-Mart reinforces its SPO is in how it applies discipline to make processes work (see "The Discipline Difference" box). Above all, it commits to measures of performance that are focused and consistent. Everyone knows the goals to be achieved, and everyone uses facts, not opinions, to arrive at conclusions.

THE DISCIPLINE DIFFERENCE

Strong-Process Organization	Weak-Process Organization
• Performance measures are focused and consistent	• Performance measures are scattered and inconsistent
• Results are valued	• Effort is valued
• There is a bias for information and knowledge	• Company drowns in data without useful information
• Accountability is high; consequences (positive and negative) are imposed	• Accountability is low; consequences are meted out erratically

At the highest levels, when Wal-Mart executives talk about performance measures, they highlight four: comparative-store ("same-store") sales, operating-income growth compared with sales growth, inventory growth compared with sales growth, and return on assets. The first simply measures growth, the second and third determine whether Wal-Mart has sold more for less during the growth, and the fourth reveals profitability.

These measures then influence the more detailed measures for employees throughout the organization. To contribute to higher operating income growth compared with sales growth, for example, employees everywhere know that they need to focus on costs—which, of course, is the point of the productivity loop.

As an example, Wal-Mart builds several distribution centers each year. Each covers more than a million square feet and costs tens of millions of dollars. Every time one opens, managers measure costs, and employees try to figure out how to reduce them. In the 1990s, the staff of one center wondered if they could postpone buying their entire $2 million pallet inventory by a week. The math supporting such a decision is straightforward. Given the time value of money, at prevailing interest rates, the delay would have saved roughly $4,000. The staff postponed pallet acquisition.

At Wal-Mart and other SPOs, executives value results—effort is irrelevant. Everyone knows the measurable goals to be achieved, and there is a bias for information and knowledge as opposed to data. In a WPO, people value effort, especially when results are below plan. You will hear such comments as, "We have commissioned a study on that" as a substitute for demonstrating results. Performance measures are scattered and inconsistent, everyone has his or her own scorecard of performance, and people are drowning in data but not information.

Aldi is another retailer with measurements that illustrate the practices of an SPO. Aldi is the 700-store Chicago-based unit of the global German retailer that sharply undercuts even Wal-Mart prices with a limited assortment of good-quality, private-branded goods. An Aldi store manager's routine is highly programmed because the corporate office dictates product costs, prices, product selection, merchandising, and product placement. Therefore, Aldi store managers are evaluated on only three measures that they control: cashier productivity (items scanned per labor hour), controllable overhead expenses (e.g. labor, utilities, and rubbish removal), and shrink (theft and spoilage). Since so much of sales and gross profit are out of their control, store managers don't even receive an income statement.

Another aspect of discipline in SPOs is accountability. One of the most frequently heard mantras in the halls at Wal-Mart is "know your numbers." At Wal-Mart and other SPOs, the level of accountability is high, and consequences are imposed for both positive and negative performance. When a unit misses its measures, the question becomes, "What are you doing to make up the shortfall this period?"

In a WPO, there is little or no accountability, and even when someone is held accountable, consequences—good or bad—are meted out erratically. When a unit misses its measures, if the leader has a legitimate, believable excuse, he or she is off the hook.

When I worked at Fleming, we met monthly with the leaders of our distribution centers to review financial results. It took over a year for most people in the company to realize that having a plausible excuse for missing numbers was not an acceptable substitute for performance. Effort was not a substitute for results.

Another client of mine struggled with accountability. The company had a strong, admirable culture of dignity and respect for the individual. Unfortunately, dignity and respect frequently were mistranslated into, "I can't hold Joe's feet to the fire for missing financial results because if I do, I am not respecting him." In essence, the opposite was really true. The best way to respect Joe was to hold him accountable so that he could learn and grow in his career.

ATTITUDE

A fourth way that Wal-Mart reflects an SPO is with a set of critical attitudes that govern behavior (see "The Attitude Difference" box). Among the strongest is a bias for action.

A story about quick execution illustrates this point. In January 2006, just after the New Year's holiday, Wal-Mart executives worried that the consistency of merchandising across the chain of stores was becoming spotty. In particular, they wanted to make sure that every store had displayed treadmills, exercise bicycles, and bun-and-thigh rollers before its customers lost resolve to act on their New Year's exercise resolutions.

Executives such as John Menzer weren't happy a few weeks into January. Only 41 percent of stores had complied with the plan. Worried about missing sales, Menzer assembled his operations and merchandising staff. He told them that setting up the fitness center in each store was a "nonnegotiable." By the next week, compliance hit 91 percent. A couple of days later it hit 100 percent. Treadmills were up and running in every store, and this could only have happened in a company that values action. In a WPO, managers enamored with ad hoc management would have defeated the plan.

THE ATTITUDE DIFFERENCE	
Strong-Process Organization	**Weak-Process Organization**
• Bias is for action	• Meetings are acceptable substitutes for action
• Employees toe the line on processes and procedures	• Managers frequently call audibles
• The right people are in the right seats on the bus	• Company retains and rewards "But People"
• Complexity is absorbed upstream to make processes close to the customer simple	• Complexity is pushed downstream toward the customer

Of course, fast and purposeful execution may not always work, yet Wal-Mart and other SPOs don't get bogged down by a bureaucracy. Consider the "Gold Star Test" again. Although Sam Walton insisted on lightning-fast compliance, he coached his team to challenge him *tomorrow* if the gold star was ill-advised. For *today*, they needed to deliver. Other SPOs work in the same way as Wal-Mart. They execute consistently and precisely first and act on feedback to improve after initial delivery.

In a WPO, meetings are acceptable substitutes for action. If executives in these types of companies were faced with the fitness-equipment merchandising problem, they would talk about it until it was too late to act for the current season. Author and management professor Oren Harari could have been describing WPOs when he once remarked in a speech that some companies talk about a good idea long enough until it becomes a bad idea.

In SPOs such as Wal-Mart, employees toe the line on processes and procedures. Leaders take calculated risks, resulting in industry leadership rather than followership. When problems arise—and they always do in any organization—employees seek the root cause and fix it constructively. This is why SPOs can deliver so consistently. How does Wal-Mart open more than 200 supercenters every year and bring almost every one to profitability almost immediately? By people sticking with the processes and making quick adjustments.

The company's record tells the story of a vast team of employees committed to sticking with the process. In 1979, its sales topped $1 billion. It had 276 stores, but in only 11 states. In 1989, sales topped $20 billion. It had 1,259 stores, but still in only 25 states, mostly the south. By 1995, it had entered 24 more states, had 2,558 stores, and logged sales of $78 billion. Today, as a global enterprise, Wal-Mart's growth for just the next year will equal the entire revenue of one Walt Disney Company or one Canon. Wal-Mart owes this to an attitude of commitment to the process.

In a WPO, if managers don't like the process, they make up their own by issuing orders off the cuff. As a result, the organization often has as many processes as it has managers. Managers in a WPO generally are followers rather than leaders. It is less risky to watch which way the company winds are blowing and stay in the safe zone than to take even the most well-calculated risks. When problems occur, the tendency is to place blame either on the structure or on other people.

An SPO embodies Jim Collins's advice described in *Good to Great*, which is to get "the right people on the bus, the wrong people off the bus, and the right people in the right seats." The opposite of this philosophy in a WPO is perpetuating the careers of what I call "But People." We have all heard about "But People": "I know John treats people poorly, *but* he consistently beats plan." WPOs are willing to retain maverick managers even when the attitude they model is cancerous to the long-term health of the organization. The wins they achieve in the short term hurt the organization in the long run.

Condoning the heroics of "But People" can make the difference between success and failure for a company. In one Fortune 500 company, the incoming CEO replaced every senior manager except one long-time executive who had the closest relationships with the company's customer base. Unfortunately, that executive was one of the "But People" who paid lip service to the company's transformation strategy and then played quarterback with his own audibles. He became one of the main reasons the turnaround effort failed.

A final attitude that underpins the SPO is simplicity. A byword at SPOs could be, "If it ain't simple, fix it."

At Wal-Mart, managers fight complexity wherever it crops up: in communication, in training, in real estate development, in store operations, and in bureaucracy. Their devotion to simplicity appears in one place above all: their commitment to absorb complexity upstream to make downstream processes, those closest to the customer in the store, as simple as possible.

Take the recent changes in Wal-Mart distribution processes, dubbed network "Remix," the effort to replenish high-volume items more frequently. On the one hand, distribution centers have become more complex to implement this strategy. They have an extra-wide aisle for forklift operators to access high-velocity items such as paper towels and diapers. They have installed gravity-fed racks with pallets stored four deep. But when the goods arrive at the store, the high-volume items are right by the door of the trailer and easy to unload. Skipping a stop for storage in the back room, the staff can wheel palletized product, which is already stacked for store display, right into the store aisle. The product can be on sale 30 minutes after the truck arrives at the store.

As one Wal-Mart distribution executive says, "The goal is to give stores the merchandise on a silver platter, or silver pallet in this case."

Wal-Mart executives are especially focused on simplicity when they broadcast messages to the front lines. When Wal-Mart's stock price was sagging owing to its slipping return on assets in the 1990s, then-CFO Menzer launched a campaign to drive up asset returns in stores. He was especially concerned with $1 billion in store inventory that he felt was unneeded. Menzer crafted three goals: to increase sales on assets in place, to reduce costs (as in the productivity loop), and to reduce assets.

Instead of using the lingo of financial wizards, Menzer launched a simple three-part program that any employee could grasp regardless of educational level. A series of videos and newsletters explained what an asset was—a toy on the shelf, a pallet in the back, a corrugated box—and explained how assets cost the company money. The training enabled employees to realize that assets aren't free. And it got them asking, "How can I do my job and use fewer of these assets?"

As a result of the program, returns on assets, which had fallen from nearly 15 percent in 1990 to 7.8 percent in 1996, rebounded to nearly 10 percent by 2000.

Wal-Mart's focus on simplicity has been mimicked by others in the Wal-Mart economy. Retailer Aldi lays out its warehouses in exactly the reverse order of the layout in its stores. Pallets of product are built in the warehouse so that the store clerk can disassemble the pallet a product at a time, wasting no steps as he or she walks the store aisles.

The converse of simplicity—complexity—is a hallmark at WPOs. Executives think up innovative programs, but at the front lines, the programs puzzle employees. The new initiatives may sound smart to the top brass, but they send groans through the rank and file.

In the Wal-Mart economy, demonstrating a bias to act, being loyal to the process, getting the right people in the right roles, and promoting simplicity count big in the formula for success. They are the attitudes that give people the confidence of winners. As Mark Hansen, the former chief executive of SAM'S CLUBS, says about the SPOs: "People in weak-process companies want to win. People in strong-process companies expect to win."

PERFORMANCE

How do you know that you have an SPO? SPOs exhibit some remarkable advantages over WPOs (see "The Performance Difference" box).

One of the clearest signs that you're working in an SPO: Average people can achieve above-average results. Wal-Mart may hire many people without either college or high school degrees, but that hasn't affected its productivity. In 1995, Wal-Mart productivity, as measured by sales per employee, exceeded its competitors' by 48 percent owing to its strong-process philosophy. Over the years, as other companies copied Wal-Mart's management, it lost its lead to

THE PERFORMANCE DIFFERENCE	
Strong-Process Organization	**Weak-Process Organization**
• Average people achieve above-average results	• Stars are required around the organization to muscle results
• Leaders successfully transfer across functions	• Leaders cannot successfully transfer across functions
• Processes scale up and down well	• Processes do not scale up and down well
• Leaders are "dispensable"	• Leaders cannot leave without significant impact on the company
• SPO leaders may not be successful in WPO companies	• Stars can be successful in other WPOs

companies such as Costco, but it still sells a remarkable $173,000 per employee worldwide.

By contrast, WPOs are star-dependent organizations. They require talented managers carefully placed around the organization to make results happen. Without the stars, results crumble. Phil Jackson's Chicago Bulls shed light on this distinction. When Jackson first became head coach, the Bulls were a WPO. Michael Jordan was the star, everyone else was a backup player, and the Bulls didn't make the playoffs. As the strong-process triangle offense took hold, Jordan brought his game down a notch, he simultaneously raised his "average" teammates' games up a notch, and the Bulls achieved way better than above-average results.

The movie industry (and many NBA teams) illustrates just the reverse of "average people achieve above-average results." Hollywood is built on the star system like no other industry. Movie production, promotion, and performance are built around individual stars. Movies soar—or fail—based on the performances of celebrities. And several times a year, the stars assemble to determine which star is the biggest of them all. It is no surprise that the film industry, more than others, is marked by erratic results—and strong-process companies such as Wal-Mart, McDonald's, and General Electric are largely known for the reverse.

Another performance advantage enjoyed by Wal-Mart is cross-functional mobility. Leaders can transfer across functions because the strength of the process infrastructure supports them, enabling them to cross-train in other disciplines.

Lee Scott rose up the career ranks in distribution. He then ran merchandising before becoming CEO. John Menzer started his Bentonville career as chief financial officer and then took the reins of Wal-Mart's international unit before assuming responsibility for the U.S. business. Mike Duke led distribution before swapping roles with Menzer in late 2005 to become head of the international business.

In WPOs, cross-functional transfers can be a disaster. Leaders with deep expertise in one function can become a fish out of water when they assume leadership of totally different departments. With no relevant functional experience—and no strong processes to help them "learn the ropes"—such an ill-fated match does not serve the company, does not serve the leaders, and certainly does not serve the functional units' employees.

Yet another performance advantage of an SPO is scalability. The company can scale up, scale down, and replace people with minimal disruption. Wal-Mart's record speaks for itself. The company was a retailing footnote for many years, a regional chain even when it had $15 billion in sales. It grew through a process of contiguous expansion. In time, the saturation strategy enabled Wal-Mart to cover the globe. Its processes were scalable.

Wal-Mart shares many qualities of strong-process management with McDonald's. As McDonald's has scaled up, retrenched, and replaced staff, the integrity of the company's processes has survived. With just over 30,000 restaurants around the world,

81

McDonald's site-selection, real estate procurement, design/build, and property maintenance processes are some of the most finely honed in the world. They even survived the troublesome early 2000s when McDonald's performance dipped and executives pulled back on building new restaurants until they could fix the brand, the menu, and the operations in existing restaurants.

McDonald's added an average of over 1,600 new restaurants a year from 1996 to 2002 and then built only 162 in 2003 while it retrenched. The company has ramped up to opening almost 400 new restaurants annually since the business has turned around. Despite the roller-coaster real estate development schedule, McDonald's real estate processes scaled down as the department shrank, scaled up as the department renewed itself, and support many new faces today. This only could have happened with processes embedded in the fabric of the company.

A final advantage of an SPO is that leaders become "dispensable." They can move to new roles or even leave the organization, and the combination of strong processes and strong-process management enables the company to continue to thrive. Although some observers were surprised when Wal-Mart CEO Lee Scott took a one-month leave in the middle of a hectic 2006, it was the SPO that allowed him to do so. At McDonald's, executives are required to take an eight-week sabbatical every 10 years and are expected to build a strong process that can live without them during that time.

By contrast, processes in a WPO do not scale well, and often don't survive the departure of the leader who supported existing processes. The "star" system tends to perpetuate reliance on people more than processes. If the leader isn't able to jury-rig new and expanded processes as the business expands, or to jettison processes and/or resources as the business contracts, the processes themselves break down. Likewise, the company may suffer substantially greater business risk when the WPO leader who was muscling the results over the goal line leaves for another position—taking the processes with him.

However, SPO leaders have one notable disadvantage: difficulty with career portability. Effective leaders in an SPO often don't perform well if they leave and take the helm of a WPO because, although they know how to operate within an SPO, they don't know how to build one themselves. Several former Wal-Mart leaders have left to take the helm of WPOs with decidedly mixed results. WPO stars, on the other hand, often perform well in other WPOs because they know how to implement ad hoc processes.

The contrast between the advantages enjoyed by an SPO and a WPO can be as stark as success and failure. An SPO creates leaders; a WPO relies on them. An SPO leverages processes; a WPO wrestles with them. An SPO values shared leadership; a WPO values solitary leadership. Ultimately, an SPO focuses on the customer and grows. The WPO focuses on itself and implodes.

STRONG PROCESS, STRONG RESULTS

Wal-Mart can't claim to run processes without error. Strong-process management even can cause mistakes. It has caused Wal-Mart to open stores filled with Arkansas merchandise where it doesn't belong. When the company opened its first urban store in Philadelphia, it lined up a varied assortment of lawnmowers out front. Unfortunately there was hardly a home with a lawn anywhere nearby.

Furthermore, some of Wal-Mart's recent legal woes may be due to unfettered adherence to some SPO principles. For example, recent lawsuits alleging that Wal-Mart store managers forced employees to work off the clock and that managers used undocumented workers could have been caused by employees following performance-based measures at all costs.

But the strengths of an SPO provide the basis for success in the Wal-Mart economy. The strong-process approach is so ingrained at Wal-Mart, from clerks to CEO, that people instinctively know what to do, whom to work with, and how to beat the competition. The people at Wal-Mart may change, but the process results don't.

Management books, consulting firms, and entire industries have been built on promulgating the concepts of "process architecture" and "technology enablement." Both are at the core of an SPO. But it is making explicit choices about leadership, governance, discipline, and attitude that makes the difference between success as a strong-process leader or failure as a weak-process also-ran.

Chapter 4

Genes of a Winner
Examining Wal-Mart's Unique DNA

Ptolemy, the ancient astronomer, believed that planets rotated around the earth and developed a theory to explain and calculate that motion. As humankind's understanding of the heavens expanded, Ptolemy's theory of planetary physics had to become more complicated to explain observed motion. Then, in the sixteenth century, Copernicus advanced a theory that the planets rotated around the sun, not the earth. This model of planetary physics triumphed because it explained the motion of the planets much more accurately and simply.

In a similar way, the productivity loop reveals a remarkable simplicity behind Wal-Mart's success. The loop explains the "motion" of Wal-Mart. But the physics behind Wal-Mart, and the management chemistry of strong process that goes along with it, do not fully explain Wal-Mart's success. There is something else that drives the company with equally compelling power: its biology.

Why haven't other companies in the Wal-Mart world been able to triumph like Wal-Mart? What is the difference that makes the difference—beyond cost-cutting physics and strong-process systems? It's Wal-Mart's "genetic" makeup, what I call its *DNA*. Most other companies miss this key factor. They fail to recognize that they cannot replicate Wal-Mart's success without replicating its DNA.

The DNA of an organization refers to its internal, hard-wired character. This is in contrast to its external traits. Many executives trying to duplicate the success of Wal-Mart think that they can do so by duplicating visible competitive advantages such as Wal-Mart's everyday-low-price (EDLP) position, its low cost structure, its streamlined logistics and distribution network, its information systems prowess, and its partnerships with vendors. Yet most of these fast-follower efforts fail because they miss the genetic code.

In biology, we describe people by referring to such traits as blonde hair, blue eyes, fair skin, high cheek bones, long legs, and small feet. But we know full well that these traits are simply the manifestation of an internal code, our genes. Modern medicine, science, and cosmetics offer many ways to modify our traits— dyeing our hair, smoothing our complexion with plastic surgery, and coloring our eyes with contact lenses. Altering traits does not endow us with the underlying genes, however, and over time, our gray roots show and our crow's feet come back.

The same is true in business. Companies that replicate Wal-Mart's competitive advantages often end up with just a corporate "dye job." They find that the change often doesn't work or doesn't work well, and even if it does work, they have to reapply the fix to sustain the change. To replicate Wal-Mart's enduring operational strengths successfully, we need to start with the DNA.

Wal-Mart executives believe that perpetuating the company's DNA is one of their chief jobs. They dedicate the first Saturday meeting of every month to culture, asking one or two managers to give a prepared talk on what the culture means. They also lead mandatory cultural training for all new managers. During training sessions at the Walton Institute, they teach trainees about everything from expense control to continuous improvement.

Wal-Mart's DNA includes some potent genes that encode the leadership and work attitudes lying at the root of its competitive advantages. Of the many genes of this kind, five deserve special attention: *focus, correction of errors, constructive paranoia, thrift,* and a *"we can make it better" attitude.*

FOCUS

Few company workforces are hard wired to focus like Wal-Mart's. The gene for focus has been passed from generation to generation of managers: Never take your eye off the ball, focus on the things of highest priority, and ignore the rest. *Focus* may sound like a hackneyed time-management principle, but at Wal-Mart, it's not a principle at all—it's part of company character.

The main object of focus at Wal-Mart is pleasing the customer through effective merchandising. Sam Walton was, before all else, a merchant. He took great pride in stocking products that flew off the shelves because customers loved both the items and their low prices. The genetic code at Wal-Mart today ingrains this thinking in every manager, from the company motto, "Think like a merchant," to the "Volume Producing Item" (VPI) program, in which executives each select a specific item to sponsor and promote throughout the chain.

As retired vice chairman Don Soderquist writes, "The point is you must concentrate all your energies on satisfying every single customer on every single visit he or she makes to your store every single day."

I once asked David Glass, chairman of the executive committee of Wal-Mart's board, how he ran thousands of stores as CEO. His response echoed the Wal-Mart DNA: "I don't. I run one store at a time." In other words, Glass didn't focus on turning managerial knobs and flipping operational levers to run the apparatus of a giant corporation; he focused on running a store.

Glass was also widely known within the organization for consistently reminding Wal-Mart leaders and employees that their business is "buying and selling merchandise." This mantra was particularly helpful at refocusing passionate discussions about administrative issues that could have easily consumed headquarters personnel.

Wal-Mart managers today continue to take their cue from the managers before them. Fifteen years after the founder's death, executives still circulate Sam Walton stories to pass on DNA. When it comes to focus, they don't just scan aggregated reports by region or store format. They check store-by-store reports to spot the smallest trends and discrepancies. Buyers in Wal-Mart's home office regularly arrive at 5:30 a.m. to pore over daily sales reports from the day before—by item and by store.

Wal-Mart executives are notorious for punching the speaker phone button at a Saturday morning meeting, calling a store manager, and asking a question about sales trends in a specific department of the store. It only takes a few such impromptu calls to send ripples of awareness throughout the chain, prompting managers at every store to know their numbers just in case the next voice broadcast through the auditorium on Saturday morning is theirs.

Focus translates into daily activities at each store. At the beginning of shifts, associates gather to do the Wal-Mart cheer. The cheer, a rah-rah spelling of the Wal-Mart name, energizes employees and builds teamwork at the start of their shift. It also reminds them every day of their primary focus because the cheer ends, "Who's number one? The Customer! Always!" After the cheer, they also discuss the action plan to be addressed in the store that day. Store managers follow up with department managers during the day on that day's action list. Department managers review the previous day's item-by-item sales report to recognize trends and opportunities.

Wal-Mart observers today talk about the company losing its focus, especially with distractions from activists and incessant challenges from competing retail formats. But this kind of talk has emerged before, and Wal-Mart has succeeded despite the doubters. This is because the focus gene expresses itself not just in the stores. It also emerges in the executive suite, where the most seasoned managers guide the company's direction.

I watched the power of focus when Wal-Mart broke its string of 99 consecutive quarters of earnings growth in January, 1996. At the time, Wal-Mart performance was slowing. Its stock price was just over $20 per share. Its return on assets had dipped under 8 percent. Same-store sales had fallen from 7 percent in fiscal 1995 to 4 percent the next year.

Executives had many concerns, which I touched on in the introduction. One was how to compete with "category killers" such as Toys "R" Us and Best Buy, which aimed to dominate sales in their product categories. Another was how to compete with dollar stores, which undercut Wal-Mart's prices, albeit in small stores with a limited assortment. A third was simply how to increase traffic to boost sales past the $100 billion mark.

The executive team was uncertain. Should Wal-Mart stay the course? Should it compete head to head by copying the category killers? Should it start dollar stores of its own? Should it open new formats of its own discount stores? Wal-Mart could have gone in many different directions.

I'm convinced that Wal-Mart succeeded because the executives all remained committed to focus. Remember that the first step in making a choose-or-lose decision is choosing what *not* to do: Strategy is the elimination of options. I asked executives the question, "What are the five things we're going to get right this year?" The meeting turned into a wrestling match among leaders who all had a passion for the business and their own projects. Yet they agreed to make tradeoffs and discipline themselves to attacking just five. They took the "nice to have" priorities off the decision-making table and applied themselves just to the "must haves."

The executives in the group decided to press ahead into toy sales. They decided to ramp up sales of food. Part of the plan was to create more private-label goods—such as Sam's Choice and Great Value brands—and pocket higher profits by avoiding the marketing and branding costs of national labels. They also decided against opening dollar stores by keeping the focus on EDLP at Wal-Mart.

The focus paid off big. Over the next five years, Wal-Mart became the largest toy retailer and the largest food retailer and out-paced dollar stores by a wide margin. To anyone thinking that Wal-Mart will stumble in overcoming its current challenges, this lesson of the past is worth noting. In the Wal-Mart world, single-minded focus goes hand in hand with success.

Like any other living organism, Wal-Mart certainly isn't perfect. The strategy for SAM'S CLUB for example, exhibits a schizo-phrenic focus. In the mid-1990s, it sold most of its product to cus-tomers with business membership cards, but market research showed that over 70 percent of purchases were for personal use. SAM'S shifted to focus on consumers in 1997, wavered between business and consumer members from 1999 to 2003, and then shifted back to targeting business customers. The blurriness of focus remains to this day, partly explaining why SAM'S CLUBS generate just over half as much revenue as an average Costco ware-house store.

Despite the imperfections, no firm of Wal-Mart's scale has ever applied the energies of so many people to so narrowly defined a project: discount merchandising. Unlike other large firms, Wal-Mart executes a single-business strategy and executes it across four store formats. It doesn't confuse people by launching many strategies for many businesses. Other companies hoping to succeed in the Wal-Mart economy need to develop the same genetic compulsion.

CORRECTION OF ERRORS

A second element of DNA that makes Wal-Mart a formidable com-petitor is its obsession with continuous improvement. Thousands of times a day, employees at Wal-Mart all over the world say, "Let's do a correction of errors." Participants hold a brief meeting to evaluate how things are working and particularly how to make them better.

Correction of errors is all about identifying ways to improve customer experiences, merchandise, processes, cost structure, and the company from within—before competitors beat Wal-Mart to it. The correction-of-errors practice carries throughout the organization. Newly opened distribution centers hold a correction-of-errors meeting to share lessons and determine how to open the next center more efficiently. Home office leaders hold meetings to improve the loss-prevention process.

A cousin of quality management, correction of errors likely gained currency when Sam Walton read the works of twentieth-century quality guru W. Edwards Deming. Deming's management dictums, which Walton investigated in the 1970s, surely resonated with the Wal-Mart chief. Among Deming's best known: "Drive out fear; encourage effective two way communication and other means to drive out fear throughout the organization so that everybody may work effectively and more productively for the company."

Wal-Mart's correction-of-errors philosophy stands in stark contrast to the habits of most corporate cultures. Correction of errors isn't aimed at placing blame. As business leaders, we have all experienced—and probably participated in—the blame game. "It's not my job," "It's the system's fault," and "Well, I sent you an e-mail about that" are all examples of the blame culture rampant in corporations today. An inordinate amount of time, money, and emotional energy is spent finding someone or something to blame for the problems that plague organizations. The resources could be expended more wisely to fix problems in the first place.

Correction of errors focuses on the problem, not the person. A focus on the person inevitably spurs a prickly response: worry about being wrong, embarrassment, and fear of being fired. Our self-preservation instinct kicks in, and we find a way to divert attention from ourselves to another victim. It requires strong DNA to overcome these responses. It also requires employees throughout the organization who are willing to be vulnerable and not fear retribution. Correction of errors encourages people to drive performance by seeking improvement, not stall performance by searching for scapegoats. The savings from this habit, in both money and personal energy, are enormous.

Wal-Mart executives often visit stores to check on their operations, and they compulsively hold correction-of-errors meetings at the end of the store tour. Executives share feedback with store managers on ways to improve merchandising, store conditions, labor productivity, and customer service. At the same time, executives listen to store managers' ideas for what the home office can do to better serve them. When I consulted to Wal-Mart, if I toured a Wal-Mart store without stopping for a correction-of-errors meeting with the store manager, I felt as though I hadn't done *my* job.

Wal-Mart places so much stress on correction of errors that most top managers in Bentonville carry a three-ring binder documenting progress on correction-of-error projects in their department. Many managers clutch the binders wherever they go—to meetings, to the cafeteria, or home. Like making a last-minute check for their wallets on their way to work, they always make a last-minute check for their binders. They don't want to be caught flatfooted if asked by their bosses about progress on a correction-of-errors project.

Correction of errors is a behavior that extends from the store floor to the executive suite. When I was running strategy meetings, we would even convene a meeting after every strategy project. We wanted to know what worked and what didn't, and we wanted to incorporate the feedback into the next strategy project.

During one strategy session, the frontline department manager from a central Arkansas tire-and-lube center had admonished all the participants—from store managers to top company executives—to quit talking about pie-in-the-sky strategies. She described the day-to-day challenges she faced as a department manager: Associates weren't showing up, inventories were incomplete, and customers were complaining. How could she expect to boost tire sales if she had only three of the four tires a customer needed in stock?

Her comments provided a strategic breakthrough at the meeting. They also stimulated a strategic breakthrough afterward. We recognized in our correction-of-errors meeting that we needed to tap into a better horizontal and vertical cross section of Wal-Mart employees to enhance our strategic decision making. In later strategy sessions, we invited a broader group of associates to participate, and we came up with much smarter strategies—all because we were willing to sit down as a team, look at ourselves in the mirror, and figure out how we could improve the process continuously.

Correction of errors has swept through the company recently in response to criticism from outsiders. After visits by such people as Michael Marx (as described in Chapter 1), executives looked at corrections Wal-Mart could make in everything from excessive packaging to overseas labor monitoring. One change was the reduction in packaging for 16 private-label toys shipped from Asia. By reducing the packaging size, Wal-Mart was able to eliminate 230 cargo containers per shipment without changing any of the products inside.

The challenge for all of us as players in the Wal-Mart economy is to nurture the same level of blame-free continuous improvement. Keeping up with top competitors in the Wal-Mart world requires people who see improvement possibilities everywhere, even in themselves. It demands attitudes that help to correct any errors. It requires bosses who support and act on opportunities to change for the better, separating the action from the person, hating the sin but loving the sinner.

CONSTRUCTIVE PARANOIA

A third element of Wal-Mart's DNA is constructive paranoia. This is an intentional attitude to avoid smugness and complacency. As remarkable as it seems in such a successful organization, the assumption by people at Wal-Mart is that the monster of defeat lurks just around the corner. They have good reason to make this assumption, of course. In the world today, the durability of competitive advantage is measured in months, not years. Remember from Chapter 1 that one of the challenges for competitors in a Wal-Mart world is that competitive advantages are now built on *when* not *what*.

Constructive paranoia serves two important purposes in building sustainable competitive advantage. First, it keeps Wal-Mart focused on protecting company secrets, a practice that lengthens the time needed for competitors to copy Wal-Mart innovations. Wal-Mart is famously protective of its trade secrets. For years, employees have been discouraged from speaking at industry conferences. The belief is that the risk of giving away trade secrets far outweighs any bene-fit of participating. Store managers closely watch competitors tour-ing a Wal-Mart store and sometimes embarrass them into leaving.

The same paranoia does not pervade the workforces of many competitors. I've visited hundreds of other retailers' stores in my career. In most I can freely inspect shelf displays, pricing, and store layout, ignored by the store manager. In some stores, I've even walked unchallenged right into the back room and was able to get a quick reading of inventory levels and waste.

The second purpose of constructive paranoia is to keep Wal-Mart's associates alert and energized. Wal-Mart store managers each send staff out several times a week to cruise the competition—despite their frowning on the same practice in their own stores. In Wal-Mart headquarters, signs of constructive paranoia are everywhere. One banner displays pictures of competitor CEOs and asks, "Who's taking your customers?" At weekly meetings, merchants and operations leaders pore through observations from their visits to competing stores and implement immediate responses.

One competitor who quickly caught onto Wal-Mart's visit-others-but-don't-let-them-visit-you approach is Fred Meijer. Years ago, Sam Walton repeatedly asked Meijer for meetings to share ideas as noncompeting regional retailers. Walton admired Meijer's super-centers, which Wal-Mart had not yet launched. But Meijer shunned each of Walton's "Aw shucks" requests. His "Just say no" response probably delayed the success of Wal-Mart supercenters by at least a few years. By contrast, Sol Price, who founded the club store concept in the mid-1970s, said yes to those same visits from Sam Walton. Price ultimately merged his Price Club stores with Costco in 1993 to combat SAM'S CLUB, which by then had double the revenue of Price Clubs.

If no outside challenge shakes the complacency of Wal-Mart managers, DNA dictates that the company create its own constructive paranoia. When I embarked on a five-year strategic planning session with Wal-Mart executives in 1999, the executives were pretty pumped up. In the three previous years, Wal-Mart's revenue had grown by $44 billion, crossing the magical $100 billion mark. Earnings had jumped 17.4 percent a year. The stock price had quintupled to $106.

Our facilitator opened the session by praising the group. "Wow, the largest retailer in the world," she started.

"As big as your three closest competitors combined," she added.

"Eighty percent of America shopped in your stores last year," she continued.

The 70 participants relished the moment, until she delivered the punch line.

"That was Sears in 1973."

The frightful analogy startled the executives—1973 was the year that marked the pinnacle of Sears' power. Sears moved into the Sears Tower that year, a potent symbol of executive hubris, and in the following decades, it lost its preeminence.

In 1999, Wal-Mart had just climbed to the number three spot on the Fortune 500. Had it reached its peak also? The facilitator's message was one of caution: At many companies with giant reputations, years of peak performance breed complacency that leads to decline.

A spotlight shined on a poster-size mock-up of a magazine cover dated five years ahead: "Wal-Mart Who?" read the headline. Mr. Smiley, Wal-Mart's beaming icon, was pictured with a frown. The subtitle noted that Wal-Mart had disappeared from the Fortune 500.

The worrisome question for the executives was—and is today—can the same thing that happened to frontrunner Sears happen to Wal-Mart?

Wal-Mart executive John Menzer then posed questions to get people worried about good times turning bad. What if sales don't increase and earnings stop growing? What if our competitors merge? What if the big European companies give us a run for our money? What if, in five years, we're not the biggest or the best?

The participants even played through some unpleasant scenarios. In one, they had to anticipate French-based retail giant Carrefour merging with supermarket giant Kroger and discounter Kmart. In another, they considered Microsoft buying Costco to dominate Internet retailing.

In the end, the group rallied around the five key strategies on which it would focus. They set a goal to top the list of the Fortune 500 within five years, a goal they reached by 2004 with $256 billion of revenue. Igniting the constructive paranoia gene helped to propel Wal-Mart to this success.

THRIFT

A fourth element of Wal-Mart's DNA is the culture of thrift. Frugality was one of the most enduring and unmistakable imprints Sam Walton left on Wal-Mart. Born in Oklahoma during the run-up to the Great Depression, Walton said that he believed in the value of a dollar because he knew how hard it was to earn one. As a boy during the stock market collapse, he traveled with his once-jobless father to repossess farms for a mortgage company.

Stories about how Walton ran his nascent discount chain permeate Wal-Mart lore to this day. Walton so hated to spend money on motels that he and a group of other managers once slept in sleeping bags on the floor of one manager's house—before any furniture arrived. "When it comes to Wal-Mart," Walton wrote in his autobiography, "there's no two ways about it: I'm cheap."

The most important way that Wal-Mart perpetuates this gene is by modeling thrift right from the very top. When I first started working with Wal-Mart, I mistakenly expected to see the plush accommodations enjoyed by executives in the rest of the Fortune 500 stratosphere. The small offices, worn carpet, and gunmetal-gray desks gave me pause. The men's room on executive row gave me a graduate degree in the culture of thrift: A sink, a single commode with a weathered sign asking, "Please flush after use," and a can of Sam's Choice spray air freshener on the back of the commode taught me all I needed to know.

In the home office, employees buy their own coffee and use both sides of sheets of paper. On the road, employees bunk two to a room. They stay in budget hotels with free breakfast buffets, not luxury accommodations. They keep ballpoint pens to use at the office. If possible, they fly to cities the morning of a meeting—economy class—to avoid the hotel bill. The company, not the employee, keeps frequent-flyer miles.

One of our strategy sessions was held on the thirty-fifth floor of an Atlanta office building. Rather than flying in the night before, the company plane fleet shuttled employees to Atlanta that morning. Curious about accommodations, the arriving participants asked SAM'S CLUB executive Rob Voss where they were staying.

Voss pointed out the window. "Do you see that beautiful sandstone building with the circular drive and the pool on the roof?" The participants were dazzled by the accommodations until Voss added, "We're in the building right next door." The building "right next door" was a budget motel—including a free breakfast buffet.

In the stores, employees are reminded to pinch pennies. Corrugated shipping boxes are imprinted, "Each box costs the company about $0.80." This encourages employees to reuse boxes for up to seven shipments, and each time the store reuses the box, it gets credit. To save on labor costs, store managers frown on overtime; it is a black mark on their record. Software helps them to schedule labor without spending any more money than they have to.

With 6,600 stores and over 200 distribution centers, employees understand that thrift makes a difference. In keeping with the productivity loop, pennies saved on the front lines turn into millions of dollars on the bottom line. In one story of thrift, a distribution center employee in Brookhaven, Mississippi, reined in the "waste" of spending on ballpoint pens. He calculated that buying pencils instead of pens for the loading docks would save $25 per week. Multiplying the savings across all U.S. distribution centers, Wal-Mart could save roughly $2,000 per year. The upshot? Wal-Mart's distribution chief switched all centers to wooden pencils.

Wal-Mart's obsession with thrift doesn't mean that it fails to spend on cost-saving investments. Retired vice chairman and chief operating officer Soderquist tells the story of the Wal-Mart team dedicated to recovering money from people who have stolen from Wal-Mart. After the team recovered $2.5 million one year, he challenged them to quadruple their take. Although the team protested, it went to work and gave him a budget for the challenge that required 19 more employees and new computer programming, about $500,000 of additional costs. Soderquist gave them the money, the team delivered the $10 million, and Soderquist upped their goal the next year to $17 million.

One competing retailer I visited offers a stark counterpoint to the culture of thrift. It has a separate, palatial floor for its senior executives, private conference rooms adjacent to each executive's office, and secretarial offices that protect each executive from drop-in hallway traffic. It looks much more like a New York investment bank than a cost-conscious merchant. By the way, that same retailer is a big loser in the Wal-Mart economy.

A "WE CAN MAKE IT BETTER" ATTITUDE

A fifth and final element of Wal-Mart's most noteworthy DNA is the "we can make it better" attitude. Whereas correction of errors focuses on Wal-Mart's own internal performance improvement, "we can make it better" focuses on other companies' ideas—that is, imitating them and going one better. Some might call it "shamelessly copy and steal." Consultants simply call it "reuse."

Like other companies, Wal-Mart often has succeeded through a fast-follower strategy. Believe it or not, Wal-Mart has never actually created a new store concept. It followed Kmart into discount stores, Price Club into warehouse club stores, Meijer and Carrefour into supercenters, and combo supermarket and drug stores everywhere into Neighborhood Markets. It then did all of them one better.

Sure, Wal-Mart innovates, too. But deep in its DNA are genetic instructions to borrow the best of everything elsewhere. Sam Walton never emerged from his competitors' stores with a self-satisfying list of criticisms. He emerged with a yellow pad and dictated notes on anything he found done better than at Wal-Mart.

As the story goes, Walton and then-executive vice president Soderquist emerged from a run-down discounter one day in 1981 in Huntsville, Alabama, and Walton asked what he thought. Soderquist was new to the company. He remembers that all he could see were the faults: empty shelves, dirty floors, boxes in the aisles.

Walton overlooked the faults. He saw a panty-hose rack that displayed goods far better than Wal-Mart's did. He had pulled the rack out, written down the manufacturer's name, and told Soderquist to order the brand for Wal-Mart. He saw an ethnic cosmetics display 12 feet long, triple that at Wal-Mart. He had written down the suppliers' names and told Soderquist to have Wal-Mart's buyer get in touch with them.

Walton could find a diamond in any rough. And he knew how to polish it. Executives at Wal-Mart today pass on this attitude and behavior. No innovation at a competitor is too small to copy. In its supercenters, it copies pallet racking from Costco to stock high-volume, easily stackable products such as paper towels and toilet paper. From warehouse-style grocery retailers such as Cub Foods, Food4Less, and Woodman's, it places pallets in the center aisle to display seasonal cooking items such as baking pans and pumpkin-pie filling at Thanksgiving.

When Wal-Mart begins to polish newfound jewels, sometimes they break. When it first tried to copy the supercenter idea from Meijer and the hypermarkets in Europe, it overspent on land and buildings. It struggled to reach a profit—and then closed them before relaunching supercenters later. For Wal-Mart, failure is a step in a continuous improvement process, not an end.

But Wal-Mart's hunt for the best in everything shows that in the Wal-Mart economy, no innovation is safe, and many innovations are free for the taking. The antithesis of "we can make it better" is the not-invented-here syndrome, the phrase managers often use to describe organizations that automatically reject any idea they did not develop themselves. Companies whose DNA fosters blind pride in their own innovations at the expense of adopting better ones elsewhere will have trouble competing in the Wal-Mart economy.

NO LESS THAN GENE THERAPY

DNA at Wal-Mart is like DNA in Lance Armstrong—hidden but critical. Armstrong has a larger heart (by 20 percent), a lower lactic acid production rate (by a third), and higher oxygen delivery rate to his legs than almost all other humans. DNA alone gives him an incredible edge. In the same way, corporate genes give Wal-Mart an edge.

In the Wal-Mart economy, copying the competitive practices of the athlete without reproducing the brains, brawn, and behaviors coded in DNA will not suffice to produce a winning company. In fact, copycat efforts may offer no advantage at all.

In the Wal-Mart economy, executives have to make a conscious choice of how to genetically reengineer. Every company is different. And each can gain an advantage in a different way. As business leaders, though, we all have to recognize how the top-of-the-line firm has created an advantage through five highly evolved genes: focus, correction of errors, constructive paranoia, thrift, and a "we can make it better" attitude. We then have to choose the right DNA for our own organizations. We can take our cue partly from Wal-Mart, but we also must take our cue from our strategic choices, the subject of the next four chapters.

PART II

WHAT DO WE DO NOW?

Twelve Smart Choices in a Wal-Mart World

So we live in a Wal-Mart world:

- A world defined by the largest retailer in history, a company that collects nearly 1 cent from every retail purchase dollar on earth.
- A world driven by the elegant physics of the productivity loop, the simple notion that prosperity starts with penny pinching.
- A world run by managers who have mastered effective processes, whether for a meeting of minds or the melding of supply chains.
- A world where competitive advantages emerge from unique and powerful DNA, a genetic code that favors focus and self-improvement.
- A world that will never be the same—and will never cease to challenge all comers.

So what do we do now?

We can all profit in the Wal-Mart world, and in the next four chapters, I'll show you how. I'll share the secrets for surviving and thriving by crafting new strategies as competitors, as suppliers, as employers, and as community members.

Each of the next four chapters begins with the story of a company that struggled in one of these roles. I then share three choices we must make to win, and I close with case studies of different companies—local firms, regional players, and multinational corporations—that exemplify successful strategies.

By the end of this book, you will have the insight, the knowledge, and the confidence to be a winner in any industry with a dominant competitor—a winner in the Wal-Mart world.

It's up to you to choose—or lose.

Chapter 5

Differentiate, Emulate, Dominate

The Competitor's Conundrum

When Mark Schwartz took over as president of Kmart in March 2001, he had a simple plan in mind: Beat Wal-Mart at its own game. Schwartz should have known what he was up against. He had, after all, worked for Wal-Mart for 16 years and then worked as CEO of two other big retailers: Hechinger, a home-improvement chain, and Big V, operator of ShopRite supermarkets. Yet, apparently he didn't believe that trying to beat the giant could prove futile, even for a seasoned player.

In an effort to level the playing field with Wal-Mart, one of Schwartz's early moves at Kmart was to champion a program called "BlueLight Always," in which Kmart lowered prices on many of the store's best-selling items, such as toothpaste and diapers. Schwartz meanwhile loaded up on inventory—$850 million worth by some estimates—ready to imitate Sam Walton's "stack 'em high, watch 'em fly" philosophy. Many, including both Kmart's board and me, cautioned Schwartz against battling the bear head-on.

To Schwartz's chagrin, the inventory didn't fly. Sales actually fell. In December 2001, while Wal-Mart's sales rose 8 percent from the year before, Kmart's dropped 1 percent. With the heap of idle merchandise, inventory costs soared. Cash flow shriveled. Profits evaporated. On January 17, 2002, CEO Charles Conaway fired Schwartz. Five days later, Kmart filed for bankruptcy, a victim of its strategy to roll out Wal-Mart-style everyday low pricing on 30,000 Kmart items.

For anyone who wants to compete with Wal-Mart or any other dominant player, Kmart provides a cautionary tale. Schwartz copied a page from Wal-Mart's EDLP strategy because he wanted to attract customers and boost volume, as well as cut marketing, sales, and supply costs. But Kmart didn't have the economic engine, the strong-process organization, or the DNA to make the program work. As one analyst joked, Kmart operated with an "unproductivity loop."

The EDLP binge damaged the company like no other single decision. In its bankruptcy reorganization, Kmart had to retrench radically. In Texas, a Wal-Mart stronghold, it closed more than 80 stores, including every one of its 11 Dallas–Fort Worth stores. Nationwide, it eventually shuttered close to 600 stores. Tens of thousands of people lost their jobs.

Jim Adamson, the former CEO of both Burger King and Denny's and the Kmart board member who took over as CEO in March 2002, turned off the BlueLight program. He returned Kmart to hi-lo pricing across the store. He began publishing circulars to advertise bargains again. Kmart began to operate like the promotional retailer its customers expected—and wanted. As Adamson commented later, "When we got into bankruptcy, we were losing 10 to 15 percent of our customers every month. We needed to immediately get customers back into the stores, and we needed to do that by returning to what our customers expected: hi-lo promotional deals."

The lesson from Kmart is not that other companies cannot compete with giants of industry such as Wal-Mart. Competing is eminently possible. In the retail sector, Target, Kohl's, and many local, family-owned businesses compete very successfully against Wal-Mart. The lesson is that as competitors, we can—and must—make specific choices to compete wisely in the Wal-Mart economy. In this chapter we'll examine the challenges we face as business leaders in any industry with dominant competitors and describe the triad of specific choices any competitor must make to survive and thrive.

IN THE LAND OF THE GIANTS

As leaders in any industry in this new economy, we face the stiffest competition from dominant players. The giants have the power to set the rules of the game. They choose the dance step; we have to choose how to dance around them.

Giant competitors typically retain their power for several reasons. To begin with, they have well-defined customer value propositions. Although some characterize Wal-Mart's goal as driving competitors out of business, its primary intent is to introduce a retail experience that is far more appealing to consumers than anything else available. This focus on the customer is ultimately what gives Wal-Mart and many other dominant companies their competitive edges. One of the main reasons Kmart's EDLP drive failed is because Kmart's focus was on Wal-Mart. Wal-Mart's focus, on the other hand, was on customers' wallets. Ironically, Kmart's strategy accelerated Wal-Mart on another lap around the productivity loop: Wal-Mart reduced prices to maintain its price spread versus Kmart.

The Coca-Cola Company is another example of a firm that stays focused on a customer value proposition. Ten years ago, then-CEO Roberto Goizueta noted that the average human drinks 64 ounces of liquid every day, and Coca-Cola was responsible for less than 2 of those ounces. The company's goal was to capture a greater share of the other 62 ounces. Since then, Coca-Cola's innovations and acquisitions have reflected that focused goal, adding products such as Dasani water, Full Throttle, Coca-Cola Zero, and the Coca-Cola Blak coffee-fusion drink.

Second, dominant players develop and nurture several sustainable competitive advantages. We mentioned a number of Wal-Mart's competitive advantages in the first half of this book, including its low price perception, its efficient distribution system, and its information-technology capabilities. In the new economy, though, competitive advantages are now built on *when*, not *what*. Wal-Mart's strong-process organization and its unique DNA give it the ability to stay steps ahead of the competition by quickly developing and deploying tomorrow's competitive advantage.

Third, giants tend to push industry market boundaries. As their market share reaches capacity in their served markets, they redefine those markets to sustain their leadership position. Almost 35 percent of Wal-Mart's revenue expansion since 2000 came from its international business, an example of expanding the served market. Its expansion into the grocery sector over the past 10 years—and threatened forays into everything from car sales to banking—further pushes boundaries beyond the company's defined industry.

As a result of these characteristics, dominant players traditionally have left many weaker players in their wake. For example, in the United States, competing discounters from Ames to Zayre are out of business. In Canada, the venerable Saan chain was driven into bankruptcy restructuring. Scores of music stores have gone bankrupt, while Wal-Mart scooped up 20 percent of the U.S. market for all CDs. Toy retailers KB Toys and FAO Schwartz have gone bankrupt, while the once high-flying Toys "R" Us chain's share of the toy market has dropped from 25 percent in the 1980s to 17 percent today.

Academic studies verify that Wal-Mart stores drain business from other stores—including stores well beyond its immediate locations. One study by Iowa economics professor Kenneth Stone showed that in the 10 years after a Wal-Mart opened, general-merchandise sales in Iowa towns with Wal-Mart rose by 25 percent (mostly from Wal-Mart), whereas general-merchandise sales in surrounding towns plunged by 34 percent. Meanwhile, in both Wal-Mart towns and surrounding towns, sales for both specialty stores and apparel stores fell by 15 to 28 percent.

Experience also suggests that retailers of other kinds may be even harder hit, especially grocers. Market research firm Retail Forward predicts that two supermarkets will go out of business for every new supercenter Wal-Mart opens. In Newcastle, Oklahoma, just outside Oklahoma City, family-owned Spencer's IGA Superthrift found itself hammered by Wal-Mart's march into its market. "When they came in, they got 45 percent of our volume immediately," reports Jim Spencer, the store owner who opened his store in 1987. He closed it just one month after the supercenter opened.

But all is not lost. Competitors who survive and thrive in industries with dominant players capitalize on the giants' limitations and vulnerabilities. One limitation is the inability to capture entire markets. Even without national and international antitrust laws, market share for any player has practical limitations. Even when Wal-Mart saturates a market, its share bumps into a ceiling. In the state of Oklahoma, where Wal-Mart has blanketed the landscape with all four store formats, its grocery market share is about 50 percent. Its grocery market share in saturated Dallas, as mentioned in Chapter 1, is 28.5 percent. The reason is quite simple: Wal-Mart can't be all things to all people, as much as it would like to be.

A trip to a big mall or a healthy downtown reveals the broad variety of retail formats that attracts shoppers, and Wal-Mart simply can't provide all that variety. In essence, to focus enough to be successful, Wal-Mart generally has to cede the majority of most retail markets to others. It cedes the part of the market that craves more fashion selection in apparel to competitors such as Target, Kohl's, and J.C. Penney. It cedes the segment of the market that desires higher-end home fashions to Crate & Barrel and Pottery Barn.

Wal-Mart's focus remains on price-sensitive shoppers buying mainstream consumer items. Although it does attract high-income shoppers, its biggest fans remain those in lower- and middle-income segments. Its value proposition is very appealing, but it doesn't appeal to everyone. It probably won't appeal to Macy's shoppers who want to sample perfume at a classy counter. It probably won't appeal to lower-income consumers who want rock-bottom prices in a convenient neighborhood store such as Dollar General or Aldi.

Furthermore, all companies have vulnerabilities, including dominant players. In Wal-Mart's case, its approach to low-cost, efficient product delivery ensures that its customer service falls short of that at many other retailers. While it does focus on service in some categories—jewelry, tire and lube, pharmacy, and optical—its levels of face-to-face customer handholding remain limited in other categories.

Other limitations of Wal-Mart include the ability to merchandise local products effectively in local stores. Wal-Mart buyers in Bentonville, Arkansas, can only do so much to procure products that consumers in each local community want. One of Wal-Mart's biggest local merchandising fiascos occurred in the Cleveland Heights, Ohio, store, which opened with a set of standard merchandise in a neighborhood dominated by African-American and Jewish customers. The noticeable lack of such items as African-American health and beauty care products or kosher foods was the wake-up call that spurred Wal-Mart to create its "store of the community" local merchandising program.

Wal-Mart also has limitations in other areas. It falls short compared with other retailers in nurturing one-on-one customer relationships, in offering locations convenient to every neighborhood, and in providing a shopping experience that doesn't overwhelm a segment of customers put off by 200,000-square-foot supercenters. David Glass, the chairman of the executive committee of Wal-Mart's board and formerly Wal-Mart's president and CEO, was well aware of the company's vulnerabilities when he used to say, "If our competition only knew how many mistakes we make!"

The good news here is that successful, dominant players simply can't succeed in all aspects of appealing to all customers because they generally have finely-honed strategies and customer value propositions. To be focused, they have had to say "no" to some products, services, and markets, which creates opportunities for other companies.

At the same time, dominant players have proven to actually boost certain segments of their markets. For example, Jim Spencer expects that his other IGA store in Purcell, Oklahoma, will experience a significant sales drop in some categories when another supercenter opens 1.5 miles away, but he figures that the drive-by traffic will increase his butcher shop sales. His butchers, who cut Oklahoma beef the way customers like it, can beat Wal-Mart on meat products and service any day.

Spencer's expectations have some basis. A recent study of retail sales in Mississippi showed that five years after Wal-Mart entered a market, sales to other retailers in the same county rose 4.2 percent. One beneficiary was furniture stores in Mississippi counties with Wal-Marts, which gained 2.5 percent in sales after five years.

In other industries, companies of all kinds have devised ways to compete with industry giants. In the package-delivery industry, behemoths UPS and FedEx dominate the market. But local, regional, and international players still thrive. Global player DHL thrives by trying to offer more service options. Regional player California Overnight competes by underpricing the giants and striving for better service. Many local messenger services distinguish themselves by delivering faster.

To succeed in the Wal-Mart economy, however, these companies did not prevaricate when it came to shaping strategy. They made explicit choices. Many retailers who have failed in the wake of Wal-Mart did not make choices to alter their approach when Wal-Mart came to town. Surprisingly, in a study of 62 small retailers in southwestern Virginia, researchers found that 52 percent of store keepers did not adjust their product lineup, 42 percent did not adjust pricing, and 21 percent did not adjust service levels. The researchers noted that store owners didn't seem to make a conscious effort to vary their product assortment away from Wal-Mart's.

FORMULA FOR WINNING

So what is the key to competing successfully against Wal-Mart or a dominant industry competitor?

Don't compete against them.

Instead, the key to profiting as a competitor in the Wal-Mart world is to make three explicit choices relative to the dominant industry player:

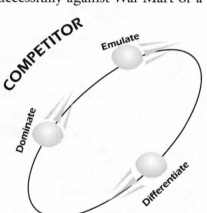

- How to *differentiate*
- What to *emulate*
- Where to *dominate*

Differentiate. Emulate. Dominate. These three imperatives form the triad of choices we all have to make as competitors to profit in the Wal-Mart economy.

Differentiate

One military historian studied the 280 major military campaigns that shaped Europe over the last 25 centuries and discovered that only 6 of those campaigns achieved victory with a direct frontal assault against the enemy. In the Wal-Mart economy, the odds of any business winning with a similar all-out, full-frontal assault against a dominant industry player are slim. As competitors, we can't take on the bear by running at it head-on, playing its game, in its habitat, with its rules. Just ask the leaders of Kmart circa 2001.

To succeed, we have to act differently, albeit with the same focus and discipline as industry giants. My favorite example of blurry focus appears in a common genre of company strategy statements that all can be summarized as follows: "We will be good to our customers, good to our employees, good to our vendors, good to our communities, and good to our shareholders." This is certainly an admirable mission. However, if a company's employees can't use their strategy statement to say "No" to the many reasonable initiatives that arise, then the organization will be at best unfocused and at worst irrelevant.

One media company asked my firm for advice when its ratings stagnated. When we arrived, the company's programming was an eclectic mix of news, features, interviews, and several genres of music. Because executives had not chosen a specific focus, they included something in the mix for everyone. The company was stuck because it hadn't said "No" to enough things. It didn't stand for anything specifically.

Since the successful giant says "No" to some set of products, services, customers, or value propositions, it leaves plenty of opportunity for competitors in the industry to *differentiate themselves in one or more of those areas.* Wal-Mart competitors have many opportunities to differentiate, and companies in other industries can differentiate themselves similarly.

- *Micromerchandising.* Stock more local products, exotic products, upscale merchandise, hand-made items, or ethnic products such as clothing in brighter colors and smaller sizes that are popular in Hispanic neighborhoods.

- *Service.* Offer expert advice and training, make deliveries, customize products, extend credit, extend hours, or get to know customers' names. Many family-owned small businesses win with a premium-service approach.
- *Convenience.* Be closer and easier to shop at than the competing supercenter. Walgreens has blanketed the country with well-located, convenient neighborhood pharmacies.
- *Niche products and services.* Narrow product and service lines to sell only in specialty markets, such as luxury, ethnic, elderly, teen, or hobbyist.
- *Niche geographies.* Locate stores in carefully chosen urban, rural, or suburban markets, serving customers with specific demographic or lifestyle needs. Dollar stores such as Aldi and Dollar General often locate in strip malls near high-traffic grocers and retailers to capture the purchases of families on a tight budget.
- *In-store experience.* Enhance the experience inside your stores by means of displays, demonstrations, decorations, layouts, and entertainment. Soriano's, a growing Wal-Mart competitor in Mexico, marks grand openings with a Mariachi band.
- *Marketing approach.* Mix and match EDLP and hi-lo pricing to stimulate urgency and trips. Studies show that retailers can win different customer segments with both.

Speaking on behalf of the dominant players in the Wal-Mart world, Sam Walton recognized as much in his autobiography: "I don't care how many Wal-Marts come to town, there are always niches that we can't reach—not that we won't try."

Emulate

In the Wal-Mart economy, dominant players get where they are because they do at least a few things right. As competitors, we should adopt a "we can make it better" attitude, picking and choosing attributes from these giants to emulate. If we compete in an industry without a dominant competitor, we should remember that rising stars often accelerate their ascents by studying the winners in other industries.

As competitors to Wal-Mart, we have a wide array of competitive advantages, business practices, and other managerial strengths from which to choose. The first half of this book enumerated the most powerful. We can use a productivity loop to lower prices. We can implement a strong-process organization to streamline the supply chain. We can grow using a saturation strategy. And, of course, we can—and must—consider which of Wal-Mart's cultural genes to splice into our own organizations to ensure that we can sustain the emulated attributes.

Yet, to be successful competitors in the Wal-Mart world, we need to be smart and selective about what we copy from dominant players. In the same way that economists talk about the "Goldilocks economy"—not too hot to create inflation, not too cold to create unemployment, just right for sustained growth—we may find some of Wal-Mart's attributes too hot, others too cold, and yet others just right for our own sustained growth. Emulating the dominant player in every attribute creates a second, me-too player in a habitat that is only big enough for one.

Companies must choose to *emulate those attributes of the industry giant which are consistent with their own differentiated position in the market.* Meijer chose to emulate Wal-Mart's low cost structure when it removed over $400 million of annual operating costs. But Meijer did not choose to emulate EDLP. Instead, it invested those savings in a combination of permanent price reductions *and* lower pricing on promoted items because it wanted to maintain its differentiated position as a hi-lo supercenter retailer. Texas-based retailer H-E-B emulates Wal-Mart's saturation strategy to fill in markets, but it differentiates itself with more fresh foods, ethnic foods, and higher-end concept stores—which also take advantage of Wal-Mart's local merchandising vulnerabilities.

Dominate

As market segments in the new economy are left open by the just-say-no decisions of industry giants, we are faced with the third strategic question of our triad: Which segments do we choose to dominate? More simply, in which pond will we choose to be the big fish? Ninety percent of Americans and over 95 percent of global consumers vote to shop somewhere other than Wal-Mart every day. If we are retailers, we must choose to dominate a carefully selected subset of those other markets. We accomplish this by analyzing the market, identifying underserved customer segments, and attacking those segments where we can shine.

Several authors including Stephen Covey have described the contrast between people who view life (and business) through a lens of scarcity versus those who view it through a lens of abundance. Players with the scarcity mind-set believe that there is not enough to go around, define themselves based on what they lack, and believe that when others gain, they lose. By contrast, the abundance players look for the opportunities, let go of baggage, believe that there is more, and believe that there is enough to go around.

Winning competitors in the Wal-Mart economy find the abundance in their markets. They recognize that there is plenty of opportunity for a strong number two by choosing to *dominate the remaining market the giant doesn't and can't occupy.* Remember Fred Meijer's message to his executives: You don't need to outrun the bear; you just have to outrun other competitors. There are numerous industries and markets with strong number two players—Coke and Pepsi, McDonald's and Burger King, Dell and Apple. Battling in Columbus, Ohio, Wal-Mart and Meijer both consolidated their market shares when weaker competitor Big Bear went out of business in 2004.

Even Wal-Mart executives have confided that they need strong competitors in their markets, probably to feed their constructive paranoia gene and to avoid antitrust concerns. The point, however, is that we have to consciously choose what segment of the market we will master. The jack of all trades, to rephrase the old saying, is the profitable player in none.

WINNING COMPETITORS IN THE NEW ECONOMY

Winning competitors in the Wal-Mart economy are the ones who consciously make—and, if necessary, remake—this triad of choices as competitors. By choosing how to differentiate, what to emulate, and where to dominate, they create a compelling vision for their businesses. They are the ones who keep a sharp lookout for competitive threats and act early to mitigate them. They leave it to laggards to bear the brunt of the bear attack.

A traditional retailer such as Jim Spencer can't outrun Wal-Mart supercenters across the street simply by lacing on some new tennis shoes (probably bought at Wal-Mart) and picking up the pace. He has to come up with a different plan and avoid a slow, costly competitive siege. Let's look in detail at a few success stories from competitors in Wal-Mart's own industry. These competitors' well-articulated strategies demonstrate how differentiating, emulating, and dominating are the platform for winning.

Marra Drug Store

Darin Marra, the third-generation pharmacist of family-owned Marra Drug Store, knows the threat of the Wal-Mart economy. In recent years, a SAM'S CLUB, a Wal-Mart, and a CVS all have opened nearby his family-owned retail store in Secaucus, New Jersey. He attributes some of his lost sales on items such as school notebooks to the arrival of the big chains.

Marra has long dedicated himself to running a far better drug store than a big box could, however. He refers to Marra's as "a health care facility." Part of his competitive strategy is to emulate the inventory-control practices of the big chains. Recently, he has started to track inventory vigilantly. He is determined to make sure that he is never out of stock of his top 300 to 500 items, such as Benadryl, Dimatab, and Fleet Enema. "We make damn sure that we've got the stuff we're supposed to have," he says.

Marra also more carefully follows the store layout plans he receives monthly from a drugstore-merchandising advisory service. He and his staff take apart and reassemble aisles to promote new items with new signage. He also takes his subscription service's advice on products, pricing, and placement for the skin care, eye care, hair accessories, beauty aids, and other categories in his 7,000-square-foot store.

Marra always has run his store differently from the big chains, but these days he makes sure to market the store's advantages like never before. Although for decades the 80-year-old operation has offered drug compounding, prescription delivery, professional counseling, and clinics for osteoporosis, diabetes, heart disease, the flu, allergies, and so on, he now runs ads every week to advertise his services to make sure that his customers understand how much he differentiates himself.

"We've been doing it for years," he says. "So we're trying to tell people we're doing it, to get the word across. It's like writing propaganda . . . when there's a war going on."

Marra maintains that the chains simply can't compete with him when it comes to prescriptions. He stocks far more medicines than CVS or his other competitors. He figures that he fills triple the orders they do. The CVS actually sends him its drug-compounding business; many competitors even refer simple work to Marra that any druggist could fill. A local doctor likes to prescribe a simple mix of two liquids, Maalox and Donnatal, for stomach cramps. The chains, he says, couldn't be bothered with dealing in such low-margin medicines.

"They're not really pharmacy-focused," he argues. "They're focused on selling umbrellas, because that's where the money is."

Marra's approach attracts lots of loyal customers. No matter what the drug, he will get it in no more than six hours. He gets four deliveries a day and even can tap his contacts at a local hospital. Customers also like seeing the same faces across the counter every time they come in for service. Marra says that his employees stay on the job for decades compared with the short tenures of chain-store staff, who turn over every few months.

"You come back in 2020, and I'm going to be here," he says. "We're making careers out of it."

Marra has made some product changes to capture sales in higher-margin categories. He has dabbled in housewares, which his customers are requesting. He is also considering installing a chiller so that he can offer water and soft drinks rather than send customers to CVS. But he continues to bank on his prescription business and his position as a health care provider as a way to bring in the customers who also will buy higher-margin items such as Valentine's Day gifts.

Marra may seem to have competitors assaulting him left and right. But in fact, he believes that he has dominated one market: When customers need anything special, they simply come to him, whether it's a stomach-cramp drug mix or a knee brace or a wheelchair. He's the only game in town for those products and services. With his unique approach, the giants in the Wal-Mart economy simply can't touch him.

Abt Electronics

Abt Electronics' president Mike Abt lives squarely in the Wal-Mart world. There are 12 Wal-Mart, Circuit City, and Best Buy stores within 10 miles of his single giant Glenview, Illinois, store. There are also 12 SAM'S CLUBS within 25 miles. But Abt Electronics, founded in 1936 in Chicago by Abt's grandfather, survives with a daring strategy that makes it the dominant electronics retailer in its market.

The Abt family has long emulated some of the tactics of big-box stores. The Abts offer a huge assortment under one roof—appliances, electronic goods, kitchens, and furniture. They price wares competitively, although not rock bottom. They maintain a store and warehouse of colossal proportions for a "mom and pop" outfit: 350,000 square feet, almost twice the size of an average supercenter. Contrary to conventional retail wisdom, the Abts have never opened a branch store. They have simply moved their single store to bigger and bigger locations. Their current location, opened in 2002, is their fifth and employs 1,000 people.

Vigilantly focused on reducing costs, Abt generates its own electricity during the day when local commercial electric rates are more expensive, switching back to the local power grid at 5:30 p.m. when rates go down. Since Abt is left with heaps of Styrofoam packaging after its daily deliveries to customers spread over a three-state area, it recently installed compressors to crunch the Styrofoam to one-fiftieth its original size, reducing waste volume and generating revenue from selling the compacted cubes.

Differentiation has been the key to success. "Since we have one store, we can control the total customer experience," says Mike Abt. "We have our own drivers, our own installers, and even our own in-house wood shop to make special installation panels for customers. Neither the big chains nor the mom and pop stores can do that."

"Plus, our in-store experience sets us apart. It's entertainment!" adds Abt.

This is an understatement. The Abts differentiate themselves by astonishing shoppers. The size of the store sets it apart. It is divided into showrooms for everything from refrigerators and washers to home theaters and mobile electronics. As customers walk through the front door, they spy a mammoth 25-foot-wide water fountain in a sun-bathed atrium at the back of the store. The backdrop to the video-camera display is a 7,500-gallon saltwater aquarium. The electric-colored tropical fish offer background to help customers compare camcorder color vividness and fidelity. In the atrium, computers are preloaded with video games and links to cartoon-network.com, engrossing the next generation of Abt customers while granting mom and dad time to shop.

Among the store showrooms are several dedicated to single premier brands: Sony, Bang & Olufsen, Sub-Zero, and Apple. These stores within a store allow customers to see manufacturers' broad product lines. In the 1,000-square-foot Apple store, customers can hold and test computers and iPods. In an adjoining miniauditorium, they can get software training and operating system tutorials from knowledgeable staff. The store's showroom is so remarkable that *Newsweek* called Abt Electronics "a cross between a Las Vegas hotel and a children's museum."

The Abts have developed a very well-informed, highly motivated but soft-sell workforce. Employees soak up hours of training and product information to sell the high-end products in which Abt specializes. This includes freshly minted products available nowhere else, which are provided to Abt because manufacturers have learned that the retailer will take a chance on bleeding-edge goods—and will give manufacturers honest feedback on winners and duds. Employees are also authorized to go the extra mile to win sales, even inviting negotiating to make sure that customers don't leave simply because they think prices are too high.

If this weren't enough to set the store apart, Abt also fields the most expert and extensive installation and repair crew of any store in the region. It operates 70 delivery trucks, 38 custom-installation vans, and 46 service vans. It makes 6,000 service and delivery calls a week. If a family is wondering if its den can be turned into a home theater, Abt will find a way. Its commitment to customer service is displayed on signs all around the store: "The answer is always 'YES' to any reasonable request."

By so sharply differentiating itself, Abt dominates high-end sales of scores of product categories for shoppers from all over Chicago. The Abts say that up to 10,000 customers visit on a weekend, 20,000 during special sales events. Abt reaps over $200 million in sales per year from its one store, ranking it in the top 20 appliance retailers in the country—including chains. Its customer testimonial wall displays autographed pictures and letters from many of Abt's more famous customers such as former Chicago Bear's coach Mike Ditka.

Trader Joe's

Trader Joe's is one supermarket chain that has sharply distinguished itself from the pack. The chain was launched in 1967 by Joe Colombe in the Los Angeles area. Colombe offered hard-to-find boutique-like and gourmet foods and beverages at low prices. He decorated his stores in nautical decor, asked staff to dress in Hawaiian shirts, and called store managers captains.

In 1979, the cofounder of global retailer Aldi acquired Trader Joe's, but the trademark approach to grocery retailing remained. Like Wal-Mart, Trader Joe's offers low prices and focuses intently on its customers' tastes. One of Trader Joe's signature products is Charles Shaw wine, available in merlot, cabernet sauvignon, shiraz, chardonnay, and sauvignon blanc. It is nicknamed "Two-Buck Chuck" because it costs just $2 per bottle in its native California (although slightly more elsewhere).

Trader Joe's can sell products cheaply because it sells in huge volume. Charles Shaw wine, a quality California table wine, costs so little because Trader Joe's buyers took advantage of a global glut of fine wines. Sales of "Two-Buck Chuck" have exceeded a million cases in some weeks.

Trader Joe's also has emulated Wal-Mart's expansion pattern. Still based in Los Angeles, it now has over 200 stores. It has grown by spreading out and filling in. It first filled in on the West Coast. Then it jumped from the West to the East with two stores in Boston in 1996. It now has over 80 stores in and around the major cities of Boston, Washington, and Chicago and recently opened a store in Manhattan.

Trader Joe's differentiates itself so completely that many customers wouldn't consider it a competitor to the big supermarkets or supercenters. Trader Joe's stores mainly stock unusual gourmet and specialty goods, and 80 percent of them sell under the Trader Joe's private label. Stores carry only about 2,500 items. Trader Joe's introduces about 20 items a week and removes about 20 slow movers. Shoppers never know quite what will appear. The store even breaks accepted supermarket rules of publishing weekly ad circulars, opting for a quarterly "infozine," the *Fearless Flyer*, that runs stories about Trader Joe's products.

The 10,000-square-foot stores are far smaller than supermarkets, which stock, on average, 30,000 to 60,000 different goods. The Hawaiian shirt–clad staff often prepares new items for sampling, soliciting direct feedback from customers. This practice is key to keeping a conversation going in the store. Conversation flows easier because customers are urged to give staff honest opinions of Trader Joe's products.

Trader Joe's target customer is well educated and affluent, health conscious and choosy, likely to read labels and value the global search by Trader Joe's buyers to find interesting new items. Trader Joe's prides itself on offering organic, kosher, vegetarian, and luxury items—each with a story to its appearance on the shelves.

As Trader Joe's expands, it increasingly dominates the market for high-end, healthy, bargain-priced gourmet and exotic foods. It is likely to continue to succeed with national expansion as it out-classes supermarkets with exotic offerings, underprices specialty shops with gourmet foods, and out-entertains most competitors with chatty salespeople and products that intrigue and educate.

Costco Wholesale

An even larger-scale success story in the Wal-Mart economy is Costco Wholesale. Costco emulates many of the same industry strategies as Wal-Mart's SAM'S CLUB. Both initially targeted small businesses as their core constituency before expanding to individual consumers. They sell a limited number of goods in bulk quantities, use their huge volume to win better prices from suppliers, and sell memberships both to earn more income and to encourage loyalty.

Like Sam Walton, Costco founder Jim Sinegal remains obsessed with lowering prices. As a result, both SAM'S CLUB and Costco use advanced systems to order, ship, and distribute products. They both press suppliers for the lowest possible cost. Cardinal rule number one at Costco is limiting the markup on products to 15 percent—compared with the supermarket convention of 25 percent and department store practice of 50 percent or more.

To keep its cost structure down, Costco doesn't advertise, has no public relations department, and offers little sales help. Just the savings on advertising amounts to 2 percent of costs. Its total selling, general, and administrative expenses are under 10 percent, compared with Wal-Mart's overall figure of 18 percent. Sinegal takes a salary of only $350,000, a pittance for a company of Costco's size (although he holds or has options on four million shares of Costco stock).

But Costco has differentiated itself enough from Wal-Mart and SAM'S CLUB that many of its customers wouldn't consider shopping at the other stores. Like Trader Joe's, Costco goes after customers who make more money. The average household income of customers is $66,000, compared with $60,000 at SAM'S CLUB. A quarter of Costco's members earn over $100,000. For these customers, Sinegal offers not just low prices but also a mix of higher-quality merchandise.

Costco demonstrates how a big competitor in an industry with one dominant player can win its own place in the market by taking a somewhat different approach. Although price remains the most important element in Wal-Mart's value proposition, value remains the cornerstone of Costco's. Shoppers can expect terrific prices for quality dog food as well as quality diamonds. Costco also recognized years ago that its primary customer was the consumer—as opposed to the business member—and oriented its product selection accordingly. It differentiated itself from SAM'S CLUB, which has flipped back and forth between consumers and business members as the primary target.

Lest the low prices of Costco goods by themselves fail to keep customers interested, Costco stresses the "treasure hunt" in its stores. It stocks only about 4,000 items, and it rotates about 1,000. Every time a shopper visits, the store will have new and irresistible unadvertised deals. Along with the omnipresent pallets of toilet paper, batteries, and copier paper, the store recently offered 19-foot-long inflatable water slides, a pergola, and even caskets! In search of surprises, shoppers come back to Costco stores once every 4.7 weeks on average compared with once every 6.5 weeks at SAM'S CLUB.

Despite the dominance of Wal-Mart in discount retailing, Costco dominates warehouse-style discounting. Costco enjoys a 47 percent market share even though it operates less than one-third of the club stores in this country. That compares to SAM'S CLUB, which owns over half of the U.S. club stores but has a lower 44 percent market share. Costco's annual member renewal rate is 86 percent compared to an estimate of the mid-70s at SAM'S CLUB. It sells $909 per square foot compared with $542 at SAM'S CLUB and $442 at BJ's Wholesale Club. In this retail niche, Wal-Mart is runner-up.

Tesco

Another example of a major retailer giving Wal-Mart a run for its money is Tesco, the largest retailer in the United Kingdom. Wal-Mart's U.K. chain, ASDA, trails Tesco in total U.K. retail grocery market share by 31 percent to 16 percent. In a delicious irony for American competitors, Wal-Mart actually called on the U.K. government to launch an investigation of Tesco for its domination of the U.K. supermarket sector. Tesco is so powerful that 60 percent of U.K. shoppers said in a recent survey that Tesco's growing power worried them.

In the United Kingdom, Wal-Mart has not won a resounding victory with its trademark EDLP approach. It recently removed its chief of U.K. operations, the implication being that he hadn't come up with a winning strategy against Tesco. Meanwhile, Tesco has expanded in recent years from its grocery base into nonfood items, Internet and mobile phone services, and even a pure-play discount store in 2005. It is forcing Wal-Mart to fight an uphill battle as ASDA expands its food business.

Two factors sharply differentiate Tesco from ASDA. One is that Tesco runs a sophisticated loyalty-card operation. Although it emulates Wal-Mart's knack for gathering mountains of data on individual customer buying patterns, it differs in one noticeable way: Tesco knows who is pushing the cart, not just what is in the cart. It then awards Clubcard points, which at certain thresholds trigger the issuance of vouchers and coupons tailored to each shopper. The company can offer 80,000 different combinations of special deals.

Tesco has 12 million cardholders. It divides them into customer groups of "mainstream," "finer foods," "healthy," or "price sensitive." Clubcard members also can join one of five special clubs—for healthy eating, kids merchandise, baby products, wine, and food. They then get additional special offers—along with free magazines, money-off coupons, recipes, and even free gifts for kids.

Another differentiating feature is that Tesco sells three lines of private-label goods: a "value" brand, a Tesco brand, and an upscale "Finest" label. With such extensive private labeling, Tesco believes that it delivers greater value to shoppers across the economic spectrum. Its higher margins on the Finest brand help it to lower prices on the value brand. Both brands have been highly successful. The company says that 80 percent of shoppers buy its value brand and 70 percent its Finest brand. Most buy both.

With 1,900 stores in the United Kingdom (and a total of 2,700 worldwide), Tesco is indeed the dominant U.K. retailing power. It earned £1.6 billion on sales of £39.5 billion in 2006 and announced plans to launch a chain of convenience stores on the U.S. West Coast. On the one hand, Tesco demonstrates that competitors can challenge Wal-Mart and thrive, even on a nationwide basis. On the other hand, it shows that the Wal-Mart economy is a global economy, although in the United Kingdom it might go by another name—the Tesco economy. In this case, Wal-Mart is in the position of figuring out how to differentiate, emulate, and dominate.

SMART COMPETITOR CHOICES

We cannot simply blame the demise of companies in the Wal-Mart economy on fierce competition. Dominant companies have succeeded by making clear choices. Competitors need to do the same—explicitly and intentionally—to win in this economy.

Avoiding choices puts every business at risk.

The Kmart of the 1990s didn't choose to differentiate. Instead, it sometimes tried to be the price leader, like Wal-Mart. Other times, it tried to be a product trend setter, akin to Target, through relationships with brands such as Martha Stewart. In the months before bankruptcy, it tried to do both.

Kmart didn't consistently select a subset of Wal-Mart's best practices to emulate either. It tried to implement a perpetual inventory system with computer-based ordering, but it didn't have the strong-process organization to execute the system by keeping inventory counts accurate.

And Kmart didn't select a segment of the market to dominate. It had many valuable urban locations. It could have chosen to become the favored retailer for urban America, a niche that has been wide open for a mass retailer like Kmart to address efficiently. As Adamson, the turnaround CEO remarked, "Its strategy should have been catering to inner-city customers and differentiating itself in the market. That was Kmart's point of difference."

The lessons from Kmart are appropriate for businesses of all sizes. The imperative of making choices is urgent. Digging in, redoubling efforts to do more of the same, and taking a run at the giant head-on do not constitute a workable approach whether for big, midsized, or mom-and-pop businesses. Instead, we must choose to differentiate, emulate, and dominate.

When we don't choose, we risk not only failure but also embarrassment. When Kmart, under Mark Schwartz and Charles Conaway, settled on the strategy to run directly at Wal-Mart, the company flaunted its challenge at its Rogers, Arkansas, Super K store. The company trumpeted the renaissance of BlueLight pricing just 10 minutes from Wal-Mart headquarters and across the street from a Wal-Mart supercenter.

Instead of showcasing its savvy—instead of carving out its own identity and its own market—the company brazenly bulled its way onto the home turf of its industry's dominant competitor. On January 14, 2003, as part of Kmart's bankruptcy reorganization, Kmart announced that it would close hundreds of stores. On the closure list, the Rogers Super K was number 13. Kmart had lost its way—right under the eyes of its biggest rival—all because the company didn't make smart choices in the Wal-Mart economy.

Chapter 6

Leverage, Invest, Diversify

The Supplier's Bargain

Not long after he took over as chief executive of Levi Strauss & Co. in 1999, Philip Marineau prescribed five key strategies to turn around the ailing company. The situation certainly required a galvanizing new regimen. In 1996, Levi's sales peaked at $7.1 billion. By the time Marineau arrived, the number had plunged to $5.1 billion. A major global apparel icon was struggling for life.

With Levi in the corporate intensive-care unit, Marineau and his team began emergency treatment. They stressed efforts to improve innovation, operations, retail partnerships, and financial strength. They also announced a new marketing and sales strategy: "Sell where people shop."

Sell where people shop?

It's one of those simple ideas that companies often never fully grasp. The once-hip maker of jeans and casual wear had not kept up with the way people buy clothes. So much so that when Marineau arrived, Levi was selling its denim in only 50 percent of retail markets where people buy jeanswear—mainly in department stores, specialty stores, and Levi Strauss storefronts. The company was absent from the other 50 percent of the market.

Amazingly, the once omnipresent 150-year-old brand of blue jeans, the choice of cowboys, Bruce Springsteen, and just about everyone else, was entirely missing the chance to put itself in front of the 160 million people who at that time shopped mass merchants such as Wal-Mart every week.

Levi Strauss executives had reasons for avoiding Wal-Mart. They fretted that sales at a mass-market retailer would cheapen the Levi brand image. They worried that the big discounter would squeeze them for thinner margins. Further, they were concerned that selling economy-class slacks would cannibalize sales of their higher-end denim products.

The company brass's marketing vision, however, was something shy of 20/20. Fewer and fewer people were visiting department and specialty stores. Surveys at the time showed that sales at such traditional outlets were shrinking, drawing only 14 percent of women's casual sportswear buyers compared to 19 percent at the mass merchants. Levi couldn't possibly ramp its sales up in markets where sales were ramping down.

The story of the near collapse of Levi Strauss illustrates a dilemma faced by all suppliers in the Wal-Mart economy. If they don't sell to the giants, they can get forced into markets with subpar growth. If they do, they can get caught degrading their brand and whacking their margins. Stories abound about Wal-Mart making impossible requests of its suppliers: "Give me a lower price every year, or I'll give all my shelf space to your competitor." Suppliers have to be wary.

Marineau and his team took a risk. They knew that they had been shutting themselves out of a growing market. By opening the mass-merchant door, they could supply sales channels accounting for 80 percent of the jeanswear market versus the 50 percent they currently served. Thus, in the summer of 2003, they began shipping jeans to Wal-Mart. They introduced the new Signature brand into 3,000 stores.

Of course, nobody can say whether Marineau deserved a pat on the back or not. In the company's annual report to the Securities and Exchange Commission, Levi executives admitted that the decision might "adversely affect the perception and appeal" of the Levi brand.

They conceded that Levi Strauss might "face demands from mass-channel retailers for wholesale prices ... we cannot offer on a ... profitable basis."

Confident the company's turnaround is heading in the right direction, Marineau planned to retire at the end of 2006. But the long-term fate of Levi Strauss is unknown. What we learn from the company's decisions is that suppliers to the giants of industry such as Wal-Mart have to make some tough choices. Although the deck is stacked in favor of the giants, we can make smart choices to thrive by feeding the bear *and* keeping it at bay.

In this chapter we look at the challenges faced by Levi and other suppliers in the face of dominant customers. We examine the triad of specific choices we all must make as suppliers to win. And we meet some highly successful suppliers who have made smart choices to survive and thrive.

THE SCALES OF ECONOMIC JUSTICE

Harvard Business School Professor Michael Porter developed a compelling way to view the dynamics of industries with dominant players. Porter argued that the competitive structure within an industry is a function of five specific forces: the threat of new entrants, the threat of substitute products, rivalry among existing competitors, the bargaining power of buyers, and the bargaining power of suppliers. Among other things, he said, "industry structure ... determines who keeps what proportion of the value a product creates for buyers."

Levi Strauss discovered the stark reality of Porter's model. In an economy with dominant players, the bargaining power has shifted dramatically in favor of the giants, the buyers, relative to the bargaining power of vendors, the suppliers. The buyers, namely, Wal-Mart and other giants, are in a position to get an outsized say in determining who captures the bulk of value in the marketplace. The scales of economic justice are not equally balanced.

One of the reasons Wal-Mart and other dominant players have such bargaining power is that they concentrate buying in just a few firm's hands and they buy in huge volumes. Bain & Company research, for example, studied 38 publicly traded companies that sell more than 10 percent of their product through Wal-Mart. The companies included American Greetings (13 percent of sales to Wal-Mart), Atari (26 percent), Clorox (27 percent), Del Monte (29 percent), Kimberly-Clark (13 percent), Hasbro (21 percent), Leapfrog Enterprises (28 percent), and Revlon (21 percent).

Wal-Mart claims such a huge share of sales in some markets that many companies simply have no choice but to woo the giant. Wal-Mart holds 36 percent of the market for dog food, 32 percent for disposable diapers, 30 percent for film, 26 percent for toothpaste, and 21 percent for pain remedies. Wal-Mart is the place where consumers buy 32 percent of their wireless phone handsets, 37 percent of their DVDs, and 22 percent of consumer electronics. Every supplier knows the rule of thumb: To the volume leader goes the bargaining power.

Another reason dominant players such as Wal-Mart have such bargaining power is that they can switch to other suppliers easily. The giants' cost of switching generally is low. In retail, the cost for a buyer to switch to another vendor's offering of a brand-insensitive product such as maraschino cherries or wooden pencils is the cost of printing one new purchase order. With so many suppliers vying for such a big chunk of business, new vendors always are willing to lowball the business to get their feet in the door. While over 61,000 suppliers do business with Wal-Mart today, thousands more probably would like to if only they could get an order.

As dominant players expand their economic habitats, integrating backward up the supply chain gives them further bargaining clout.

With every passing year, Wal-Mart edges up its supply chain to displace suppliers' businesses. Wal-Mart is growing organic cotton in fields in Turkey. It is developing and pitching new product ideas back to vendors. It is increasing its direct sourcing of overseas apparel and home furnishings. For example, Wal-Mart's direct sourcing of bed and bath products grew by 40 percent in 2005 and the company plans to assume an additional 30 percent over the next few years. In such a world, no vendor wants to get on the wrong side of the giant.

Despite the awesome bargaining power of dominant players such as Wal-Mart, we would make a grave mistake to view them as omnipotent. Wal-Mart and other titans in the Wal-Mart world absolutely depend on their suppliers for success. Wal-Mart admitted as much back when it launched its first supplier partnership with Procter & Gamble. The two companies' executives sat down and discussed intimate details of each other's operations to see where they could improve quality and cut costs together.

Because Wal-Mart depends on its suppliers, it leaves room for suppliers to take the initiative to increase their share of the bargaining power. For one thing, giants depend on suppliers to consistently deliver a flow of great products and new innovations. When Faultless Starch discovered from Retail Link data that sales of its spray-on starch were higher along the Mexican border, it proactively developed a line of starch for the Mexican market. Faultless now claims a one-third share of the U.S. starch market and a 10 percent global share.

Dominant players also rely on suppliers to whip up consumer demand for products. Apple Computer is a good example of a supplier creating demand that no dominant industry player could ever hope to generate. While Apple runs its own retail stores, it also sells iPods and related accessories through Costco, Radio Shack, Wal-Mart, and other retailers. The buzz Apple spawned over its iPod technology created such demand among consumers that retailers vie to court Apple for the right to sell limited allotments of the hottest Apple products.

A third way giants depend on suppliers is to supply top-quality brands that shoppers demand. Wal-Mart executives have repeatedly reaffirmed the company's merchandising strategy to attract shoppers with national brands, whether those brands come as diapers or dishes or DVD players. Wal-Mart executives know that there is no substitute for the drawing power of great brands. While Apple creates incredible technology, it also wields a brand that enhances Apple's value and pulls shoppers into Wal-Mart stores. The iPod brand is so strong that one Apple store manager confided to me that the majority of first-time Apple computer buyers last year were converted to Apple by their experience with their iPod players.

The power of any dominant player, including Wal-Mart, is kept in check to the extent it depends on vendors to create and build strong brands. Not all brands are the same, of course. There are the traditional national brands, such as Tide and Crest, that are heavily advertised by Procter & Gamble and highly demanded by shoppers. There are global brands, such as Jumex and Goya, that offer a wide range of products appealing primarily to Hispanic consumers. There are regional brands, such as CDM, a chickory-accented coffee popular along the Gulf Coast. There are controlled brands, such as President's Choice, that are minimally advertised but well stocked by specific retailers. And there are private-label brands, such as Wal-Mart's Sam's Choice or Costco's Kirkland, that are made expressly for single retailers.

A giant such as Wal-Mart needs these brands to be relevant to its customers. If we manufacture "Bill's Laundry Detergent," which has no brand recognition among consumers, we largely depend on Wal-Mart. But if we are Procter & Gamble and make Tide, the perennial number one laundry detergent brand in 11 countries, Wal-Mart needs us. Since Wal-Mart could not satisfy its own customers if it left Tide off the shelf, Wal-Mart doesn't retain all the bargaining power for detergent.

A fourth way that dominant players depend on suppliers is to create unexpected value for the giant. General Electric's managing of light bulb inventories for Wal-Mart reduces the giant's inventory cost without incremental overhead. Wal-Mart vendors such as Elizabeth Arden and Manco both serve as category advisors, managing assortments in the cosmetics and hardware categories, respectively, to generate the most profitable product mix.

Despite the dependence of dominant players on suppliers, the bargaining power still balances in favor of the giant. Earlier in my career I advised debtors and creditors in multi-billion-dollar debt-restructuring deals. I observed a phenomenon I call the *greed-versus-fear tradeoff.* When each party's level of greed reached a balance with its fear of what it could lose if it pushed negotiations further, the negotiation reached equilibrium. In the Wal-Mart economy, Wal-Mart and other dominant industry players can instill more fear than suppliers.

At bargaining sessions, the dominants simply have more threats to bring to the negotiating table. Wal-Mart, for example, can threaten to award the business to another supplier, launch its own private label, or contract directly with Chinese factories. Like tough older brothers choosing sides in a pickup game of soccer, Wal-Mart buyers and buyers for other dominant companies will readily overlook relationships to choose the best player for the team.

One of the most threatening things Wal-Mart does is require vendor transparency. Wal-Mart buyers will ask to see suppliers' costs and other data. Buyers then rate suppliers with vendor scorecards, evaluating everything from inventory levels to on-time delivery rates. Good grades get awarded when vendors show steady progress in eliminating wasted spending, including materials, manufacturing, and shipping costs.

The risk to suppliers comes from exposing so much data. The industry giant can learn the secrets of the supplier's business—and use the valuable inside information to creep backwards up the supply chain. Levi Strauss CEO Marineau no doubt wrestled with the risk that Wal-Mart would launch its own private-label products to compete with Levi. Wal-Mart, after all, became privy to Levi Strauss sourcing procedures, cost structure, and marketing secrets.

The private-label threat is hardly an idle one. After Wal-Mart learned about the dog-food business from Purina, it launched its Ol' Roy brand. Made by Doane Pet Care (recently purchased by Mars, Inc.), Ol' Roy long ago displaced Purina Dog Chow as the alpha dog of canine chows by outselling Purina in volume. The Ol' Roy dog-food coup is a tale told repeatedly to remind suppliers of Wal-Mart's competitiveness. When Ocean Spray began supplying a 64-ounce bottle of white cranberry juice, Wal-Mart launched a Sam's Choice brand version, at $1.98, underpricing Ocean Spray's $2.50 bottle by 52 cents.

As suppliers in a Wal-Mart world, we face an uphill battle. The scales of economic justice tilt in favor of dominant industry players like Wal-Mart. But we have plenty of flexibility to win because we do control some of the variables in the supplier-customer equation. Our challenge is to make conscious, intentional decisions to shift those variables in our favor—and shift the scales of power back to our side.

FORMULA FOR WINNING

Even before we think about *how* to do business with Wal-Mart or other dominant players, we have to weigh one other explicit choose-or-lose decision—*whether* to sell to the industry giant at all. The risks of giving up proprietary information and strategies, of overinvesting in plant and equipment, and of becoming beholden to the giant may far outweigh the potential returns. Some suppliers have consciously elected to keep certain product classifications and entire lines out of the discount channel. Examples are high-end Sony electronics, luxury fashion brands such as Armani and Akris, and department-store cosmetics brands such as Clinique.

So we face an important decision right from the start, another greed-versus-fear tradeoff. Do we take the chance of playing with the bear, at the risk of getting eaten?

If we decide that supplying to companies such as Wal-Mart is important to the success of our business, we then can devise our strategy for *how* to supply the dominant player in our industry by making three explicit choices:

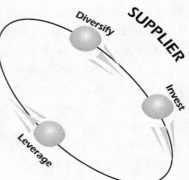

- What to *leverage*
- How to *invest*
- Where to *diversify*

Leverage. Invest. Diversify. These three imperatives form the triad of choices we all have to make as suppliers to profit in the Wal-Mart economy. By anticipating those choices, we can first decide whether to supply the giant at all. By making and committing to them, we can craft a new strategy to win.

Leverage

During NASA's Apollo missions to the moon, the spacecrafts' flight paths and rocket-engine burns were carefully designed to leverage the moon's gravity both to pull the spacecraft early in the mission and then to slingshot the spacecraft back toward the earth upon its return. In the event a spacecraft became disabled, this "free return" trajectory would enable the astronauts to return safely to earth with virtually no propulsion — a feature that probably saved the lives of the Apollo 13 astronauts. In the same way, we can use Wal-Mart or another dominant player's strengths to amplify our own.

The first critical choice for suppliers is *what strengths of the giant to leverage*. We need to determine which strengths fit our strategy. We then need to take advantage of those strengths to drive value into our own businesses. Whereas the choice to emulate best practices in the last chapter enabled us to compete against industry giants, the choice to leverage the giant's strengths actually enhances our own performance and therefore our relationships with other customers besides the giant.

Many suppliers find that leveraging a superb operator's practices gets everyone's motivational juices flowing. As a very amateur golfer with a 23 handicap, I notice that I generally raise my game a few notches when I play with much better players. Suppliers similarly can leverage the dominant player's strengths to raise their business operations game, accelerate momentum for self-improvement, and even gain an advantage over the giant.

In a study for the Grocery Manufacturers Association, McKinsey & Company found that winning consumer goods suppliers in the Wal-Mart world perform at a peak level in three or more of six categories: pricing, running an effective supply chain, in-store execution, promotion, sales organization and processes, and managing key accounts and channels. The first three of these six attributes clearly leverage Wal-Mart's core strengths. Companies that outperformed their peers in three or more of the six categories raised operating margins twice as fast on all of their business—not just Wal-Mart's—without spending any more on selling. In addition, winning companies delivered outsized gains in productivity, selling $4.6 million per full-time equivalent (FTE) versus $2.0 million for other organizations.

McKinsey also found that winning vendors leveraged Wal-Mart's extensive information technology strengths. Eighty-six percent of winning suppliers in the retail sector receive store-level data compared with only 67 percent of other companies. Eighty-six percent of winners get share data compared with only 27 percent of other companies. One hundred percent get data on stock-outs; only 73 percent of others do. The winners not only look at sales and market share, but they also monitor pricing, promotion, and in-store execution.

A multiyear study of supplier relationships by Bain & Co. found that Wal-Mart suppliers who are able to retain healthy sales margins succeeded on four variables. Two of those four variables, making the most of Wal-Mart's supply-chain expertise and using a sales team in Bentonville to manage a lean cost structure, confirm the importance of leveraging the giants' strengths.

Invest

We had a saying in the troubled debt-workout business: "If you borrow a little, the bank owns you. If you borrow a lot, you own the bank." In other words, when a loan is not material to a bank's portfolio, the bank plays hardball with you and pushes you to the wall because it holds the cards. However, when your loan *is* material to the bank, the bargaining power shifts. If your company fails, the bank suffers a significant hit to its earnings. As a result, the bank is much more amenable to negotiating an amicable modification to the loan terms.

The lesson is just as applicable to us as suppliers in any industry with a dominant player. If the giants rely on us a little, they own us. If they rely on us a lot, the bargaining power shifts back toward us. The key is to *make the giant need us more by determining how to invest to rebalance the scales.* We have to play to their dependency on us for building end-user demand, for building brands, for creating unexpected value, and for innovating.

Building end-user demand effectively bypasses the giant to appeal directly to its customers. Pharmaceutical companies have achieved significant growth by advertising maladies (from erectile dysfunction to acid reflux), positioning their products as the cure, and then pulling the demand through giant health care systems and physician groups. Cable TV networks advertise niche channels such as ESPNU, marketing them directly to consumers in the hope of fueling a grass-roots consumer effort to demand the channel from local cable providers.

Brand building is another investment that tilts the bargaining power back in our favor as suppliers. Strong brands create emotional connections with customers. These connections "pull" products through the giants' supply pipelines. Established companies such as Procter & Gamble continue to invest in their well-known brands so that customers will continue to demand them from retailers. Other suppliers invest heavily to stimulate new demand. Intel's reputation with computer users, burnished with "Intel Inside" advertising, pulls significant chip production through industry giants such as Dell and Apple.

Sometimes brand building actually involves brand winnowing: Less is more. Global consumer goods manufacturer Unilever marketed 1,600 brands in the 1990s. Today it markets just 200, names such as Dove, Hellmann's, Lipton, and Ben & Jerry's. By jettisoning brand weaklings, it could invest much more in building awareness, knowledge, and image of its big names.

We also can invest in services that create unexpected value for the giants. One supplier to the claims departments of major auto insurance companies developed a unique Web-based service that enables the insurance claims adjuster to satisfy an auto theft claim instantly while handing over the repairs to the supplier. The service created value for the insurance companies by closing claims more quickly—and thereby satisfying the insurers' customers.

Private-label soft-drink bottler Cott is an example of a supplier that innovates to create value for retailers. Cott Corporation began working with Wal-Mart in 1991, offering a cut-rate, premium-quality Sam's Choice brand cola based on the venerable RC brand formulation. Cott not only owns its beverage formulas, but it also employs its own talent for developing retailer packaging, graphics, labeling, and brand image—valuable services sought out by giants such as Wal-Mart.

Of the four critical variables in the Bain & Co. study of successful Wal-Mart suppliers, two underscore the importance of investing to rebalance the scales: understanding and targeting pricing to Wal-Mart's specific customers and innovating constantly to keep products and brands unique and in demand.

Diversify

Every supplier faces a choice that is critical to survival: *where to diversify away from the industry giant*. Because industry concentration is a fact of life in the Wal-Mart economy, we always face the problem of selling too much to a single big player. More simply, we have put too many eggs in one basket. We not only become beholden to one customer, but we often also put our entire business at risk. The first question to ask is, How many eggs in one basket is too many? The second is, How do we find other baskets?

I know firsthand that putting too many eggs in one basket can have devastating consequences. When Kmart canceled its supply contract with Fleming after I left, Fleming was unable to withstand the loss of 20 percent of its business and filed for bankruptcy. Although Fleming had done its best to balance its bargaining power with Kmart, successfully anticipating the problem was small consolation when Fleming collapsed owing to Kmart's woes.

When is concentration with one customer too much? Simply put: When we need the giant so much that we can't walk away from the business and survive. There is a good rule of thumb for determining how much is too much. We cross that threshold when the loss of the gross margin from any customer would cause our operating profit to turn negative.

The choice of where to diversify as a supplier requires an explicit effort to look at alternatives. We can evaluate new markets in which the giant doesn't play. We can seek out channels of distribution that bypass the giant. We can design an exclusive product with additional value-added features to sell through those alternate channels. We can develop or acquire products the giant doesn't need and sell them elsewhere. In every case, our objective is to increase our total sales more rapidly than the giant's share.

Levi Strauss created its Signature brand jeans for distribution in Wal-Mart's mass segment, but it still works to expand sales of its Dockers and Levi brands through its own stores and higher-end retailers. While Henkel Consumer Adhesives (Manco's successor) still sells duct tape through Wal-Mart and other giant retailers, it bought Ohio Sealants, Inc., a firm that makes sealing and caulk products for the building industry to diversify sales into new markets.

Incidentally, to keep pushing the negotiating balance back in our favor as suppliers, we always should have a well-planned exit strategy. The strategy should include not only plans to pursue alternate channels and customers but also plans for immediate shutdown of facilities, cancellation of outsourced capacity, and reductions in workforce. If we are not prepared to walk away from even our biggest customer, with a plan to survive the crisis, the scales will be tipped against us forever.

Vendors who maintain huge shares with Wal-Mart or any other single dominant player run a calculated risk. Cott is one of them, with 41 percent of its production shipped to Wal-Mart. Hasbro is another. If Hasbro were to lose its sales to Wal-Mart, it would have to nearly double sales to its next two biggest customers, Toys "R" Us and Target, to maintain the status quo. Given the near impossibility of that challenge, the choices of leveraging and investing become all the more important.

WINNING SUPPLIERS IN THE NEW ECONOMY

Despite horror stories in the press about the collapse of suppliers in the Wal-Mart economy, we can survive and thrive in the face of giants. Let's look in detail at a few supplier success stories from the Wal-Mart world. Together they demonstrate how winning companies have succeeded by using the triad of strategic choices, deciding what strengths to leverage, how to invest, and where to diversify.

Michael Farms

Todd Michael manages Michael Farms in Urbana, Ohio, along with his two brothers, a sister, and a brother-in-law. The farm, started by Michael's father in 1958, covers 2,300 acres. It supplies potatoes, corn, cabbage, beans, beets, and other vegetables to supermarkets and supercenters such as Meijer, Wal-Mart, and Kroger.

Michael is the largest potato farmer in the state. As a past president of the National Potato Council, he also helped to navigate the Mr. Potato Head helium balloon in its debut in the Macy's Thanksgiving Day Parade in New York City. He grows Reba and Superior potatoes, two round, white table varieties.

The Michael family was one of the first to leverage the increasing sophistication of the shipping operations of various retailers three decades ago. Taking advantage of nearby retail distribution centers, the Michaels arranged vegetable shipments on the back-hauls of retail truck fleets, now a common practice. Seventy percent of the Michaels' potatoes are cross-docked, a process whereby pallets of product are unloaded from a truck at a retailer warehouse and loaded directly onto a truck bound for a store. This process cuts freight costs, avoids warehouse handling costs, and speeds shipment while extending the shelf-life of the vegetables.

The Michaels have invested in new shipping techniques to create value for their giant customers. The Michaels stack their potatoes on double pallets, each pallet piled with a hundred 10-pound bags stacked only 2.5 feet high. The pallets make attractive and convenient displays for grocers to wheel directly from truck to store floor, avoiding the handling of bags a second time. Both Meijer and Wal-Mart use the double pallets, now a common sight at nearby markets.

The Michaels sold their potatoes under the Buckeye brand for 60 years (starting with Todd's grandfather) but began to receive pressure from retailers to cut prices—the stores can get potatoes from many suppliers. Michael and his two brothers, all graduates of nearby Ohio State University (OSU) in Columbus, decided to invest in branding their potatoes under their beloved OSU Buckeye logo. The OSU Buckeyes are the only major university football power in the state.

The Michaels landed the first OSU license to sell produce under the Buckeye brand, and they have sold potatoes for two seasons with the university's scarlet and gray mark. Their investment in the brand—an 8 percent royalty to OSU—shifted the bargaining power back in their favor. Many Ohio-based consumers prefer the locally grown appeal of the brand, so the Michaels were able to increase prices 10 percent. Ultimately, selling under this OSU brand also helps them to compete with the big national brands such as Green Giant and Dole that enjoy greater consumer trust.

During the first two years, sales convinced Michael that he had a winner. "One customer reported a 30 percent increase in sales the first week and 13 percent over standard the second week," he says. "That's what showed me we could generate increased sales with packaging."

Fall 2006 was his third year selling the OSU brand, which he uses for 25 percent of a roughly 10,000-ton harvest. "Our marketing season is during the fall, so it works pretty well with all the enthusiastic football fans over in Columbus," he says. The new branded bag "stimulates some increased sales without discounting the price."

Michael has joined with Wal-Mart for two seasons to highlight the big retailer's purchase of local produce. Ohio State cheerleaders and the "Buckeye Man" mascot have kicked off a week-long promotion at a Columbus supercenter, which included sponsorship from the state of Ohio's "Ohio Proud" program to sell state produce. The "Ohio Proud" chef of the year prepared two potato recipes. Michael plans to continue the promotion.

The Michael brothers may be small suppliers in the eyes of big retailers, but they realized that they could sell potatoes not just as a commodity but as a branded product. They even sought to follow up their OSU brainstorm by launching a Cleveland Browns versus Cincinnati Bengals brand bag—featuring the two big pro-football teams in the state. But the National Football League's upfront $75,000 royalty payment was cost prohibitive.

Like many farmers, Todd Michael and his brothers are naturals at diversifying their sales. In addition to operating its own retail outlet, the Michaels sell about 25 percent of their crop to Meijer, 10 percent to Wal-Mart, and the rest to Kroger and other grocers. Investing in their brand, an Ohio namesake burnished with the logo of the state's favorite footballers, is key to Michael's strategy to keep the business healthy.

Manco

Jack Kahl received his first order from Wal-Mart in 1976, after he and Wal-Mart buyer Gary Broach met at a trade show. The CEO of Manco, who in Chapter 2 struggled with bonded towers of duct tape, followed a disciplined strategy to build his business from under $1 million in sales when he purchased Manco in 1971 to over $180 million when he sold it to The Henkel Group in 1998. By riding the coattails of Wal-Mart's growth, Kahl presided over the business as it grew over 22 percent annually for 27 years.

Besides partnering with the world's most successful retailer, Kahl credits his success to how he leveraged the culture, strategies, and systems of Sam Walton. His efforts won the company five Wal-Mart "Supplier of the Year" awards in the hardware, stationery, paint, and housewares categories. His leveraging efforts also won him "Vendor of the Year" awards from Ace Hardware, Target, and Staples.

Along with embracing the productivity loop, one of Kahl's key moves was embracing Wal-Mart tools, especially Retail Link. His company was one of the early vendor pioneers connected to the system and he took pride in leveraging its information. On the wall outside the executive offices is a sign: "The war is between assets and information. The nerds have won."

Manco was so good with information that Wal-Mart appointed it category advisor for several categories, including hardware. With Wal-Mart's point-of-sale data, Manco isolates hot sellers, manages inventories to keep them in stock 24/7, and takes steps such as positioning the best-selling products (from any manufacturer in the category) at eye level on shelves so that customers can snatch them quickly. By leveraging its early experience as a category advisor, Manco was better able to serve both Wal-Mart and its other retail customers with sophisticated category management capabilities.

Manco and Wal-Mart once investigated why one of its winterizing products sold great in some places and languished elsewhere.

Stores in Texas and Oklahoma sold thousands; stores in Minnesota, Ohio, and Michigan sold only a few. Kahl's team discovered that building codes in the North had certain requirements that made the Manco product superfluous. In southern markets, homeowners rushed to Wal-Mart to buy the product at the first sign of cold weather. Through such investments in research, Manco was able both to understand consumer behavior and to shift Wal-Mart's inventory closer to where it was needed.

As Kahl built on Wal-Mart's culture and systems, he invested heavily in his own brands, especially the Duck brand of duct tape. He didn't have the money for big-time advertising, so he adopted guerilla marketing tactics. Four times a year, the unit mails cards to store managers featuring a duck in a funny cartoon (incidentally, the Thanksgiving card can never show a cooked bird). The company sponsors a duct tape festival in Avon, Ohio, featuring duct tape sculptures, games, and a comedy show by the "Duct Tape Guys." It runs an annual duct tape prom dress competition, for which a best-dressed couple modeling outfits made of duct tape receives a $3,000 college scholarship per winner.

Kahl strengthened his business by diversifying. He diversified his sales to other retailers, such as Ace Hardware, Office Max, and Lowes. He diversified by investing in new brands, growing beyond adhesives into stationery and housewares. As mentioned earlier in the chapter, Manco's successor, Henkel Consumer Adhesives, recently continued the diversification by acquiring Sovereign Specialty Chemical and its Ohio Sealants, Inc. division.

One example of brand diversification is the Duck brand of mailing supplies, which Kahl built from scratch. Kahl first partnered with Sealed Air Corporation to leverage and utilize a line of padded packaging and envelopes. He coupled that with a line of mailing supplies from 12 manufacturers—36 products ranging from cutters and kraft paper to sealing tape and mailing tubes. All the products sell under the Duck brand. The popular line helped Kahl balance his bargaining power by diversifying away from Wal-Mart; he also sold the line to office supply retailers such as Office Max and Staples.

Kahl's former Manco unit has continued to blossom, now offering 600 base products which it packages into 2,500 SKUs to suit different retailers. The unit is a model of how suppliers can thrive in the Wal-Mart economy: It leverages the retailer's culture of thrift, its productivity loop, and its information systems. It invests in strong, independent brands that compete with the likes of 3M. And it maintains a strong base of business with diverse customers, products, and sales channels.

Procter & Gamble

Procter & Gamble (P&G) is probably the most written about supplier to Wal-Mart. Articles in the press often focus on the Cincinnati-based company's partnership with Wal-Mart, how it leverages Wal-Mart's best practices, its Retail Link expertise, and its office near Wal-Mart headquarters. But the more useful story is how P&G has employed all three parts of the triad together, consistently leveraging, investing, and diversifying at the same time to balance its bargaining power with the giant.

P&G is at the forefront of a trend that blurs the boundaries between merchandiser and manufacturer. It has combined its own data-analysis expertise with Wal-Mart's rich transaction data to find ways to boost sales one store and one customer at a time. In its own lingo, P&G works together with customers "to improve the in-store presence of our products and win the 'first moment of truth'—when a consumer is shopping in the store." Like other manufacturers, it has found that it cannot build brands just by running ads on a few national television networks. Network viewership is too fragmented. Therefore, it uses the store itself as a platform to build awareness and knowledge of brands.

P&G meanwhile is investing in an extreme form of brand building to keep bargaining power balanced. It is creating a select group of superbrands, such as Pampers, Olay, Tide, Folgers, Iams, and Pringles. In stores today, it faces merchants who are increasingly limiting shelf offerings to three brands, the number one and number two best-selling brands and a quality private-label brand. P&G thus understands that as a supplier, it must produce robust, competitive brands that stand above all others in the eyes of consumers, pulling product through retail stores.

P&G's strategy is to develop "billion dollar" brands that produce or are capable of producing $1 billion in annual sales. If P&G cannot push its brands into the top two slots, it is divesting them. It sold Jif brand peanut butter and Crisco brand shortening in 2002. It sold its Sunny Delight brand fruit juice line in 2004.

With its remaining brands, the company invests in constant innovation to win the "second moment of truth," or what the company refers to as the point "when a consumer uses the product, evaluates how well it met his or her expectations and whether it was a good value."

Of course, P&G has little choice but to build its brands. It is running a branding race, and at times, its fiercest competitor is its own customers. As Wal-Mart—like all retailers—creates powerful private-label brands, manufacturers have to bulk up the brand appeal of their own products.

Wal-Mart can play a tough game. P&G abandoned its White Cloud toilet paper brand in 1993 to focus on its Charmin brand. Wal-Mart subsequently bought the trademark and relaunched White Cloud in direct competition to the pricier Charmin in 1999. P&G now competes with what at least some consumers perceive as its own brand. Some P&G executives at the time called the

Wal-Mart brand takeover a betrayal. I would call it the new reality of competition in a Wal-Mart world.

The tenor of that competition is one factor that forces P&G to diversify customers, products, and channels. It recently acquired the Clairol brand from Bristol-Myers Squibb and acquired Gillette Company, including superbrands such as Mach3 razors, Braun shavers, and Oral-B toothbrushes. It has long sold to a broad roster of customers, from mass merchandisers to grocery stores, membership club stores, dollar stores, and drug stores. As one way to expand its channels, though, it is now making a fresh push into what it calls "high frequency" neighborhood stores that serve consumers in developing markets. As a result of its proactive diversification efforts, P&G's business concentration with Wal-Mart has fallen by 1 percentage point per year from its peak of 18 percent in 2003.

P&G, certainly considered one of the giants in consumer goods manufacturing, still has to play by the rules of the new Wal-Mart economy. Its experience is a reminder of how tough the game and choices remain. It has been at the forefront of leveraging Wal-Mart's leading practices, investing in brands, and diversifying. But it still bears the scars of tangling with the bear—as in losing the White Cloud brand.

SMART SUPPLIER CHOICES

In some ways, suppliers in the Wal-Mart world face a challenge just as formidable as that faced by competitors. If we choose to sell to Wal-Mart, we cannot blame our travails on the dominant player any more than competitors can. We must respond in the same way to make three clear strategic choices. We must leverage, invest, and diversify to garner our share of the bargaining power in the industry.

Yet our choices should not tilt us too far in any one direction. If we leverage too much without diversifying, we can become too beholden and interconnected. Vlasic, the maker of pickles, ended up producing a gallon jar of pickles to satisfy Wal-Mart's yearning for huge volumes. In a story related by author Charles Fishman, it agreed to price it at under $3, shaving its margins to almost nothing. The deal goosed its volumes but cost it millions in profits while nicking the premium image of its brand.

Arguably, Levi Strauss is beginning to leverage, invest, and diversify in a way that makes it a winner in the Wal-Mart world. It dedicated 100 people at its headquarters, along with 12 in Bentonville, to leverage Wal-Mart's supply-chain expertise. It has long invested in a strong brand—which is why Wal-Mart and other discount channel retailers were clamoring for a Levi's branded product in the first place. And after a long delay, it has diversified out of established but declining retail channels.

But Levi shows that by not choosing explicitly and boldly in the first place, we can put our businesses at risk. By the launch date of the Signature line, Levi Strauss's sales had fallen over 40 percent from its peak to nearly $4 billion. It looked like company executives would preside over an eighth year in a row of rapidly sliding sales.

As it turned out, Signature brand jeans generated $336 million in their first full year, 8.2 percent of total company sales. Total sales for the company stayed steady at about $4.1 billion. The next year, the Signature line brought in $361 million in the United States, 8.8 percent of sales. Total sales remained steady again, whereas profit rebounded from a mere $7.3 million in 2002 to $156 million by 2005.

The maker of the classic jean with the two-horse trademark, symbolizing the down-to-earth toughness of Levi's riveted clothing, almost got trampled for want of making the right strategic choices in the Wal-Mart world. It was a supplier that waited until the last minute to choose to win and therefore almost lost.

Chapter 7

Reward, Impassion, Grow

The Company's Compact with the Worker

obbin Franklin worked at the Wal-Mart in South Haven, Michigan, from September 1990 until June 2001. Her starting pay was $5 an hour—less than the $5.40 an hour she had made in 1978 when she began working at a union grocery store. She started at Wal-Mart as a customer service manager, dressed in a red smock, helping cashiers at the front of the store. Within a year, she moved to the layaway department, which she eventually ran for nearly 10 years.

Franklin, a single mother whose children are grown, reminisces about the days she worked at the local grocery store. Although the store has since closed, she at one time earned $8.35 an hour, received full medical coverage, and earned double time on Sunday, thanks to a contract with the United Food and Commercial Workers Union Local 951. She sympathizes with single mothers now working at Wal-Mart, mothers whom she describes as desperately needing a job and suffering daily stress from jobs in which they barely scrape by.

Franklin maintains that Wal-Mart has the public in a death grip—in which working people can't afford to shop elsewhere because their wages aren't keeping up with the cost of living. As far as she's concerned, Wal-Mart's culture of thrift has not helped the average worker's bottom line at all.

"Wal-Mart will do anything to avoid paying its workers decent wages and benefits," she says. "If employers would just treat people fairly. An employee does not want to harm a company by forcing them to give too much. But just be fair."

Traditionally, Wal-Mart's definition of fairness was to strike the best economic deal it could get in a free market. Wal-Mart set wages and benefits at a level to attract the number and quality of employees it needed—and it now hires over 700,000 employees annually around the world. For years, Wal-Mart thrived by offering entry-level wages to low-skilled, often inexperienced workers in an industry not known for rich paychecks. Its thrifty employment practices matched its strategy and fulfilled the needs of part-time and temporary workers while offering advancement opportunities to meet the aspirations of those seeking longer-term careers.

But Wal-Mart's former free-market way of thinking has increasingly caused the retail giant to teeter. The world is now filled with ardent competitors such as Target, Tesco, and Carrefour battling over the same worker base—as well as vocal citizens disenchanted with the imbalance between what Wal-Mart provides and what workers expect. Wal-Mart executives have found that operating according to free-market economics alone is inadequate. Even if the company might win its case for fair and equitable treatment of employees in the free market, it can lose in the court of public opinion.

The leaders of Wal-Mart have conceded as much. In October 2005, chief executive Lee Scott gave a seminal speech to employees in which he committed Wal-Mart to taking a lead in corporate responsibility. "Our most vocal critics do not want us to stop doing business, but they feel [that] business needs to change, not just our company, but all companies," he said. "People expect a lot of us, and they have a right to."

"What would it take for Wal-Mart to be ... at our best, all the time?" he asked an assembly of managers. "What if we used our size and resources to make this country and this earth an even better place for all of us: customers, associates, our children, and generations unborn?"

One of the critical issues with which Scott is struggling challenges all of us as employers in the Wal-Mart economy—creating a new employment compact that rebalances the needs and expectations of both employers and workers. This compact, forged in the heat of the fiery debate over Wal-Mart, must take into account competitive strategy, economic reality, and public sentiment. Workers such as Franklin, who have braved the public spotlight to press for a new kind of compact, are a reminder of the urgency of rising to this challenge. Although now retired, Franklin has worked to give testimonials for several years—voluntarily. Voices such as hers, ardent and persistent, ring out in the Wal-Mart economy—they cannot be ignored easily.

And they don't have to be. Even in the fast, efficient, hyper-competitive Wal-Mart economy, we as employers *can* develop such a new compact. In this chapter we'll find that instead of leading change, Wal-Mart itself is struggling with change. Nonetheless, as the defining company in this economy, it illustrates the challenges we all face today as employers. In the second half of this chapter we describe the triad of specific choices any employer must make to survive and thrive by crafting a new compact with workers.

REBALANCING THE COMPACT

Dominant players have created a furor over employment issues around the globe and throughout history. At the dawn of the twentieth century, both unions and governments reacted to unfair pay and working conditions imposed by trusts dominating the meat-packing, steel, coal, sugar, and other industries. From the shipping docks of Poland to the mineral mines of South Africa, workers have rallied to upend the unfair labor practices of economic giants.

This is not to say that multinationals have not also promoted employee economic well-being around the world. The Coca-Cola Company, for example, does business throughout Africa and employs 60,000 across the continent. For every job Coca-Cola creates directly, another 16 jobs are created indirectly, making the company responsible for one million jobs on the continent. They also provide financial benefits to the economy, tax revenues to governments, and major charitable contributions to help solve problems such as the AIDS crisis.

But the actions of companies such as The Coca-Cola Company have been viewed by many members of the public as first steps and not as the ultimate solution. Politicians and civic leaders thus are calling on corporations to do more. As the company that defines this global economy, it is no wonder that Wal-Mart has been assailed by a volley of criticism for falling short. The scope and intensity of attacks on the world's biggest company—by workers, advocacy groups, lawyers, and the media—have reached a critical mass.

We should not view Wal-Mart's travails as unique to one company, however. They are a sign of the times. They reflect the challenges facing many leaders in business, especially when issues of public policy arise. In the Wal-Mart economy, fair wages and benefits for entry-level employees, work scheduling that supports the well-being of families and communities, training policies that build the skills of every worker, and a multitude of other worker-related issues have become fodder for the debate over the future of corporate employment practices both in the United States and globally.

Under the world's microscope, Wal-Mart executives have faced an onslaught of testimonials about managerial failings that highlight the most divisive issues of the Wal-Mart economy. Current and former workers complain of inflexible work scheduling, discrimination, unaffordable health care, pressure to work through breaks, and much more. Such criticism abounds in the media and on Web sites sponsored by union-backed groups such as Wal-Mart Watch and WakeUpWal-Mart.com.

Franklin, who makes her case on the AFL-CIO's own Web site, complains in interviews that accusations of her insubordination by Wal-Mart managers were baseless. "You would think they were little gods," she says of two managers insisting on her obedience. "They get a little bit of power, and they're awful. Just treat me as an equal human being."

As one of the largest employers in the world, Wal-Mart has attracted a spate of employment-related lawsuits that contribute to the perception that it operates with subpar standards. In late 2005, a jury awarded $172 million to 116,000 Wal-Mart employees in California who claimed they were denied lunch breaks. The lawsuit was filed by a handful of employees in 2001 but mushroomed into a class-action suit. The whole affair cast doubt in the public's mind about Wal-Mart's fairness in dealing with its workforce.

As academics, activists, and politicians have criticized Wal-Mart for low wages, it has highlighted the question of what amounts to appropriate wage levels in an affluent society. In April 2004, a number of academics held a conference in California to examine Wal-Mart's wage practices. They subsequently published the proceedings as *Wal-Mart: The Face of Twenty-First-Century Capitalism*. One paper described Wal-Mart's approach as resembling "the model of Ebenezer Scrooge instead of Benjamin Franklin."

Several studies confirm that Wal-Mart workers earn about a third less than some of their colleagues in similar stores. University of California professor Marlon G. Boarnet and three others estimated Wal-Mart wages in the unionized Bay Area region to be $9.60 per hour compared with $15.30 at unionized grocers. With benefits added, the Wal-Mart package was nearly half the unionized one, $11.95 versus $23.64. Many union workers understandably consider Wal-Mart a threat to their way of life.

Another study by Global Insight, which was commissioned by Wal-Mart, concluded that Wal-Mart pays market rates. Its average full-time hourly wage in 2006 for store employees was $10.11. In urban sites it was higher, $11.49 in Boston, $10.78 in New York, and $10.29 in Los Angeles. Global Insight found no evidence that Wal-Mart pays significantly lower than retail industry averages. In fact, it found that Wal-Mart paid modestly higher.

Studies over Wal-Mart's wage levels have not silenced critics, however. One reason is that wage rates in the retail sector share the bottom rungs with arts, agriculture, and lodging in a list of sectors tracked by the U.S. Bureau of Labor Statistics. Wages at the top end, in utilities, mining, and information, are twice those in retail. If one were to trust the Consumer Price Index as a wage deflator, retail earnings adjusted for inflation have fallen 34 percent since the 1970s, whereas the weekly earnings of workers in such sectors as mining, manufacturing, and utilities have risen at least marginally.

It is not clear from these statistics whether Wal-Mart is just the beneficiary—or actually the driver—of this decline in relative wage rates. But the statistics do underscore a problem both Wal-Mart and other companies face. Given low wage rates, many workers have to supplement their pay with public assistance. This has led to the argument that "wealthy" firms such as Wal-Mart don't pay enough to keep their people off welfare. In Wal-Mart's case, critics argue that the company doesn't offer enough health coverage to pay for all medical expenses, and the result is that the company transfers its wage and health care bills to taxpayers.

Wal-Mart is not the only company whose lower-paid employees use public assistance. Many other big companies, such as McDonald's, are often on the list too. As the world's biggest private employer, Wal-Mart often draws the most attention—and its employees draw the largest share of public-assistance funds.

A study on the impact of Wal-Mart stores in Ohio by Michael J. Hicks of the Air Force Institute of Technology and Marshall

University actually quantified the amount of assistance Wal-Mart workers obtain. Hicks found that the presence of Wal-Mart drives up both Medicaid expenditures and earned-income-tax-credit claims (tax credits for the working poor). According to Hicks, Wal-Mart's presence boosts Medicaid expenditures by roughly 16 cases per county, the equivalent of an added expense of $651 for every Wal-Mart worker. To give the number perspective, this amounts to about one-half to three-quarters of a percent of total county Medicaid expenditures.

Another study, this one by Arindrajit Dube and Ken Jacobs at the University of California, concluded that in some markets, families of Wal-Mart workers use about 40 percent more taxpayer-funded health care and 38 percent more in food stamps, subsidized school lunches, subsidized housing, and other monies than the average family at all other large retail employers.

The public furor over these hotly debated topics has elevated to center stage the compact between the employer and the worker. The challenge for us as employers in the Wal-Mart economy is to grasp the nature of the needs and expectations for both our companies and our employees, gauge the imbalance between the two, and establish a new balance—a *new* compact. The rebalancing may take the form of actually satisfying current needs, changing the understanding of those needs between worker and employer, or shifting expectations.

SEISMIC FORCES

The rebalancing required won't be easy because numerous forces continue to shake the compact's balance. One is the social pressure applied by corporate outsiders. The second is the unrelenting increase in benefit costs. The third is the pressure to upgrade the quality of workplace life.

Corporate outsiders such as employee rights advocates, politicians, and the public continue to work hard to trump free-market dynamics. A good illustration emerged in a tale of two Chicago Wal-Mart stores. The story of the first one was simple: Wal-Mart, assailed by politicians unhappy with the company's employment practices, abandoned plans to anchor a retail development in an economically depressed neighborhood. Yet the free market was alive and well 16 months later when Wal-Mart opened a store in Evergreen Park, Illinois, four miles from the abandoned site. At this site, two blocks outside the Chicago city limits, Wal-Mart accepted applications for 325 positions paying an average $11 hourly wage. Twenty-five *thousand* people applied.

Despite similar demand for Wal-Mart jobs elsewhere, workers, union organizers, and activists are unimpressed. The heart of their argument is that Wal-Mart and others don't pay a "living wage," a wage level that enables a family of four to maintain a prescribed standard of living. Some business people argue that many of these entry-level jobs are filled by teenagers, unskilled entrants to the workforce, and part-time wage earners who do not "need" such a prescribed living-wage level.

In the Wal-Mart world, executives can't push the argument for free market dynamics too far. For example, Chicago's City Council passed the "Big Box Ordinance" in a hotly debated vote. The ordinance required all stores greater than 90,000 square feet in size that are part of $1 billion or larger retailers to pay a minimum hourly wage of $10 and minimum benefits of $3 per hour by 2010. The Big Box Ordinance affected 35 stores already operating in Chicago such as Target, Home Depot, and Kmart. Lowe's and Target responded by announcing plans to curtail or cancel new store development until the ordinance was overturned. Although the law was ultimately vetoed, the debate over the Big Box Ordinance forged unlikely alliances, such as between pro-business mayor

Richard Daley and local citizens desiring jobs who sported "Don't Box Us Out" T-shirts. On the opposite side of the debate were two-thirds of the City Council, organized labor, and various community groups.

Wal-Mart CEO Scott, addressing these issues in a speech in Los Angeles, showed that he had come around to thinking about the compact as going far beyond a question of free-market economics. A "vital debate," he said, "will be how business, government, and individuals should best share the burden of financing a decent society." Wal-Mart is now actively wrestling with these issues, testing new compensation plans that trade off higher minimum wages for wage caps by job classification.

The second force rocking the balance of the compact with workers is the steady upward pressure on benefits costs. A Towers Perrin study showed that health care costs in 2006 alone were set to rise by 7 percent, or $582 per worker. This puts health care costs at $8,448 per worker, 76 percent higher than in 2001. At such a cost level, health care coverage is hardly a "fringe" benefit, and companies have responded by requiring employees to assume a higher burden to pay for and contain health care costs.

Workers and employee rights advocates see it differently. The heart of their argument in this case revolves around whether health care coverage is a benefit or an entitlement. Companies have a long history of funding health care, and employees in big organizations have come to expect it. Some politicians encourage this notion, especially in the United States and other developed countries. In a highly critical report on Wal-Mart by staff reporting to Congressman George Miller, the authors wrote, "The promise that every American can work an honest day's work, receive an honest day's wages, raise a family, own a home, have decent health care, and send their children to college is a promise that is not easily abandoned. It is, in short, the American Dream."

This dream is widespread, even for unskilled and uneducated workers, no matter where in the world they reside. An added difficulty in negotiating a new compact while that dream floats in the wings is that workers often don't understand the economics of employment. They often don't distinguish between what's economically feasible for business and what's economically desirable for themselves. This lack of understanding will undoubtedly persist and make the development of a new compact a contentious process.

The third force rocking the balance is pressure to upgrade the quality of workplace life, spanning everything from child care to instilling a greater sense of purpose among the workforce. In a worldwide survey of 86,000 workers, Towers Perrin sought to quantify how many workers in medium and large businesses are "engaged" in their work—that is, willing to regularly go the extra mile for their employers. The firm found that the number of people fully engaged amounted to a mere 14 percent.

Towers Perrin also found that four workplace practices were core to boosting the engagement number. One was visible senior leader involvement—and the firm found that corporate leaders rated poorly for their accessibility, visibility, inspirational leadership, and communication. A second was emphasis on learning and career development. A third was effective frontline supervision. A fourth was a thoughtful reward strategy tailored to segments of the workforce.

Studies by research firm Walker Information confirm the scale of the challenge. In its recent study of employee loyalty, Walker found that although 75 percent of employees said that they were satisfied, only 34 percent considered themselves truly loyal—willing to go beyond the call of duty in their jobs. Walker found reasons similar to Towers Perrin, but it also found that an appealing compact had to include such items as a strong company brand, a good reputation, and a company that cares about the community and society.

In some ways, the pressures for change in the employment compact are like the forces created by tectonic plates in the earth's crust. The plates grind and push against each other in a constant but virtually unnoticed ebb and flow of conflicting pressure. Few people grasp the tremendous buildup of forces until the earth's crust convulses, erupting into fissures and triggering disasters. Industry giants such as Wal-Mart have been surprised to find that they were standing on the fault line of the resulting earthquake.

Wal-Mart executives got a harsh reminder of this lesson when the Maryland legislature passed a law requiring companies with over 10,000 workers in the state to devote 8 percent of salary costs to health care (criteria that made Wal-Mart the only target). Although the law was later overturned, at least 30 other state and local jurisdictions have considered similar legislation. One could argue that if Wal-Mart had rebalanced the rewards in its compact before activists painted that target on its chest, government would not have intervened. Combined with an internal company memo disclosing that fewer than 45 percent of Wal-Mart's employees received company health insurance, Wal-Mart instead became a symbol of a corporation trying to duck its health care responsibilities.

Executives at smaller companies might think this lesson doesn't apply to them. But several executives of smaller firms confided to me that if the trend marched across state legislatures, the threshold would keep dropping, and they would all be caught in the dragnet. Such is the reality we all have to deal with in the Wal-Mart economy.

In this tumult, we cannot fail to take the initiative. We must recognize the forces of employment advocates, surging benefit costs, and unsatisfactory workplace life pressuring our existing compacts. We must then clarify and communicate our company's needs and expectations while discerning the needs and expectations of our workforce. We must step up and redefine how we will contribute not just to employee compensation but also to employee well-being.

When we step forward and explicitly choose a compact for the future, we avoid abdicating the responsibility to outsiders.

FORMULA FOR WINNING

If we are to develop a new employment compact, what kind of approach gives us an edge in the Wal-Mart economy? With a perpetual demand to get the best workers possible, we don't want to aim too low and simply strive for a compact that's "competitive." We want to aim high and seek to develop a people strategy that directly supports our business strategy.

The key to profiting as an employer in the Wal-Mart world is to make three explicit choices about serving our employees in the face of a dominant player:

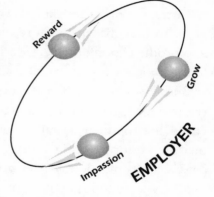

- How to *reward*
- How to *impassion*
- How to *grow*

Reward. Impassion. Grow. These three imperatives form the triad of choices we all have to make as employers to profit in the Wal-Mart economy.

Reward

The first strategic choice we need to make as employers is *how to fairly reward our employees*. The choice depends on four factors: designing reward levels consistent with corporate strategy, determining how to respond to social forces that influence the free-market balance, specifying the extent to which pay is linked to performance, and carefully crafting a portfolio of rewards beyond pay and benefits.

As for the link with corporate strategy, consider the contrast between Wal-Mart and Nordstrom. Both are retailers, but they have very different employment strategies because they have very different business strategies. Wal-Mart promises the lowest prices on a mix of basic consumable, general merchandise, and clothing items in a self-service store. Nordstrom offers service-intensive customer attention while selling designer and private-label apparel.

To create a compact with balanced rewards, executives have to factor into their decision the kinds of workers they want to attract, retain, and promote. Wal-Mart, as an EDLP retailer, will not seek to attract only the skilled variety of employee sought by Nordstrom. It has many more entry-level jobs, and its jobs require less product-specific expertise. Its economic model depends on hiring people with fewer skills, so it offers less generous rewards.

Businesses with different corporate strategies will pay higher rewards for specific purposes. Red Lobster restaurants pay employees in the top-quartile range for its industry, but it expects top-quartile performance in return. Abt Electronics from Chapter 5 pays salespeople double the going market rate, but Mike Abt expects people to bring in more than double the revenue in return.

The second factor in our strategic choice of rewards is how to respond to the many social forces that influence a basic free-market compact. One of the forces is the clash of expected entitlements with prevailing economic realities. As employers, we sit in the unenviable position of not only setting the right pay but also resetting workers' entitlement expectations. We have to reconcile those expectations with the economic pressures of global competition, pricing pressure, and outsourcing—all of which are inconsistent with workers' desire to earn more, often much more, than workers doing the same job elsewhere in the world.

We also need to include in our strategic choice of rewards how closely we want to model one of the elements of a strong-process organization: How important is it to grant rewards based on performance and not just tenure? In the Towers Perrin survey, pay for performance emerged as a sensitive issue. Views about pay were among the most negative—and they reflected workers' dissatisfaction with the frequent imbalance between pay and merit. Workers told Towers Perrin that companies were "failing to adequately differentiate performance and provide rewards that are perceived as fair, consistent and genuinely commensurate with the level of contribution that employees provide."

The choice of rewards goes beyond pay and benefits. For example, Wal-Mart managers select one employee from virtually every store to make a pilgrimage to Northwest Arkansas, for the company's annual meeting. It's a six-hour revival-like gathering of 16,000-plus employees, vendors, shareholders, and executives, and the meetings get employees' motivational juices flowing. Companies must explicitly choose the unique set of nonmonetary rewards that motivate employee behavior.

Impassion

The second choose-or-lose decision we face as employers is *how to impassion our employees to be engaged and motivated*. Before we can impassion our employees, we have to explicitly determine what most reliably enlivens their passions. At the deepest level, passion comes from providing a workplace and work tasks that fulfill employee values.

Whereas rewarding our employees primarily serves financial needs, impassioning them by fulfilling their values also serves their emotional needs. It motivates them to go the extra mile *for* the company by getting more than a paycheck *from* the company.

Winning companies in the Wal-Mart economy are the ones which recognize that financial rewards alone won't rebalance the compact or create a high-performance workforce. They invest in an equally important exchange—the emotional one—making intentional, explicit choices to match company values to employee values.

The values I'm talking about are not just lists of ethereal concepts or ethical platitudes we hang on the wall. (In fact, values posted in company buildings probably are the values the company aspires to, not the ones that currently drive business behavior.) According to Manny Elkind of Mindtech, Inc., who has spent years studying the role of values in organizational performance, values are "standards or principles that consistently have an important influence on our thinking, feelings and behaviors over time." They are the principles by which the company needs to live in order to drive employee behaviors that deliver our strategy. They guide our decisions, our priorities, the way we treat our customers, and especially the way we treat employees. Clearly stated values are not a "soft, fluffy" concept. They are a direct determinant of employee behavior.

Each employee has a set of personal values that, along with his or her beliefs, ultimately drive behaviors. When the corporation's values are consistent with our personal work values, we come home satisfied—even when circumstances may suggest otherwise. Conversely, when our work values are violated, we experience visceral dissatisfaction even when circumstances may appear positive. Conflicts over the way that employees handle situations often can be traced to a violation of their personal values.

What distinguishes winning companies in the Wal-Mart world is that they realize that corporate values must be explicit and that the employees' personal values and the company's corporate values must be matched in order to serve the employees' emotional needs and drive desired employee behaviors. For example, many people value personal integrity even over loyalty to a company or to friends. If their company's values are consistent, they feel affirmed when they tell a customer the truth, even if they lose a sale. However, if the company's values are the reverse, they might win the sale (an apparent success) by stretching the truth yet feel miserable because they violated their own values.

To impassion employees, we can't simply choose our company values. We have to prioritize them and then attract employees who will be satisfied by those values. One of the most important values of the Ritz-Carlton hotel chain is putting the customer's needs ahead of everything else. All members of the staff are expected to drop whatever they are doing to help a guest who has a need and to follow through until the guest is satisfied. If a Ritz-Carlton employee personally values punctuality over service or finishing every task before starting the next one, his or her personal work values will be violated every time a guest "interruption" occurs. Impassioning that employee will be very difficult for the Ritz-Carlton, but that same employee might thrive at UPS.

Executives also must reinforce corporate values in their own behavior. For example, a significant volume of theft in most stores comes from insiders, such as checkout clerks who don't scan a few items for "friends." Much of the loss-prevention effort by Wal-Mart and other retailers therefore focuses on reinforcing the corporate value of honesty. One of the reasons Wal-Mart publicly pursued senior executive Tom Coughlin, who pled guilty in 2006 to charges of wire fraud and tax evasion, was because he had violated this essential corporate value. Had Wal-Mart not pursued Coughlin, it would have undermined the importance of this corporate value in the eyes of 1.8 million employees globally, who had read reports of his stealing money, gift cards, and merchandise.

As another example, Chick-fil-A is a $2.0 billion chicken sandwich chain based in Atlanta that was founded by Truett Cathy in 1946. Cathy made it clear that he valued first "glorifying God by stewarding resources and having a positive influence on others," values that have been expanded to include humility, passion for service, compassion, and genuineness. To this day, the chain won't hire anyone—churchgoer or not—who doesn't match up with those values. Chick-fil-A has since grown to over 1,200 restaurants in 38 states. Management turnover is less than 5 percent per year in an industry where 20 percent is common.

Appealing to employees' values is what creates the intangible, emotional link between company and employee that leads to low turnover, high loyalty, and the desire to go beyond the call of duty. Witness the thousands of parochial school teachers who willingly accept dramatically lower pay than their public school counterparts because the jobs offer something they value well beyond a paycheck. The job of executives is to articulate the company values and the behaviors that flow from those values. They then have to find and consistently impassion people through satisfying their personal values.

Grow

The third choose-or-lose decision we face as employers is *how to grow our employees into more capable and fulfilled workers.* In other words, how do we inspire them to aspire? Growing employees takes them a step beyond impassioning them. Impassioning employees gets the most *out of them* today. Growing them gets the most *for them* tomorrow—and in turn, brings a vibrancy and performance level to the company that is hard to duplicate.

Winning companies in the Wal-Mart world have discovered the secret to establishing a new compact and getting sustainable performance from their workforce: Go beyond just making a financial and emotional commitment to employees and invest in them intellectually as well. By awakening people to their potential, by transporting them to new levels of professional and self-mastery, we can motivate them in possibly no more powerful way. Employees come alive when their leaders actually help them to make the most out of themselves.

Recall that in a strong-process organization, the goal of leaders is to work themselves out of their jobs. They want to mentor and grow their teams so that they can ultimately let their subordinates take over their jobs while they step up to other opportunities. Growing tomorrow's leaders is an essential element of strong-process management. In turn, making explicit choices to grow people—and grow them into leaders—is the third critical choice in developing an employer strategy.

Leaders in the Wal-Mart economy can assemble an employee-growth strategy from a wide array of programs. Offering a variety of education classes is a basic form of growth for employees. Most retailers have a mandatory curriculum of basic classes for new store employees, for everything from handling customer service to completing time records. Other companies invest in the mandatory cycling through a variety of job responsibilities, a formalized mentoring program, and executive coaching.

Although Wal-Mart does offer basic training and a variety of management development programs, some store employees don't feel that they grow enough with Wal-Mart. When a national home-improvement chain began interviewing potential employees for a new store in Hurricane Katrina-ravaged Waveland, Mississippi, one of every five applicants came from the recently reopened Wal-Mart. Many cited their perception of more focused functional training and broader growth opportunities offered by the home-improvement chain as the reason for the switch.

Growing employees involves every level in an organization and every walk of life. ServiceMaster, the parent company of service brands such as Merry Maids, TruGreen ChemLawn, and Rescue Rooter, is a case in point. Recognizing that many of its entry-level maid-service and janitorial jobs attract low-income immigrants, who often lack language and basic life skills, the firm offers regular classes on topics such as balancing a checkbook, changing a tire, improving personal appearance, building language skills, and registering to vote.

Management's cultural attitude toward training is just as important as the education itself. If employee attendance at training is regularly postponed by supervisors for the sake of the crisis *du jour*, the company is sending a clear message that personal growth is not really important. Conversely, when important company meetings are scheduled so that they don't conflict with growth programs, the priority of individual personal employee growth is much clearer.

To be sustainable, the three strategic choices of reward, impassion, and grow must start at the top of any organization. It is easiest to engage senior leadership in the financial reward process because salary reviews and budgets force that discipline. However, senior leadership needs to devote just as much attention to engaging with their teams emotionally and intellectually to win in the Wal-Mart world. Senior leaders need to understand their own values and model desired behaviors with their colleagues if they expect to engage the rest of the organization emotionally and intellectually.

When Meijer embarked on its cost-reduction campaign, senior leaders realized that they needed to model the value of thrift for the entire organization. The first two cost-reduction initiatives—selling a company plane and eliminating the company car program—demonstrated not only that the value of thrift was important, but that senior leadership was willing to go first. Modeling the desired behavior at the top triggered the momentum that ultimately led to the millions of cost savings the company realized.

In many ways, the imperative to make explicit choices as an employer in the Wal-Mart world corresponds with the research of psychologist Abraham Maslow. Maslow posited in his famous hierarchy that all individuals first need their physiological needs served, followed in ascending order by safety, love/belonging, esteem, and self-actualization. As soon as they meet their needs at one level of the hierarchy, they move up.

So it is with people strategy. Making choices to reward our employees satisfies physiological and safety needs. Impassioning our employees is akin to satisfying love/belonging and esteem needs. And growing our employees through educational, experiential, and other means fulfills their highest-level needs. The result for the company? People performing at the highest level, willingly, eagerly, and thirsting for more.

In the old economy, paying rigid attention to wage rates in the free market may have been sufficient to compete profitably. However, in the Wal-Mart world, a financial agreement with our employees is no longer enough. We also have to make explicit choices to serve our workforce emotionally and intellectually to craft a new compact that drives world-class performance.

WINNING EMPLOYERS IN THE NEW ECONOMY

The stories of three employers suggest how companies of any size can craft a great employment compact. These companies take their cue from the triad of employment strategy choices for rewarding employees, impassioning workers to carry out their jobs, and providing a chance for growth. They show that in a Wal-Mart world, we can all follow innovative paths to formulate a people strategy that advances business strategy.

Dancing Deer Baking Company

Trish Karter runs the Dancing Deer Baking Company in the inner-city Roxbury section of Boston. A former artist with a management degree from Yale, Karter helped launch the business with an inventive baker and her former husband in 1994. Today, she runs an enterprise with 55 employees and $8 million in sales, delivering cookies, cakes, and gourmet gift packages to stores, homes, and businesses nationwide.

Dancing Deer isn't an ordinary baking company. Like other modern-day bakers, Karter has built her company's brand on all-natural, premium-quality products, such as deep, dark gingerbread cake and molasses clove cookies. But she also has built the brand on her efforts to make Dancing Deer a model employer and a force for community good.

Karter's business strategy directly informs her employment strategy. She starts by rewarding employees in a novel way. With no skills, no experience, and no English-speaking ability, employees who pack cookies might start as low as $7.50 per hour. Although this starting rate approaches a bare-bones free-market wage, most rank-and-file employees can earn up to twice that much based on job classification and skill level. Karter gilds the compensation package by giving all employees equity options from day one on the job, with an unusual mechanism for allowing employees to monetize the growth in asset value during their tenure if they leave. This is particularly designed to help lower-wage workers develop financial assets and skills.

She also gives annual bonuses based on sales, provides automatic disability and life insurance, pays a matching 3 percent of wages into an IRA, offers a flexible paid time off program, pays almost 70 percent of employees' health plan costs, and even provides educational reimbursement. She believes that employees value the personal development, culture of respect and learning, and positive relationships even more than the monetary incentives. The entire package ensures that Karter's customers can feel confident that Dancing Deer cookies come from well-cared-for employees.

Karter has established clear values for Dancing Deer, treating her employees as she thinks everyone would want to be treated. She impassions her employees by matching the company's values to theirs: the need for respect, the desire to use their minds as well as their hands, and the desire to serve others compassionately and to be served the same way. During hiring, she targets smart people who want to work hard and have fun—and who care about others.

"That standard of caring about people... permeates the organization," she says. "There are a lot of people who care to care."

Typical of the company's flexibility is the ability for employees to take long leaves to their native countries, with their jobs intact and guaranteed on their return. A young woman, who initially had no work skills and spoke no English, left for Columbia to retrieve her young son and to move him to Boston. Years later she has risen to a management level and according to Karter has "added significant skills and value to the organization."

Karter often goes the extra mile to respect inner-city workers. She employs many immigrants who initially speak no English and invests to promote them through the ranks. She gives them extras, such as a 25 cent per hour raise for every English course they finish.

One unique component of every Dancing Deer employee's goal sheet is the first item: "Contribution to deer [employee] happiness and effectiveness." The goal sheet places a quantifiable measuring stick on company values. Employees' success at contributing in this way counts 15 percent toward their bonus. Working to uphold company values and making it a "fun and wonderful" place to work, says Karter, are part of every employee's job description.

Karter also has made explicit choices in her employment strategy to help people grow personally and professionally. She says that helping others grow is simply something she learned from her parents. While contribution to happiness ranks as the first item on the company's employee goal sheet, achieving personal growth—often totally unrelated to work—ranks as the final one. It counts 5 percent in the performance rating.

Dancing Deer offers a variety of development courses designed to help workers in their jobs and in their personal lives, including anger management, speaking to others, and having honest conversations. Karter also invests in strictly personal growth outside the company. One employee came to Dancing Deer just shy of his college degree. Achieving additional credits toward the degree is now part of his personal goals. If he doesn't get the credits, he loses part of his bonus.

Through such unique employment choices, dovetailing with the company's business strategy, Karter sets Dancing Deer apart in the competitive packaged-food business.

Wegmans Food Markets

Wegmans Food Markets, based in Rochester, New York, is among the supermarket chains that have learned to thrive in the Wal-Mart economy.

It thrives in part because of its competitive strategy: It differentiates itself with the design of its stores. At 130,000 square feet, they are three times the size of a typical supermarket and offer a European-style open-market atmosphere, in-store dining, sub shop, cappuccino bars, and employee-staffed children's play areas for ages three to eight.

But it also thrives through employment strategy. Wegmans stands apart for the knowledge and passion of its employees for food—how to choose it, how to prepare it, and how to serve it. Reminiscent of a high-tech executive, third-generation CEO Danny Wegman says that Wegmans delivers service to customers through employee knowledge. His customers won't buy many of his products, including 400 kinds of specialty cheeses, if they don't know how to serve those products. So Wegmans workers show or tell them how.

Because employee knowledge is all-important, Wegman says that the company's people strategy *is* its business strategy. By building the business on people strategy, Wegman and his daughter are steadily expanding the chain. It now has over 70 stores, extending from New York to Virginia. The largest ones average nearly $1 million in sales a week, triple that of an average grocery store. Its operating margins are roughly 7.5 percent, double the average of the nation's largest grocers. Annual sales in 2005 were $3.8 billion.

Although Wal-Mart does pose a threat, Wegman doesn't believe that going head to head on labor costs for his 35,000 employees is the way to respond to the competition. Instead, the company offers a range of rewards to attract and retain the people who will support its mission: To help others prepare great and easy meals to live healthier and better lives.

Robert Wegman, the former company chairman and Danny's father, introduced profit sharing and full medical coverage in 1950. The company now offers a buffet of other benefits more typical of

Fortune 500 companies, such as adoption assistance, although employees now have to help chip in for their medical care. The average wages and benefits offer a richer deal than competitors. The higher per-person costs are offset by far lower turnover, about 6 percent for full-timers compared with 19 percent for similar-sized chains.

Wegmans has made a point to impassion its employees. The choice of values makes the difference. Wegman's strategy demands the hiring of employees who value being recognized as experts, being able to pass knowledge on by teaching others, and caring. Such employees guide customers in making delicious, nutritious, and easy meals.

Why do such values matter? "Let's take caring," says Wegman in an interview for *Training & Development* magazine. "When employees have a problem of some kind, we step forward and help them solve it. Permission to do that doesn't have to come from me."

In recent years, Wegman has focused on the idea that when each employee improves, the whole company improves. He asks his people, "What are you learning this year that's going to help you improve as a person and as a team member?"

In keeping with its strategy to win through knowledge, Wegmans invests heavily in individual growth through training and education. Wegman says that the company supports education, whether for the job, career advancement, or personal development. Wegman has specifically made a choice to spend millions to help employees grow—such as when he chartered two planes to fly employees from the company's new mid-Atlantic stores to Rochester to meet and learn from veteran employees.

On the job, employees receive a clear map of how to advance through a grocery-related career. A chart outlines five job families and the courses employees need to take to advance in various ways. Wegmans also offers scholarship money. It has awarded $59 million to more than 19,000 employees since the program started in 1984.

About 2,500 students study with the help of Wegman money each year at colleges nationwide.

In 1987, the Wegmans also established a program to apprentice Rochester youth in the grocery business while reducing the high school dropout rate. The Work-Scholarship Connection sponsors 1,000 middle and high school students each year, who must strive to attain goals in academic standards, job-skill attainment, and relationship building. Those who keep up at least a 2.0 GPA and 90 percent attendance rate and meet on-the-job performance standards get a Wegmans scholarship of up to $1,500 per year toward a degreed college program.

The Wegmans' investments of $40 million in the Scholarship Connection to date have paid off big financially. The youth program costs about $2,500 per child. But about 80 percent of those who graduate from high school stay employed with Wegmans. Given that training a new employee costs roughly $4,000, the program is a good business deal. At the same time, it is an investment to inspire youth to aspire—aspire to much more than they could achieve alone.

S.C. Johnson

Few Wal-Mart suppliers offer a more explicit employment compact than 120-year-old S.C. Johnson, the $6.5 billion Racine, Wisconsin, maker of cleaning, insect-control, storage, air-care, shaving, and other household products. S.C. Johnson, best known for old-time favorites such as Windex brand window cleaner and Pledge brand furniture polish, has played a lead role in workplace strategies since it introduced paid vacations in 1900 and a company pension plan at the height of the Depression in 1934.

To attract and retain the innovative employees needed to invent and make new and reformulated products, S.C. Johnson's rewards strategy focuses on balancing work and family life. It offers tangible benefits such as expanded maternity/paternity/adoption benefits, onsite banking, company-owned recreation facilities, and paid sabbaticals. It also offers flexible work schedules and telecommuting. It actually forbids meetings every other Friday to allow people to get their work done and not take it home on weekends. It has repeatedly won top grades as a best place to work not just in America but in nine other countries.

Today's chairman and CEO, H. Fisk Johnson, offers a statement in the company's public report that would strike someone who is unfamiliar with the company as human resources fluff: "By working in partnership with each other, bringing fairness and respect to work every day, celebrating differences and truly enjoying the fun and friendship of being a family company, the people of S.C. Johnson make the company a success."

Yet this statement serves as the basis for engaging people passionately. S.C. Johnson targets people with specific values—those who thirst to make a difference in other's lives, who want to raise standards of society, who value role-modeling moral and social leadership, and who prize credibility, respect, fairness, camaraderie, and individual growth. In short, as the company's statement of beliefs reads, they are people who prize earning "the enduring goodwill of the people."

S.C. Johnson has made an explicit choice of the values that underpin its competitive strengths. People thus come to work each day reaffirming the values they were hired for—and bettering company performance as a result. According to surveys, 82 percent of the company's people believe in the values of the firm. The company has an annual turnover rate of only 2 percent.

Like Wegmans, S.C. Johnson makes huge investments in employee growth initiatives that inspire people to aspire to their best. For salaried workers, it groups curricula under the Johnson Learning Initiative, and course work ranges from conflict resolution to manufacturing best practices. It also sponsors a one-week executive program each year at INSEAD outside Paris.

For hourly workers, it runs the LINK program, a partnership between the company and the local Gateway Technical College. LINK offers hundreds of onsite courses for academic credit, making it one of the rare accredited college campuses on a work site. S.C. Johnson also runs an online learning program, which offers 174 topics for study via computer 24/7 anywhere in the world.

The company makes no bones about its people strategy. It likes to quote former Chairman Herbert F. Johnson, Sr., who made a speech on a profit-sharing day in 1927: "The goodwill of the people is the only enduring thing in any business. It is the sole substance... the rest is shadow." Johnson grasped early on the value of the three critical strategic factors—employee rewards, values, and growth opportunities—to long-term, profitable success.

SMART EMPLOYER CHOICES

In a world of dominant companies, developing an employment compact is essential to winning. Whether we run a small bakery or a multinational conglomerate, we can use the same triad of choices—how to reward, how to impassion, and how to grow—to craft a compact that survives the social and economic tensions that make the compacts of other employers crack.

The risk for many employers today stems not so much from substandard or uncompetitive employment practices but from substandard strategic reasoning. As employers in the Wal-Mart economy, we have to ask: Does our compact reflect our changing business strategy? Does it reflect realities of the free market for labor? Does it reflect the expectations of our society, a society whose vision of corporate responsibilities expands with every uptick in affluence and downtick in perceived corporate behavior?

For years, Wal-Mart thrived by offering an employment compact that fit its strategy. Its offer of spartan wages to some of the least employable workers for some of the least lucrative jobs in one of the lowest-paid industries made perfect sense. Its compact matched its EDLP strategy. It fit the local labor markets. It dovetailed with rural communities' expectations for entry-level and second-wage-earner work. Wal-Mart honed its compact to deliver the rewards, impassion its people, and offer worker growth opportunities to win hands down in its competitive niche. It was even ranked among the top 100 places to work in America as recently as 2002.

But now Wal-Mart has a black eye. The criticism suggests that the employment compact should have been rebalanced—as worker needs and expectations shifted—but Wal-Mart was not ready. Outsiders reading about sex-discrimination lawsuits, off-the-clock working, and a climate of inequity in the stores have a right to wonder if Wal-Mart lost its way on people strategy.

As employers in the Wal-Mart world, it is only a matter of time before the forces that caused the tremors in the habitat of the world's biggest company shake the foundations of our own employment compacts. By choosing today how to reward, how to impassion, and how to grow our employees, we can reinforce an employment compact that not only can withstand these tensions but also can position us to thrive in a tumultuous global economy.

Chapter 8

Belong, Align, Engage
Terms of Community Endearment

In the evening of January 12, 2006, Wal-Mart looked like it would soon secure approval to build a supercenter from the planning board in the southern New Hampshire city of Nashua. Despite more than 10 hours of testimony over three meetings, in which not one member of the public spoke in favor of the store, the board clearly was swayed by the expert testimony of engineers hired by Wal-Mart.

The week before, the board had deadlocked 4–4 on the plan. But this week, one board member opposing the store was absent. A second opponent disqualified himself from voting after citing possible conflicts of interest. Chairwoman Bette Lasky, a Democratic state representative, affirmed her intentions: "My vote is in favor of the project." The political runway seemed clear for approval: Wal-Mart was coasting to a 4–2 win.

But Wal-Mart lost.

Remarkably, just before the final vote, board member and city engineer Steve Dookran switched sides. In slow, measured sentences, Dookran described what amounted to betrayal by his engineering colleagues. He said that he initially had trusted the conclusions of Wal-Mart's traffic engineers. Then he had doubts. After poring through the details, he ultimately distrusted their findings. He distrusted traffic counts that seemed suspiciously low. He distrusted road-upgrading estimates as out of line. He distrusted accident figures, which appeared undercounted.

"The claims made by the applicant are less than believable," he said. "As the city engineer, I just don't see your traffic plans working." Dookran was executing an about-face. It was a gutsy move. He publicly endured put-downs by fellow board members for expressing his reservations at the eleventh hour. He defended his reputation against what he called "professional character assassination." When the final vote came on January 18, he voted no. With the absent board member returning for the final vote, the final tally was 4–3 against Wal-Mart.

Evaluating Wal-Mart's proposal was an emotional roller-coaster that spanned five planning board meetings. Chairwoman Lasky had reprimanded the audience periodically with raps of her gavel for obscene mutterings and outbursts mocking Wal-Mart. The same audience sat in stunned silence at the final meeting, as if in wonder at the storm of human emotions that had just echoed through the old New England auditorium. After a pause, opponents applauded.

The Nashua story raises questions about how, in a Wal-Mart economy, companies should relate to municipalities and society. An observer could ask: How could a company of Wal-Mart's size, skill, and financial depth get sidelined at the last minute by losing the trust of an engineer? How could it have completely alienated whole segments of a community—with a proposal for a store on a commercial strip already dotted with the likes of Sears, Target, and Home Depot? Did Wal-Mart fall asleep at the switch? And what does Wal-Mart's experience mean for other companies in the economy it has created?

These are good questions. In the Wal-Mart world, they apply not just to the giant retailer; they apply to all of us. Today, the evidence suggests that we all have to adopt new and broader responsibilities, or we will get caught flatfooted in our role as community members. We have to view ourselves as good stewards, responsible for the care and well-being of more than our customers and the bottom line.

Ultimately, making smart choices in how we act and respond to communities will separate those of us who profit and win from those who lose.

How broad must our response be? We must consider stewarding relationships with local citizens, stewarding environmental resources, and stewarding the legacy of equity and social opportunity championed in free markets and by free nations. In the past we learned to leave such stewardship to the government and nonprofit leaders, but the evolution of our society suggests that those days are past.

As business leaders, our stewardship responsibilities include crafting a strategy for our role as local community members, as the Nashua story illustrates. As we affect societies around the corner and around the globe, though, our strategy must provide for regional, national, and global communities. Wherever we operate our offices, plants, and stores, wherever we spread our influence with our products and services, wherever we consume the resources of the environment, and wherever we have an impact on society, we have to make smart choices to win as corporate citizens. In this chapter we'll examine the challenges we face as members of these multiple communities and the triad of strategic choices we need to make to be leaders in the Wal-Mart world.

OUR RESPONSIBILITIES TO MULTIPLE COMMUNITIES

Dominant corporations attract an inordinate amount of attention in this economy. They field the complaints of mothers whose children play next to their offices and of monarchs whose citizens work in their plants. They draw fire on issues from child labor to animal testing. They receive blame for the impacts of every chunk of ore extracted from the world's mines and every piece of plastic waste generated—not to mention the air, land, and water in between.

Dominant players today can't escape their role as community members, especially when they are culpable for actual and even perceived injustices. The debacle of the *Exxon Valdez*, the tragic loss of life near Union Carbide's plant in Bhopal, India, and Nike's overseas labor transgressions sparked outrage from both local villages and the global community. Similar crises since these milestone events have triggered a fresh call for longer-term changes to minimize future impacts on communities at all levels.

The problems of giants who are under the spotlight for questionable behavior amount to a clarion call to all companies. The ranks of well-funded, effective critics have swelled beyond unions who press for higher wages and better working conditions. They include women's rights and human rights activists, environmentalists, and community organizers. They include powerful personalities and passionate advocates of social causes with plenty of money—often money invested in shares of the companies themselves.

One of the triggering complaints for long-term change comes from labor and community advocates. They raise the alarm over companies destroying jobs, whether at home or by exporting them abroad. In Wal-Mart's case, the advocates decry most passionately the destruction of existing local jobs and businesses. A recent McKinsey & Company study commissioned by Wal-Mart and leaked to the press cited public concerns that Wal-Mart "is too aggressive and is hurting local companies."

It's easy to see why. As the marketplace evolves, familiar and often well-liked local competitors go out of business. Studying Wal-Mart's effect on communities, Emek Basker of the University of Missouri found that four retail stores with fewer than 20 employees close within five years after Wal-Mart opens. An average of 0.7 stores with 20 to 99 employees close within two years. Wal-Mart has become today's icon representing the decades-old trend of chain stores replacing local shops.

The ultimate effect of big companies on local employment is often harder to determine. David Neumark, Junfu Zhang, and

Stephen Ciccarella of the University of California–Irvine found that Wal-Mart destroys jobs. Writing in a National Bureau of Economic Research working paper, the economics professor and two associates found that, on average, Wal-Mart stores reduce retail employment by 2 to 4 percent.

But Basker found that Wal-Mart initially creates 100 new retail jobs per county, net of losses. Over five years, the net gain shrinks to 50. Global Insight, in its study funded by Wal-Mart, found a similar trend but different end results. The opening of a typical store raised retail employment by 137 jobs at first, leveling off at 97 jobs over time. Wal-Mart eliminates jobs in competing food, apparel, and accessory stores but creates them in building materials and garden supply retailers, as well as in its own stores.

Whether or not Wal-Mart increases or decreases jobs, we can safely say that it does shake up the configuration of community job rolls. Concurrently, Wal-Mart and other big companies attract another complaint among communities—that the entry of dominant firms damages community character and living conditions. William Beaver of Bentley College examined some 25 cases where Wal-Mart proposals met opposition. He found traffic as the most common complaint, followed by pollution (noise, air, water, and light), sprawl/aesthetics, and harm to local businesses.

A third complaint about dominant companies is that they shift costs onto the taxpayers. One means of doing so is by accepting public subsidies for plants, offices, and other facilities. Wal-Mart has received subsidies for some of its stores and distribution centers—property tax breaks, discounted land, infrastructure assistance, income-tax credits, tax-exempt bond financing, and so on. Although these subsidies are aimed at stimulating local economic growth, the size of the breaks appears excessive to some people.

Activist group Good Jobs First tallied the value of the subsidies for 91 Wal-Mart stores and 91 distribution centers. It concluded that

Wal-Mart had taken handouts of more than $1 billion for just these 182 facilities. The distribution center in Sharon Springs, New York, alone raked in subsidies worth $46 million. In Oklahoma, Wal-Mart received significant tax subsidies from the state to build a new distribution center. When it then blanketed the state with its stores, many higher-paying supermarket jobs were in effect exchanged for lower-paying jobs at Wal-Mart.

A fourth complaint about dominant companies comes from corporate watchdogs who track conditions of overseas workers making products destined for global markets. When it comes to Wal-Mart, aid group Oxfam International has blasted the company for driving working conditions down globally. Oxfam says that overseas subcontractors, despite lip service to the contrary, find ways to work people overly long hours to meet production targets, pay less than a living wage, fire those wishing to unionize, and tolerate sexual harassment.

A final complaint about dominant companies comes from environmentalists, who have attacked industry leaders on issues ranging from poor waste disposal to greenhouse gas production. Wal-Mart has taken hits for energy consumption, contribution to urban sprawl, excess packaging, water pollution (from runoff), and even its impacts from fish farming. The attacks have put the retail industry—which used to float below the environmental radar screen—in the limelight, and global opinion makers have taken notice.

The tenor of the attacks on Wal-Mart and other big companies is daunting. Executives express frustration that the complaints ignore many corporations' positive effects. In Wal-Mart's case, the company benefits many, especially shoppers. "We find the effects of supercenter entry and expansion to be sufficiently large…that overall we find it to be extremely unlikely that the expansion of supercenters does not confer a significant overall benefit to consumers," wrote Jerry Hausman of MIT and Ephraim Leibtag from the U.S. Department of Agriculture in a National Bureau of Economic Research paper. Economic consulting firm Global Insight calculates that from 1985 to 2004, Wal-Mart lowered overall consumer prices by a cumulative 3.1 percent, saving every American household $2,329 a year.

Another positive effect of dominant companies is charitable giving. Wal-Mart gave $200 million to more than 100,000 organizations in 2005. Ninety percent of the money went to cities and towns with Wal-Mart stores. The remaining aid went to national charities. In 2006, it gave Sesame Workshop $1 million to create an outreach project to help children of U.S. military personnel deal with the stresses of military life.

On top of dispensing charity dollars, companies such as Wal-Mart encourage their employees to volunteer. It made a name for itself following Hurricane Katrina. It arrived on the scene with tractor-trailer loads of bottled water and other supplies before government agencies could respond. Wal-Mart's employees donated more than a million hours of time last year. The company's Volunteerism Always Pays program donates cash to charities in proportion to the time employees spend working at them. Wal-Mart donated $5 million through the program in 2004.

Despite many contentious store approval cases such as that in Nashua, New Hampshire, Wal-Mart actually has an admirable record in many communities. Less than four miles away from the proposed Nashua store, a nine-year-old Wal-Mart supercenter in Amherst, New Hampshire, won a commendation from town officials for its generosity to the town. The Amherst selectmen praised Wal-Mart "not only for its community commitment in the town of Amherst, but around the United States."

When it comes to Wal-Mart, Professor Basker of the University of Missouri underscores perhaps the key point that all businesses should heed: "The small magnitude of the estimated net effect of

Wal-Mart on retail employment is striking in light of the level of public discussion on this topic."

And therein lies the message for us as business leaders in the Wal-Mart economy. While the level of impact may not be significant, the level of public angst, if not anger, often is. Sometimes we cannot even sort out the positive and negative because of the heated opinions on both sides. That's why, whether the issue relates to employment, human rights, or the environment, and whether our business affects a local community, a region, the nation, or the globe, fighting advocacy facts with company facts only gets us so far as community members. A lot of company outsiders don't care about the facts; they simply want companies to step up and make a bigger contribution to the betterment of the world around them.

DOING THE RIGHT THING

Several trends have driven all business leaders to the front lines of the battle over finding the correct strategy as community members. One of the most pervasive trends is the ineffectiveness of government at solving social issues. The institutions that once held the great society together have struggled to retain funding, staffing, and legitimacy. With the growth of entitlement spending, discretionary programs aimed at social good have been squeezed and cut. Even Head Start, a program for underprivileged toddlers that has received broad bipartisan praise for years, initially was threatened with a 2007 budget cut that would have slashed 35,000 slots.

Meanwhile, corporate power has been ascendant, fueled by its demonstrated ability to grow, adapt, and generate wealth. But with ascendancy comes expanded responsibilities. As the saying goes, to whom much is given, much is expected. Today, as the Wal-Mart furor demonstrates, the public expects corporations to address a whole new range of issues relating to the community, the environment, poverty, health, human rights, and economic justice.

The trend is so strong that executives across industries have recognized its staying power. In McKinsey & Company's global survey of executives, a remarkable 79 percent of executives said that they expected companies to either share with government or take on added responsibilities for handling social and political issues.

One of the reasons corporations have been tagged with accepting this burden comes from a parallel trend—the growth in the numbers and power of nongovernmental organizations (NGOs). These include small community activist groups such as Citizen Action of Southern New Hampshire, based in Nashua, which fought the Wal-Mart supercenter proposal. They also include national groups such as Michael Marx's Business Ethics Network (introduced in Chapter 1) and global groups such as Amnesty International, which now press companies on human rights issues in China and elsewhere.

These groups can be incredibly effective in setting the agenda, in particular tacking one new item after another onto the corporate responsibility program. Like Marx, the leaders of these groups may work partly behind the scenes to lobby for change—successfully getting Wal-Mart to reconsider its approach to salmon farming, for example. But they also may work as traditional activists, organizing boycotts, lobbying legislators, and bashing the company's reputation.

The trend of rising consumer expectations continues unabated. Consumers have come to care not just about products but also about how they are made and who made them. A Cone corporate citizenship study showed that 86 percent of shoppers say that they are likely to switch to a brand if it's associated with a cause. A solid brand now includes elements of price, quality, value, safety, design, and convenience. It also includes a company's citizenship program, environmental record, community policies, and sourcing practices.

As business leaders, we face constituencies almost daily that make it hard for us to ignore these trends. Company outsiders remind us repeatedly that we are members of multiple communities in which we have a responsibility as good stewards. They sound a consistent message: We can't just operate for the short term. We have an obligation to pass on to our children a full complement of the human and natural assets entrusted to us without compromising them for future generations.

As Ian Davis, head of McKinsey & Company, wrote in an article about corporate social responsibility in *The Economist*, "Companies that treat social issues as either irritating distractions or simply unjustified vehicles for attack on business are turning a blind eye to impending forces that have the potential fundamentally to alter their strategic future." Leaders in the Wal-Mart world are recognizing that the communities within which they operate have the power to affect the bottom line.

The lack of thorough thinking sets business leaders up for plenty of missteps. In the McKinsey study, many leaders recognize their deficiencies in executing a social and community strategy. When asked by McKinsey how well their companies anticipate social pressure, including criticism, only 3 percent of the more than 4,000 executives responding said that they were doing a "good job."

"Most executives view their engagement with the corporate social contract as a risk, not an opportunity, and frankly admit that they are ineffective at managing this wider social and political issue," said the report.

In the past, few companies had the foresight to get in front of the wave of community action. But today, forward-thinking companies focus on doing the right thing for communities in the first place. Recalling the minority relations—and public relations—nightmare he inherited from the pattern of racial discrimination at Denny's, turnaround CEO Jim Adamson says, "Denny's came to the table of enlightenment by force. It is nice to see companies not coming to the table by force today."

Responsible stewardship as community members in the Wal-Mart economy requires more than doing things right; it requires doing the right thing. The public often gives credit to companies that do things right. But it gives praise to and builds admiration for companies that choose to do things that make lasting, sustainable changes in our local and global communities. As an example, Frito Lay took the lead in removing trans fats from its snack foods. It didn't spin the story of unhealthy fats to make it go away. It fixed the problem before it could become a crisis. Like the executives at Frito Lay, we must all make explicit, intentional choices as community members to satisfy our economic, social, and environmental responsibilities in the Wal-Mart economy.

FORMULA FOR WINNING

As business leaders, we can't control the overall political, social, and environmental climate, the agenda of social crusaders, or even the demands of people at the fringes of community opinion. But we can make choices that put us at the forefront as stewards in our local and global communities. And we can use successful stewardship to drive competitive advantage and enhanced shareholder value in the Wal-Mart economy.

The key to profiting as community members in the Wal-Mart world, whether we

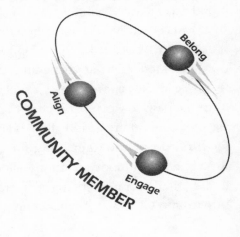

dominate our markets or not, is to make three explicit choices about community strategy:

- Where to *belong*
- How to *align* strategies
- How to *engage*

Belong. Align. Engage. These three imperatives form the triad of choices we all have to make as community members to profit in the Wal-Mart economy.

Belong

Before we can make a lasting difference as community members, we first must belong to the communities that matter, explicitly and intentionally. *Belonging* means having a presence—a face—and staying actively involved. As the first part of our community strategy, we have to proactively choose *where to belong to the community to have the greatest impact.*

Just as we can't choose to be everything to everyone as competitors, vendors, or employers, we can't choose to belong to every community our companies affect. We must eliminate many possible options. Like retailers who have learned that success depends on connecting customers with locally-relevant merchandise, we must connect with locally-relevant organizations and causes that will create a sustainable difference for our companies and communities.

Wal-Mart itself has grasped the opportunity belatedly. It has chosen to create connections with onetime antagonists, among them Conservation International and Natural Resources Defense Council. These two environmental groups advised Wal-Mart on how to reduce its impact on the environment. In addition, the group Business for Social Responsibility helped Wal-Mart to connect with groups monitoring work conditions in overseas plants.

At the local level, it has instituted a process for creating dialogue and partnerships where it hopes to site stores in local communities—something that perhaps would have helped the company in Nashua.

What do we gain strategically from belonging to various communities? First, we satisfy our responsibilities as civic leaders, as stewards in our communities. Second, we create an invaluable intelligence network for better understanding the panoply of issues affecting our business. Third, we create a new pipeline to acquire business intelligence, possibly providing ideas for new products, services, or markets. Lastly, and as a result of the human touch, we moderate the risk of a public relations backlash. Company outsiders always find it easier to criticize a faceless company than to criticize a face that has a name, a voice, and a personality.

Experience shows that going narrow and deep when choosing where to belong creates more sustainable advantage than going broad and shallow. PetSmart focused its community stewardship activities beginning in 1991 on stopping the euthanasia of companion pets. To date it has saved over 2.5 million pets via adoption services. Red Lobster ensures its suppliers follow sustainable fishing practices to protect the health of our oceans, and has led the seafood industry in developing environmentally friendly aquaculture so it can have safe, reliable supplies of top-quality shrimp and fresh fish for generations. These companies have narrowed their focus to the communities of interest most connected to their businesses.

To reap the rewards of a strategic choice of where to belong, we have to belong in three ways: physically, financially, and emotionally. Physical belonging starts with devoting time and talent to be in the community, dealing with issues company outsiders care about. This may include helping with solutions—leading initiatives to address industry-specific environmental problems, providing employees to teach inner-city school classes, or organizing local fund-raising events. The starting point is sitting down with members of the outside community to listen—and then act.

Financial belonging simply means funneling money into the community, as opposed to draining it. It also goes well beyond charitable giving and includes implementing a business structure to strengthen the communities to which the company belongs financially. The Coca-Cola Company and its bottlers have 900 plants in over 190 countries, but it is a very local business. The vast majority of the revenue generated in a country stays in that country. The company repatriates only its profits from selling concentrates to its local bottlers. The product is made in the country, mainly from local ingredients, and sold in the local currency.

Emotional belonging means connecting with needs and issues the community is passionate about. Applebee's connects emotionally through the Neighborhood Wall in each restaurant, which celebrates local life, events, and people. Starbucks connects to groups in support of raising wage levels for global coffee growers. Wal-Mart connected emotionally with many communities through its Hurricane Katrina relief response.

Last year, Tyson Foods, Luxottica Group (parent of LensCrafters, Pearle Vision, and Sunglass Hut), and Ty, Inc. (maker of Beanie Babies stuffed animals) found a compelling way to belong on all three levels. They worked together through the Lift Up America humanitarian aid organization to distribute 2.25 million meals of Tyson chicken, 40,000 pairs of eyeglasses, and 300,000 Beanie Babies to needy families via 27 professional and college sports teams in 23 cities.

The in-kind donations by Tyson, Luxottica, and Ty certainly constituted financial belonging to the community. Since the events were targeted to specific, heartfelt needs in local communities, the food, eyeglasses, and stuffed animals helped the donating corporations and sports team to connect emotionally. Since key leaders such as John Tyson (chairman of Tyson), Kerry Bradley (COO of Luxottica), Wayne Huizenga, Jr. (owner of the Miami Dolphins), and Dan Snyder (owner of the Washington Redskins) personally delivered the donations to local citizens and aid organizations, they physically belonged to the community as well.

The key to belonging is going beyond simply writing charitable checks to outside groups. It means that we empathize with and invest ourselves in serving specific needs in our communities.

Align

A sea change is occurring in the Wal-Mart economy. Business leaders are realizing that their involvement as community members can be entirely consistent with their strategic and profit objectives. As good stewards, we can *align our business strategy* and *our community strategy*. We can satisfy economic, social, and environmental responsibilities at the same time.

For many organizations in the old economy, charitable giving and community involvement were viewed as necessary evils of doing business—the price we paid to look like good corporate citizens, to get choice seats on the boards of our favorite charities, and to mitigate pressure from special-interest groups. In the Wal-Mart world, however, our challenge is to find the intersection where we can both enhance shareholder value *and* fulfill our role as community members—and be intentional about it.

Aligning our business and community strategies requires us to simultaneously solve some problems as business people and as community members. What are the most pressing needs of those communities to which we have chosen to belong? What effect would meeting those needs have on the long-term shareholder value of our company? How are our customers likely to respond? What core competencies and assets do we have that enable us to contribute better than others to satisfying those needs? How do we make a noticeable, sustainable difference rather than a perfunctory contribution?

The Ronald McDonald House is a great example of aligning business and community strategy. McDonald's understands that one of the earliest consumer decisions a child ever makes for the entire family is to say, "Let's go to McDonald's." McDonald's set up the Ronald McDonald House to serve the communities where it does business, fulfilling the needs of parents who require an affordable place to stay while their children are hospitalized. McDonald's is simultaneously serving the community needs of these families *and* enhancing its brand in the all-important competitive battle over trips, not loyalty.

The efforts of PetSmart Charities to avoid euthanasia of companion pets clearly serves a noble goal in the community. But it is entirely consistent with its business strategy: It enhances PetSmart's perception among both its pet-loving customers and employees, not to mention that there are 2.5 million more pets who now need food, training, and others products and services. Red Lobster's focus on long-term ocean preservation builds its brand image among its target market but also promotes a steady, healthy supply of its critical ingredients for years to come.

Wal-Mart even has discovered how to align business strategy with community stewardship. At first glance, its environmental initiatives may look like they contradict the productivity loop. Conventional wisdom says that environmental initiatives cost money. But the answer from Bentonville is that store-level environmental efforts actually *reduce* costs. Store employees are encouraged to find ways to reduce or eliminate anything in the dumpster, such as excess packaging or damaged products, because it reduces the impact on landfills. That same waste also represents non-value-added costs, the key target of the productivity loop.

Alignment demands some effort, but it returns a strategic advantage. It can strengthen our brand, differentiate our business, reaffirm employee values—in fact, it can add value in multiple ways. It calls for forward thinking and imagination, adeptly merging corporate and civic interests.

Engage

In the movie, *The Second Chance*, Jake Sanders is the pastor of an inner-city church who deals every day with the drug, gang, and crime problems facing his congregation. He is invited to speak to a wealthy suburban congregation that supports his church financially but seldom sends anyone into the inner city to help urban church members through real-life problems. Sanders admonishes the comfortable congregation, "This is how we solve problems in America. We roll down our window, throw out some money, then drive off.... If you're not willing to come down and get a little gravy on your shoes, keep your damn money."

Sanders's frustration speaks to the passive approach company executives often take to the issues that rock their communities. As community leaders, we have to make a third choice: *how to engage in the public debate as leaders of the agenda, not followers.* As McKinsey's Davis wrote in *The Economist*: "[Business leaders] need to shape the debates on social issues much more consciously. This means establishing ever higher standards of integrity and transparency within their own companies. It also means becoming much more actively involved in external debates and in the media on social issues that shape their business context."

Roberto Goizueta, the late chairman of The Coca-Cola Company, echoed these sentiments in his classic quote, "We cannot for the long term exist as a healthy company in a sick society."

Engaging involves picking the pressure points where we as community members can have the greatest impact in moving our agenda to align community and business strategy. What issues will we choose to put our weight behind? Are we harming communities with any of our policies and strategies? With which trade groups and business think tanks will we ally to draft agendas, generate new thinking, and set new standards? On what issues will we speak out to shape opinion? When will we get proactively involved at local, state, national, and global levels? In short, what choices will we make to define and influence the debates over the role of companies in society?

One can argue that Wal-Mart stumbled by failing to make an explicit choice for engaging in a public debate. It got caught letting other people shape the business context. While the company's leaders convinced themselves that saving consumers money and disbursing charitable dollars to communities were enough of a social strategy, outsiders convinced the public and politicians otherwise. The film, *Wal-Mart: The High Cost of Low Price,* by Robert Greenwald, for example, posited that Wal-Mart's social conscience had not evolved to a level of maturity of which society approved.

Hillary Clinton, a former Wal-Mart board member, turned her back on Wal-Mart. When Wal-Mart sent her a $5,000 campaign contribution in 2005, she returned it. Amid a storm of negative stories on Wal-Mart appearing in film, broadcast, and print media, her spokesperson cited "serious differences with current company practices."

Choosing how to engage isn't a call for us as business leaders to become politicians or to press for self-serving legislation or short-term market advantage. It is a call for us to become activists in public life, to shape the agenda, to lead the business solution, and to influence public policy. Although perhaps late to the game, Wal-Mart is energetically entering new areas of debate. It submitted a plan for mandatory global-warming controls to the Senate Energy Committee. The company committed to doubling the fuel efficiency of its truck fleet by 2010, which would eliminate millions of tons of carbon dioxide emissions.

Danny Wegman, CEO of Wegmans Food Markets, has made himself part of the debate for a number of years. He testified before a committee of the House of Representatives in 2002. He urged Congress to amend and reauthorize the Workforce Investment Act, legislation that to this day facilitates and funds local training and employment programs. The Act provided part of the funding for Wegmans' apprenticeship program for Rochester youth, a program benefiting both the community and Wegmans.

Although leaders of small businesses may think that this doesn't apply to them, they duck the debate at the risk of losing a seat at the decision-making table. To retain authority, legitimacy, and a say in our future, we all have to make a genuine effort to find a way to fulfill our roles as stewards at a public-policy level. If we forego making an explicit choice to engage, we shut ourselves out of a powerful means to succeed in the Wal-Mart economy.

WINNING COMMUNITY MEMBERS IN THE NEW ECONOMY

When we fail to make smart choices to belong to the community, align our corporate and community strategies, and engage actively in policymaking in our various communities, we run a risk—abdicating the opportunity to manage our future and instead letting our business and social environment manage us. As community members, we don't have to follow the trends: We need to get ahead of them.

For many business leaders, approaching community and social strategy is like going to school all over again. For one thing, the issues are very broad. They draw leaders onto foreign turf from the start. How many of us have training in global environmental change, social justice, and human rights? For another, social strategy frequently forces us as leaders into unfamiliar roles—as corporate emissaries, diplomats, and advocates. Even so, many leaders have faced the risks and risen to the challenge. At Procter & Gamble, leaders refer to their work as "corporate social opportunity."

Leaders at Wal-Mart have recognized that opportunity. CEO Scott has put on the mantle of public-policy mediator. While activists have succeeded in convincing the public that workers with little health coverage, few skills, and little earning power are company problems, Scott has sought to convince others that they are national problems. In 2006, he addressed the National Governors Association. "So, let's commit ... to working together to solve these problems," he urged.

The stories of three corporate community members demonstrate the extent a robust community strategy can play in companies of different sizes. The strategy is far more than a defensive play, as it became for Wal-Mart in the mid-2000s. It can become central to competitive strategy.

University Bank

David Reiling runs University Bank in St. Paul, Minnesota. He bought the struggling institution with his father in 1995 and today operates a local bank with 35 employees and $115 million in assets. The bank's strategy is to revitalize run-down urban neighborhoods in the Twin Cities by offering a variety of programs to finance affordable housing, small-business development, and urban nonprofit groups.

In 2001, Reiling's bank earned the designation as a Community Development Financial Institution (CDFI) from the U.S. Treasury. Reiling was able to leverage the designation to obtain $1.5 million in low-cost capital, increasing the bank's equity base enough to expand loans to distressed neighborhoods by about $20 million. With the help of the CDFI designation and funding, University Bank has made over $130 million in loans just for renovating run-down housing since 1996.

Reiling's strategy starts with explicit choices to belong to the community physically, financially, and emotionally. When he took over, he marched his tellers down the street, asking them to introduce themselves to every small-business owner and resident along the way. Outside their assigned duties, all employees can elect to take time during the workday to volunteer. Starting in 2005, tellers decided to volunteer for Meals on Wheels. They now make lunchtime deliveries to the elderly once a week.

Reiling requires every bank officer to make 500 calls outside the bank each year and actively participate in a local nonprofit group. Today, the bank's 15 officers spend a collective 3,000 hours per year volunteering for local nonprofits, contributing invaluable financial and management expertise. This works out to nearly four hours per week per officer.

"The giving of time and talent is probably more important to our local community organizations than just the cash," says Reiling. Meanwhile, he says, employees get to know the needs of customers. "When you have all these people out in the community bringing this information back, we can innovate, mold, and shape products and services to meet community needs."

Reiling has closely aligned his business strategy and community strategy. The bank attracts deposits because 82 percent of them go to projects with a community or social benefit. One of his first big initiatives was a partnership with the city of St. Paul, which lent the bank $1.25 million in loan guarantees for lending to immigrants. The guarantees, principally to Hmong and other Southeast Asians, have rolled over multiple times. They have enabled the bank to satisfy business goals by expanding lending and satisfy community goals by getting immigrants into houses and businesses they could never have afforded otherwise.

Another initiative is the Houses to Homes program. Launched in May 2000 to rehabilitate an ambitious 1,000 homes in five years, it reached its goal two years early and to date has renovated more than 1,300 homes. University Bank lends 100 percent of the home's acquisition price to renovators with a track record for successfully buying, fixing, and selling homes in poor communities.

A third initiative is the Urban Revitalization Fund, launched in June 2002, now totaling $66 million. Customers depositing in the fund earn a traditional, competitive return on their bank deposits. Meanwhile, the bank lends their money solely for revitalizing distressed neighborhoods. Today, socially responsible investors nationwide can deposit in the fund by buying certificates of deposit offered through Charles Schwab.

Reiling likes to tell customers that they achieve a "double bottom line." "We can offer a financial return as well as a social return," he says. "It's a broader definition of value; it's a broader value proposition."

In some cases, the community actually has come to Reiling. The City of St. Paul, hoping to revitalize economically distressed neighborhoods, designated a portion of its investment portfolio for socially responsible deposits. University Bank now targets lending of the city's money to the distressed areas that worried city officials.

As for engaging publicly on behalf of the community, Reiling speaks often on the social impact of banking. In 2005, he defended fee-based stored-value cards when the Minnesota legislature sought to ban all fees on the cards. He testified that the cards provided the poor with a terrific bridge between check cashing and bank accounts. They offered social good, but they weren't a financially sustainable product without fees. The ban did not pass.

Reiling also publicly advocates socially minded investing, the bank's bread and butter. "Tell the CEOs of companies ... that their fiduciary duties go beyond maximizing profits to ensure that some corporate assets benefit all stakeholders—customers, neighbors, employees—not just shareholders," he wrote in the *Minneapolis*

Star Tribune. "If every reader of the *Star Tribune* invested 1 percent of their assets in a socially responsible mutual fund, stock, or bank, the impact on our Twin Cities neighborhoods would be stunning."

Reiling's choices to belong to the community, align the bank's needs with the community's needs, and engage in the public debate are not tangential to his business strategy: They *are* his strategy. Such strategies define a unique way to win in the Wal-Mart world.

Clif Bar

Clif Bar is another example of a business riding a wave of success while pursing an explicit community strategy. The Berkeley, California-based food company was founded in 1992 by Gary Erickson (and named for his father) and today sells $100 million of energy bars, gels, and drinks. Clif Bar holds the number three spot in the $1 billion energy bar business.

Although Erickson always sought to run a business helpful to the community and environment, over the years the company formalized his strategy. In fact, the company's strategic vision now explicitly focuses the workforce on the sustainability of the community and the planet. Erickson has repeatedly emphasized that supporting environmental and social causes is an integral part of the company's identity.

The challenge for Erickson and chief executive Sheryl O'Loughlin is to continue to integrate business and social strategies to sell Clif bars, Luna bars, and other products against giants such as Nestlé and Kraft. The company does so in part with a vibrant strategy to belong to a select group of consumer, charitable, and other nonprofit communities; align business and community strategies to generate good money and good deeds; and engage outsiders in debates that shape a favorable context for Clif Bar's communities and brands.

The company's Luna bar demonstrates how Clif Bar made an explicit choice to belong to the community devoted to women's issues. Luna was produced as the first nutritional bar just for women, formulated to taste great and serve women's dietary needs. Clif Bar committed from the start to donate part of Luna proceeds to the Breast Cancer Fund, a group focused on breast cancer research. Luna, guided to market by O'Loughlin, benefited both the company and a constituency about which the company cared.

Clif Bar strengthened its efforts to belong to the women's community—and strengthened the Luna brand—by adding clever marketing. It funded the Luna Chix team, four professional female mountain bikers, riding under the Clif Bar name. Clif Bar then launched LunaFest, a traveling film festival for and about women, covering health, body image, sexuality, sports, relationships, and so on. Part of the proceeds goes to the Breast Cancer Fund.

"Luna came to represent more than a nutrition bar," writes Erickson in *Raising the Bar*, his story of Clif Bar. "Luna also symbolizes women's wellness, power, and a place for women to feel comfortable." It also represented a tight alignment between business and community strategies.

Clif Bar's alignment between business and community strategies is so tight that sometimes there is little distinction between the company's marketing initiatives and its engagement in public policy. Clif Bar often promotes products associated with its new vision for corporate social and community strategy. It favors grassroots venues such as bike races, ski events, and film festivals.

For example, the company has made a particular effort to lobby for lower greenhouse gas emissions. Clif Bar sought to offset the carbon dioxide emissions from its manufacturing plants by buying renewable energy credits funding a Sioux wind farm in South Dakota. Clif Bar sells "Cool Tags" for $2 each to its customers, promising to invest proceeds in wind farming. Each tag will save the planet 300 pounds of carbon dioxide emissions, about the equivalent of driving a car 300 miles.

Clif Bar has devised many ways to use the tags to promote lobbying for climate policy change. In an effort called "Start Global Cooling," it sells the tags at sports events and on the Web. It has even teamed with ski areas and touring rock bands to sell tags that offset emissions created by customers who visit their venues.

Clif Bar meanwhile has engaged in drives to educate the public, obtain petition signatures, and pass legislation limiting greenhouse gas emissions. In a recent effort, it partnered with stopglobalwarming.org, where visitors can join a "virtual march" on Washington by signing onto a drive to call attention to what the organization calls this "most urgent threat facing humanity."

Like University Bank, Clif Bar meshes business and social responsibility as a way to build a strong, highly differentiated brand. The effect is that Clif Bar customers today consider it a cool company and not just because Clif Bar makes tasty food with organic ingredients. It represents an enterprise with a vision of making the world a better place.

Starbucks

Starbucks is one of the icons of social strategy among the world's largest companies. The $6 billion chain has more than 11,000 locations around the world. Starting with a cup of coffee, founder Howard Schultz aimed not just to please customers but also to build stronger communities, improve the well-being of people around the world, and take care of the environment.

The company even claims that its work has led to the coining of a new phrase, the "Starbucks effect," shorthand for Starbucks' beneficial impact on communities around the world. (The term also is used by some people in other ways, for example, to characterize Starbucks-caused traffic congestion.)

The company has come a long way since the mid-1990s, when protesters picketed Starbucks outlets over the dreadful working conditions of Guatemalan coffee farmers. Starbucks, in a foreshadowing of the forces buffeting Wal-Mart today, responded with guidelines to improve farm conditions, the first initiative of its kind for a big importer of farm commodities.

"One reason we're a successful company is the quality of our coffee and our real estate," Schultz once said in an interview. "But a large part of it is the trust the customers have about how Starbucks does business."

Starbucks is explicit and intentional about where to belong in the panoply of communities its business affects and how it aligns its business strategy with the needs of those communities. Its emerging-issues council, composed of 18 senior company leaders, examines new issues regularly to be sure that the company meets not just business objectives but the expectations of stakeholders such as suppliers, community members, environmental groups, and humanitarian groups. Recent critical topics addressed by the council concerned nutrition, cocoa sourcing practices, and Starbucks' impact on climate change.

The council also engages in public policymaking by convening formal conferences of stakeholders on particular topics. It hosted a session in Lausanne, Switzerland, collecting feedback from European policymakers, NGOs, and trade groups on Starbucks' coffee sourcing practices. It hosted a session to gather feedback from global NGOs, industry experts, and the U.S. Agency for International Development (USAID) on cocoa sourcing. With reports of human rights violations in some African cocoa-producing regions, Starbucks used the feedback to develop a socially responsible cocoa sourcing program.

Starbucks has aligned its business strategy and its community strategy by embracing progressive social and environmental causes that

211

appeal to the like-minded segment of its customer base. In 1998, it began working with Conservation International to protect biodiversity, devising principles for growing "conservation coffee," which is coffee grown under the canopy of bird-friendly shade trees. By 2004, it went further. It introduced its "Coffee and Farmer Equity (CAFE) Practices," guidelines to encourage the development of a supply chain producing high-quality coffee grown both to protect the environment and to give a fair shake to farmers.

Today, Starbucks pays a premium price to farmers following the CAFE Practices to help them make a profit and support their families. It also pays an annual premium for "fair-trade certified" coffee. This premium totaled $575,000 in 2005 and is set aside for community-development projects in the growing region. It also provides funds for farmers to access credit and for development projects in coffee-producing communities. The funds provided for credit total over $6 million to date.

Starbucks further distinguishes itself from other coffee vendors by intentionally involving itself in many of its communities, such as contributing directly to community improvements in poor coffee-growing regions. Starbucks gave Oxfam International thousands of dollars for, among other things, women's literacy programs in Ethiopia.

Starbucks actively engages in public-policy debates, thereby setting a corporate-responsibility standard for companies in the Wal-Mart economy. Its CAFE Practices address social, economic, and environmental principles. Farmers, cooperatives, processors, and exporters actually receive scores on their performance. The principles have a big influence on industry practices. The company also engages continuously in shaping public policy of other kinds—the hot issues today being global sourcing, global warming, and national health care policy. Chairman Howard Schultz has personally lobbied legislators for health care reform.

In the Wal-Mart economy, Starbucks stands out as a leading com-pany—a dominant company—that wins with a strong and highly differentiated community strategy. It runs counter to the contention that community-centered strategies work best for niche companies in niche markets. As Starbucks shows, they work globally.

SMART CHOICES FOR COMMUNITY MEMBERS

As business leaders, we face a historic turning of the tables. For more than a century, executives could run their companies with less account-ability than they could run their lives as private citizens. In their jobs as fiduciaries, they faced merciless accountability for finances but marginal accountability for the well-being of employees, the commu-nity, the environment, and society. They simply could let nonfinancial concerns go.

Today we face corporate accountability of a new kind. As suc-cessful leaders, we cannot bypass our nonfinancial responsibilities. In fact, we cannot achieve our financial goals without achieving our community ones at the same time. We are members of diverse com-munities—communities of citizens at local, national, and global levels; communities of special interests from human rights to animal rights; and communities representing the environment. The challenge of working within these communities can seem over-whelming—and yet it is the challenge of our era.

Leo Shapiro, senior statesman of retail marketing, says that the challenge today reminds him of the old story about an ugly and curmudgeonly prince. The prince seeks not to make himself virtu-ous, but he does seek to woo a beautiful woman. He has to wear a mask, which projects handsomeness and honor, to win this sensi-tive woman's heart. The prince begins to act like the mask, and he becomes the person he aspires to be. He makes the mask authen-tic—the mask of a good prince.

In some ways, Wal-Mart and other businesses today have put on that mask. They have received praise for changes in the handling of social concerns of all kinds. Time will tell if they actually become the princes they aspire to be. If they do, they can expect to grow and prosper in markets and communities that demand a higher standard. If they remove the mask before an authentic makeover, they may stumble.

In Nashua, an observer could conclude that Wal-Mart had put on that mask. It behaved with deference and courtesy. It changed its plan in multiple ways to meet the criticisms of Nashua planning staff. Its water-treatment system cleaned runoff not only from its property but also from waters flowing onto its site from acres of developed land upstream. It asked for no public subsidies. After widening the access highway, it proposed to deed the land to the city.

But some on the planning board, and certainly among the public, didn't feel that the mask was authentic. They not only rejected the engineering, but they also scorned the entire proposal. One board member, city Alderman Richard LaRose, called Wal-Mart's plan "offensive, annoying to the general public."

As business leaders and community members in the Wal-Mart economy, we all have to start by choosing the right mask, an authentic one in which we truly steward the resources with which we have been entrusted. We can meld business strategy and community strategy by belonging, aligning, and engaging. We can lead, rather than follow, as both global competitors and responsible community members. As we do, we may well find, like University Bank, Clif Bar, and Starbucks, that we have gained a new form of competitive advantage.

Being Wal-Smart
Find the *And*

The executives of a major processed-foods company were meeting in Atlanta to rethink their future. Recent results were causing consternation. Their return on assets had dropped below 4 percent. Their once-unique products had slipped into commodity status. Even the company's popular brands could no longer command premium prices. Dismayed by shrinking margins and feeble results, Wall Street analysts and investors vented their frustration publicly.

The company's executives felt that they knew how to resolve the problem. They wanted to craft a new functional organization structure to reverse their fortunes in the retail market and, in turn, give them a boost in the stock market. I was working with a breakout group of the executives, laboring through a planning scenario. We were trying to organize the entire company around customer segments. Since the company then was organized around products, this scenario was wrenching for the executives.

A half hour into the scenario, we were stymied. We had made no progress because every time someone floated a fresh idea, the rest of the group shot it down like a bunch of overeager hunters: "Our customers don't think that way." "Our plants are already organized by products, and we can't change that." "This scenario will never happen."

In desperation, I tried an exercise. I asked one executive to propose an idea. I asked the next to build on the idea by starting with the word *and*. We went around the table, and lo and behold, we came up with a wave of fresh thinking. Instead of critiquing ideas into a quick grave, we were connecting ideas to a new future.

Over the years, I've found that executives can get stalled in many ways while developing strategies. Some stay married to the status quo and worry about relinquishing parts of their fiefdoms. Others can't foresee the omens of change in their markets. Yet others hold out for just the right idea, the "one big silver bullet" strategy. In most cases, well-meaning executives kill potent ideas by finding just one thing wrong with them. This "gotcha" mentality can be useful to the executives' personal agendas in the short term—and devastating to the company's future.

Effective strategic thinking comes from piecing together wisdom from diverse and often disparate places. One of the things that clients value in me is "fuzzy thinking," being able to connect seemingly unrelated dots in the market or across industries to develop new strategies. Effective strategies come from making connections, from synthesizing, from melding choices in ways that no other company has—or can. When we make one choice *and* link it to another *and* link it to another, we eventually craft a mosaic that evokes a more compelling, more complete image than any strategic piece taken individually ever could (See Figure E-1).

This is what it means to be Wal-Smart. We link explicit, intentional strategic choices so that competitor strategy *and* vendor strategy *and* employer strategy *and* community strategy work together. The vision of our business that emerges is far brighter, far clearer, and far more effective than each choice standing on its own. We survive and thrive because—We find the *and*.

When the Abt family, from Chapter 5, chose to grow employees through extensive training, it also chose to differentiate in a way big-box retailers could not touch. When Manco's Jack Kahl, from Chapter 6, chose to diversify into Duck brand mailing supplies, he also chose to dominate the consumer packing-materials industry segment.

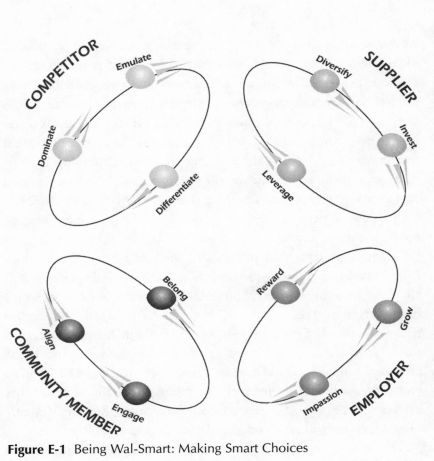

Figure E-1 Being Wal-Smart: Making Smart Choices

When University Bank's David Reiling, from Chapter 8, chose to belong to the community, he also chose to emulate certain special-purpose banking products tailored to the unique needs of low-income borrowers.

I was reminded of how powerful "Find the *and*" can be in practice when I served on an industry committee with Kim Lopdrup, the president of Red Lobster restaurants. Although the casual dining industry (and the service industry in general) is different from the retail industry, Red Lobster still has had to face many challenges of the Wal-Mart economy. Red Lobster has over 680 seafood restaurants in the United States and Canada and another 37 franchised restaurants in Japan. A unit of Darden Restaurants, Red Lobster is the largest casual dining seafood restaurant company in the world. It rings up $2.6 billion in annual sales while serving 2.8 million customers a week.

Lopdrup took the helm of Red Lobster in 2004, at a time when same-store sales and customer traffic were declining. The business was struggling even as it dominated its restaurant niche. Lopdrup helped to restore Red Lobster's forward momentum by making or reaffirming some explicit strategic choices and then—and this is the key—finding the *and* between them to magnify their effect.

Lopdrup started with a strong competitive strategy to differentiate, emulate, and dominate. He differentiated the restaurants by improving the guest experience. He focused the restaurant staff on four goals: fresh, clean, friendly, and full. By 2006, every one of 15 guest-satisfaction measures reached record levels. The biggest progress came in server enthusiasm and atmosphere. The turnaround helped to boost sales: Red Lobster posted its seventh consecutive quarter of comparable-store sales growth in fiscal 2006.

Red Lobster's global inspection network helped it to differentiate. The restaurant is known for having the highest standards in the seafood industry, which are commonly referred to as the "RL Standard." For years, it has inspected every vendor's processing plant using a quality-control process based on best practices from NASA, and has established seafood inspection labs around the world. No competitor has matched its efforts to deliver quality seafood.

When Lopdrup came on, he emulated Wal-Mart's pricing strategy, eliminating steep promotional discounting in favor of lower, more consistent pricing. He set a goal to raise prices at a lower rate than inflation while improving product quality. Because the company shifted gradually toward EDLP, it avoided succumbing to the

"Kmart syndrome," of changing the value proposition overnight and thereby confusing—and losing—customers.

"We have achieved record satisfaction scores from customers," says Lopdrup. "When we made the transition, we did lose some guests, but profits went up immediately. The reduced discounting smoothed out the volatility of our traffic, enabling us to improve our operating efficiency."

As a result, Red Lobster has been able to dominate several segments of the restaurant industry. It has been the top-rated restaurant in the seafood segment for every one of the 18 years that *Restaurants & Institutions* magazine has rated the segment. It beat its competitors in seven of the eight categories, including cleanliness, convenience, food quality, reputation, menu variety, service, and value. Ninety-two percent of those surveyed planned to return to Red Lobster — the highest score of any restaurant in the survey.

What's most interesting is that Lopdrup has created competitive advantage by finding the *and* multiple times between competitor strategy, employer strategy, and community strategy. In other words, he did not craft competitor strategy in isolation. He matched his competitor choice to differentiate the restaurant via friendly service with his choice to impassion his employees with an explicit set of values.

"One of the secrets in a service business is that the people who provide the best service to customers have a genuine desire to be of service to others," he says. "To attract and retain those kinds of people, we have to run our business in a way that they feel good about or they'll leave."

Red Lobster publishes its values in a booklet called "Our Compass." The booklet describes each value in detail and concludes each with a question. Under hospitality, the question is, "Have I made you feel special?" Under quality, the question is, "Is this over the top?" Employees who receive "Yes" answers to each question demonstrate that they are living the values the company—and its customers—expect.

Red Lobster tests all its incoming employees, especially restaurant wait staff, to make sure that their personal work values match Red Lobster's corporate values. Red Lobster has found the *and* in a way that enables one strategic choice to ensure the success of another. It can differentiate itself from its competition *because* it has impassioned its employees. As a bonus, staff retention is better than industry averages.

Another notable way that Red Lobster achieved competitive advantage was by finding the *and* between competitor strategy and community strategy. The company chose to differentiate itself by belonging to the global environmental community and committing to the sustainability of the world's oceans. Former Darden chairman Joe Lee helped draft the Law of the Sea treaty, which spells out United Nations requirements for preventing exploitation of the world's oceans and marine life. Separately, the Darden Environmental Trust belongs financially to several key ocean health initiatives, such as supporting the protection of endangered sea turtles and the restoration of delicate coastal ecosystems.

As part of its business practices as the largest casual dining seafood restaurant company, Red Lobster urges suppliers to invest in programs to ensure the long-term viability of many species. The restaurant does not sell any endangered species, such as orange roughy or Chilean sea bass. It has encouraged the Maine lobster industry to implement exemplary practices to sustain the long-term health of that important species. It also engaged with the other largest seafood purchaser in the world—Wal-Mart—to upgrade the Best Aquaculture Practices for shrimp farming.

Lopdrup believes that these environmental community initiatives are closely aligned with business strategy. After all, the company sources seafood from 40 countries via procurement offices in Orlando, Toronto, and Singapore. "We have a strong vested interest in making sure that our oceans remain in good shape and are able to support the growing world population for a long time," he says.

Taken separately, Red Lobster's choices of how to compete, how to manage employees, and how to steward the global environment could seem unconnected. Executives outside the firm could view them as "nice to haves" or even as distractions. Wall Street analysts could view them as optional expenses, transferring wealth from shareholders to employees and even to sea turtles.

But Figure E-2 tells a very different story. It maps some of the intentional connections — the *ands* — that strengthen and fortify the strategic architecture of the firm.

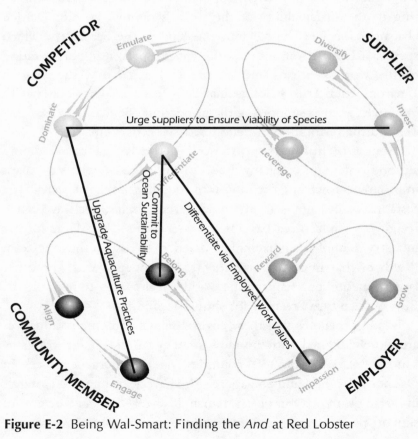

Figure E-2 Being Wal-Smart: Finding the *And* at Red Lobster

Red Lobster demonstrates how strategy as a competitor *and* a supplier *and* an employer *and* a community member works together. "Environmental sustainability clearly helps us in the long term, and it helps us attract and retain the kind of people we want as employees today," says Lopdrup. "Our environmental efforts are very well known within the industry, as well as among employees. It is a source of employee pride."

"Our competitors would have a difficult time doing the same thing—they don't have the scale we do to afford it," he adds. "It builds competitive advantage for us."

Lopdrup's comment brings us back to where this book started. How do we survive and thrive in a Wal-Mart world? How do we outrun the bear? How do we win in an economy with dominant players such as Wal-Mart that seem to own the marketplace?

Whether we are a Fortune 100 company, a regional player, or a mom-and-pop firm, our response is the same: We make explicit, intentional choices. We find the *and*. We arrange the pieces of our strategy until a colorful, vibrant future emerges with new potential for our organizations. Ultimately, the daunting challenges of a world dominated by giants such as Wal-Mart fade, replaced by a clear vision of a brave new world created by being Wal-Smart.

Postscript

As I was finishing this book, I visited Mike Abt, the president of super-successful retailer Abt Electronics. While I was waiting to meet with Mike, I scanned the wall of satisfied customers to find the testimonial that captured the benefit of being Wal-Smart. I found it in famous Apollo astronaut Jim Lovell's thank-you letter to the Abts for his home theater system. It was accompanied by a photo of "earthrise" over the surface of the moon taken from Lovell's Apollo 8 mission. Demonstrating that successful companies don't have to become engulfed in the Wal-Mart world but actually can define a world to call their own, Lovell signed the photo, "A moon's-eye view of the world of Abt."

Acknowledgments

First and foremost, I want to thank my wife, Leslie. She is my business partner, my life partner, and my absolute best friend. This book would not have been possible without her willingness to take a leap of faith with me on this project, her perseverant support, her insights into strategy and the people who deliver it, her encouragement to keep refining my ideas, her careful editing, her personal and economic sacrifices, and her unconditional love. More important, our life together would not have been possible without her believing in me when I was (and always will be) a work in progress and her willingness to share God's greatest gift with me.

I also would like to humbly thank many other people without whom this book would have been impossible.

Mark Hansen has been my client (as CEO of SAM'S CLUB) and my boss (as chairman and CEO of Fleming) and now is one of my best friends. This book was Mark's inspiration when he recognized the unique perspective I had to write a book based on Wal-Mart. Since that singular moment of inspiration, he has stood by my side through the subsequent two years of perspiration, helping me to refine my ideas, encouraging me, and adding vivid color and flavor to this book. He has been a mentor, a cheerleader, and a great friend.

Bill Birchard (www.billbirchard.com) cowrote this book with me. His contribution to this project and his collaboration exceeded my wildest expectations. Bill was able to deftly navigate me, as a first-time author, through the writing process because of his seasoned experience. This book benefited from the confluence of Bill's prior experience writing on topics such as value disciplines (Treacy and Wiersema), leadership, performance measurement, the environment, corporate social responsibility, and a host of other business topics. He worked tirelessly to get into the weeds with me on many of the topics in this book so that he grasped the subject well enough to write. He was always willing to push back on me and help me to further refine my own ideas, and he embraced feedback and edits with a passion for excellence. I would absolutely recommend Bill as a writer to anyone, unless I have another project for him, too!

Meryl Brodsky is a researcher extraordinaire. Meryl has worked with my wife and me for many years and has pored countless hours of her life into researching this book over the past two years. She was the first member of the team, as I began to explore whether there was enough information to pursue this project. If you need the GDP of Botswana (did you know that the country has the only investment-grade credit rating in Africa?), Meryl can find it. If you need to assess the market for Turkish organic cotton, Meryl can find it. My theory: If Meryl can't find it, it doesn't exist.

Leslie Nunn Reed of Nunn Communications (www.nunncommunications.com) served as my agent to help me develop the book proposal, diligently shop it to numerous publishers, and guide me along the way. Her diligent commitment to this project, her thoughtful insights into positioning and selling it, and her wise counsel have helped to make this book what it is. Sensing I was getting frustrated in the throws of final edits, she wisely reminded me that author Philip Yancey once described book writing as giving birth to a bale of barbed wire. Thanks for the visual image, Leslie—at least it helped me to know that I wasn't alone!

Donya Dickerson, my editor at McGraw-Hill, has provided insightful guidance and feedback on the book's content, its positioning, and its marketing. She rapidly caught the vision that there was a huge opportunity in the market for a book about the Wal-Mart economy that was balanced, especially one that helped other companies to figure out how to survive and thrive. She was willing to take the risk to champion a first-time author whom she recognized had something unique to say. She also rolled up her sleeves and dug into the content and flow of the book in a way that remarkably improved the end product. Daina Penikas of McGraw-Hill shepherded the book masterfully through production, and Jim Madru provided comprehensive and thoughtful copyediting. Kenya Henderson and Seth Morris of McGraw-Hill were instrumental in building interest for the book by adeptly cultivating their public relations and marketing contacts.

The team of Nancy Lovell and Julie Fairchild of Lovell-Fairchild Communications (www.lovell-fairchild.com) have served our firm, Marble Leadership Partners, with creativity and panache. They have been invaluable partners in getting this book and its insights well positioned in the marketplace.

Mark Hansen, Tom Compernolle, and Dennis Sheehan read the complete manuscript—their comments made the final book much more compelling. Dennis is battling primary progressive MS and has been an inspiration to me during this project as I have watched him struggle boldly and courageously against a disease that is crippling him. Tom is a great retail mind and has been a very valued peer, client, business advisor, and especially friend for years.

A number of my business associates through the years have been contributors to this book not only by sharing stories and insights but also by working side-by-side with me solving many real company problems. I thank Kirk Dupps, Jean-Michel Fally, Andy Fauver, Bill Godwin, Brent Knight, Rich Knust, Sue MacReynolds, John Miologos, Phil Murphy, Jim Postma, Bill Ryan, Owen Shapiro, and Jimmy Wright, as well as the entire Capgemini team with whom I worked on the Meijer project.

Jay Smethurst at Sente Corp. (www.senteco.com) designed the Wal-Smart triad graphics, and Peter Durand of Alphachimp Studio (www.alphachimp.com) provided valuable graphics insights. Chris Firestone at Trinity International University, a like-minded philosopher, assisted in developing the quotes for the front page.

Schuler's Books and Music on Alpine Avenue in Grand Rapids, Michigan, was my mobile office. I spent many long nights in the café (I highly recommend the food) and in front of the fireplace researching, drafting chapter outlines, and editing chapters.

Special thanks to my sons, Christopher and Patrick. I realized that it was time to get out of consulting for a while when they were in grade school and couldn't really understand what Dad did for a living. When I went to Fleming, they were finally able to touch and feel Dad's job, since they helped me to stock the first yes!Less store in Athens, Texas. I know you were sick of me dragging you into many retail stores over the years—the book you are now holding in your hands is the result of those sacrifices.

Finally, a word of thanks to my Mom and Dad, Marilyn and Bill Marquard. I could not have hoped for better parents to raise me, nurture me, and love me through the good times and the bad. You provided me with a role model of parental love that I hope to pass through to the next generation of Marquards. And I know that you didn't understand why I ever wanted to be a philosophy major in college, but at least I proved I could get a real job!

Sources and Notes

The following notes represent the sources of major facts in the book. Many facts and opinions which are not cited come from the author's consulting experience.

INTRODUCTION

The William James quotation is from John Cook (compiled and arranged by), *The Fairview Guide to Positive Quotations* (Minneapolis: Fairview Press, 1996), p. 316. The Confucius quotation is from Laurence G. Boldt, *Zen Soup* (New York: Arkana, 1997), p. 19. The Revelation quotation is from the Holy Bible, New Living Translation (Wheaton, IL: Tyndale, 1996).   x

For Fred Meijer, the day of reckoning...   This story about Fred Meijer and the Meijer chain of supercenters comes from the author's consulting engagement with the company from 2003 through 2006.   1

Consider that in 2002, Wal-Mart bought 14 percent...   Abigail Goldman and Nancy Cleeland, "An Empire Built on Bargains Remakes the Working World," *Los Angeles Times*, November 23, 2003.   5

It even hosts high-level envoys from Bangladesh...   Ibid.   5

5   *Wal-Mart alone accounts for 10 percent of the U.S. trade deficit…*   Robert Flint, "Wal-Mart Trade with China Goes Beyond Retail," Dow Jones Chinese Financial Wire, November 16, 2004.

5   *Once feeding on the heavy traffic flowing…*   Penelope Patsuris, "Wal-Mart's Next Victims," *Forbes*, November 11, 2004.

5   *Since 1988…13,500 U.S. supermarkets have closed…*   Matthew Swibel, "Nobody's Meal," *Forbes*, November 24, 2003.

5   *…Wal-Mart alone has been a major catalyst in the closing…*   Kathleen Parker, "Attention, Wal-Mart Shoppers," *Buffalo News*, January 29, 2006.

6   *…most bank customers have little desire to put all their money in one institution…*   Jim Cole, "Survey: Most Customers Don't Want Just One Bank," *American Banker* 170(117):2, June 20, 2005.

6   *Fifty percent of Wal-Mart's $18 billion of annual imports…*   Mona Williams, vice president of corporate communications, Wal-Mart Stores, Inc., letter to *Newsweek*, June 27, 2005.

6   *While Wal-Mart creates more than 100,000 net new jobs every year…*   From Wal-Mart Stores Web site, www.walmartfacts.com/doyouknow/default.aspx#a26.

6   *Union grocery-worker wages are often at least 30 percent more…*   Marlon G. Boarnet, Randall Crane, Daniel G. Ghatman, and Michael Manville, "Emerging Planning Challenges in Retail: The Case of Wal-Mart," *Journal of the American Planning Association* 71(4):433, Autumn 2005.

6   *More than 220 Wal-Mart sites…*   David Moberg, "The Wal-Mart Effect," *In These Times*, June 10, 2004.

7   *In a story of the tables turned…*   Mike Duff, "Older and Wiser—and Gaining Ground," *DSN Retailing Today*, June 13, 2005.

8   *…when I was executive vice president of Fleming Companies…*   Information about the Fleming Companies and Kmart comes from author's tenure as an executive at Fleming from 1999 through 2002.

9   *"There are costs and risks to a program of action…"*   John A. Barnes, *John F. Kennedy on Leadership: The Lessons and Legacy of a President* (New York: AMACOM, 2005), p. 143.

Recall a couple of the more muddleheaded comments...   Steve D. Price, *1001*   9
Dumbest Things Ever Said (Guilford, CT: Lyons Press, 2005), pp. 152, 154.

Soon after Chuck Conaway took over as chairman and CEO of Kmart...   10
The story about Kmart comes from the author's personal experience
managing Fleming's $3 billion supply alliance with Kmart and working
directly with Kmart senior executives such as Chuck Conaway and Mark
Schwartz.

One of Wal-Mart's senior leaders reduced the strategies...   Based on the   10
author's personal experience leading Wal-Mart's strategic planning sessions
from 1996 to 1999.

Wal-Mart's toy industry market share...   Greg Johnson, "The Game Has   11
Changed," *Los Angeles Times*, December 13, 1998, sec. C; and NPD
Group, "Wal-Mart's Lead Grows," *Playthings* 98 (6):10, June 1, 2000.

Wal-Mart's market share in groceries vaulted from third...   "Changing   11
the Lineup," *Supermarket News*, January 25, 1999; and Alice Z. Cuneo,
"Wal-Mart Pressure Goes Up a Notch," *Advertising Age* 73 (25):S24,
June 24, 2002.

CHAPTER 1

In 2004, Michael Marx, director of a coalition...   Michael Marx, interview   18
with Bill Birchard, October 20, 2005. Marx confirmed details of the
activist meeting, initially published on the Business Ethics Network's Web
site, http://businessethicsnetwork.org/goalsandstrategies.php.

...nearly one of every 100 workers...   The 2006 figure is 1 of 110 workers.   19
In 2006, the Bureau of Labor Statistics reported that total U.S. employment was 144 million. Wal-Mart Stores, Inc., 2006 Annual Report (Form
10-K) reported that the company employed approximately 1.3 million
workers in the United States.

Almost 9 of 10 Americans shops at Wal-Mart...   Lee Scott told analysts   19
that ". . . the last statistics I saw showed that 86 percent of all people in
the United States were in a Wal-Mart store once a year"; 2005
Wal-Mart Twelfth Annual Analysts' Meeting Day 1, Voxant FD [Fair
Disclosure] Wire, October 25, 2005.

19   *Globally, Wal-Mart already runs stores in countries where 3.9 percent...*
Based on data from International Monetary Fund, *World Economic
Outlook Database,* April 2006, and from Central Intelligence Agency, *CIA
World Factbook* (Washington: CIA, April 2006). Excludes Wal-Mart's
businesses in Germany and South Korea, which were to be sold in 2006.

19   *In December 2005 alone, it added 50,000 people...* From Wal-Mart
Stores Web site: http://walmartstores.com/GlobalWMStoresWeb/
navigate.do?catg=14.

20   *Wal-Mart's revenues of $312 billion exceed the GDP...* Based on data
from International Monetary Fund, *World Economic Outlook Database,*
April 2006.

20   *In one year alone, Wal-Mart sells more than $1,000 worth of merchandise...*
Based on $312 billion revenue, per Wal-Mart Stores, Inc., 2006 Annual
Report (Form 10-K), divided by 298 million U.S. population, per *CIA
World Factbook* (Washington: CIA, April 2006).

20   *It does more business than its next four competitors...* Based on fiscal year
2006 U.S. Securities and Exchange Commission Annual Reports (Form
10-K) by Home Depot, Kroger, Target, and Sears.

20   *...scooping up roughly 10 cents of every retail dollar...* According to figures cited by Wal-Mart executives. See, for example, Lee Scott, Speech to
Executive Club Luncheon, Chicago, May 17, 2005. The figure would be
7 cents if calculated using Wal-Mart's fiscal 2006 U.S. sales of $250 billion
per Wal-Mart Stores, Inc., 2006 Annual Report (Form 10-K) and figures
for total retail sales from the U.S. Census Bureau, which in 2005 tallied
$3.8 trillion. Scott's comments may have excluded some segments of
retail sales included in the U.S. Census Bureau figure.

21   *...Wal-Mart's share of the entire global economy approaches 1 percent.* The
2005 figure was 0.7 percent based on data from International Monetary
Fund, *World Economic Outlook Database,* April 2006.

21   *Its share of the U.S. economy has grown to 2.5 percent.* Derived from
calendar year 2005 figures from the Bureau of Economic Analysis,
www.bea.gov.

21   *U.S. Steel had a 3.1 percent share...* Calculated by dividing consolidated revenue by U.S. gross national product or gross domestic product, as applicable.

Wal-Mart has 3,900 stores...   Store count figures for the United States   21
and international business come from the company Web site.

The number of people who depend on Wal-Mart...   Figures for the num-   21
ber of people and companies depending on Wal-Mart come from the
company Web site.

Wal-Mart's influence extends directly to the 35 million...   Estimates of   21
Wal-Mart's sphere of influence derived by analyzing U.S. Bureau of Labor
Statistics employment by industry segment.

Wal-Mart's reported selling, general, and administrative...   SG&A   23
expenses for Wal-Mart and competitors come from the most recent U.S.
Securities and Exchange Commission Annual Report (Form 10-K) filings
for the respective companies, generally fiscal year 2005–2006. These
numbers may not be entirely comparable because of differences in the way
each company treats items such as depreciation and amortization, credit-
card income/expense, and the occupancy costs of warehouse and distribution facilities.

Its total distribution costs run just 3 percent of sales...   Rob Walton, un-   23
titled speech delivered to the American Antitrust Institute, June 21, 2004.

Its data center tracks an unrivaled 680 million...SKUs...   Wal-Mart   23
Stores, Inc., 2005 Annual Report, p. 9.

Its information warehouse holds 570 terabytes...   Ibid.   24

One year it discovered that about 25 percent...Barbie doll...   Based on   24
author's personal experience during the Wal-Mart strategic planning process.

It moves product through its pipeline...   Derived from financial figures in   24
Wal-Mart Stores, Inc., 2006 Annual Report, p. 31.

It has shortened its product-introduction pipeline...   Jack Neff,   24
"Wal-Marketing: How to Benefit in Bentonville," *Advertising Age*
73 (40): 1, October 6, 2003.

In a recent test with a new Gillette razor...   Michael Garry, "With RFID   25
P&G Improves Launch of New Fusion Razors," *Supermarket News*,
March 27, 2006.

General Electric manages Wal-Mart's inventory of GE light bulbs...   Rob   25
Walton, untitled speech delivered to the American Antitrust Institute,
June 21, 2004.

25 *...over 1,200 suppliers now staff offices...*   Marcus Kabel, "Wal-Mart Base Could Lure More Suppliers," Associated Press Newswires, May 25, 2006.

26 *A study released in 2005 by Emek Basker...*   Emek Basker, "Selling a Cheaper Mousetrap: Wal-Mart's Effect on Retail Prices," *Journal of Urban Economics* 58:226, Fall 2005.

26 *...Global Insight calculated...just how much Wal-Mart's continuous lowering...*   Global Insight Advisory Services Division, "The Economic Impact of Wal-Mart," November 2, 2005, p. 1.

26 *The McKinsey Global Institute concluded in 2002 that retail productivity growth...*   Bradford Johnson, "Retail: The Wal-Mart Effect," *McKinsey Quarterly* 1:40, 2002.

27 *The vice chairman of Target once remarked...*   McKinsey Global Institute, *U.S. Productivity Growth 1995–2000: Understanding the Contribution of Information Technology Relative to Other Factors* (Washington, D.C.: McKinsey & Company, October 2001), Chap. 4, p. 11.

28 *Analysts at market research firm Retail Forward found that in countries...*   Stephen Spiwak, *Strategic Focus: Global Food, Drug, Mass Shopper Update* (Columbus, OH: Retail Forward, April 2005), Fig. 8, p. 9.

28 *A study of Oklahoma City shoppers by Leo J. Shapiro & Associates...*   Leo J. Shapiro & Associates "OK 2010: Wal-Mart in Oklahoma City," presentation done in cooperation with Foote Cone & Belding, July 2003, pp. 77, 87. See also Betsy Spethman, "Small City Big Ideas," *Promo Magazine*, September 1, 2004.

29 *Ninety-three percent of households in the United States include...*   Ann Zimmerman, "Wal-Mart Sets Out to Prove It's in Vogue," *Wall Street Journal*, October 25, 2005, Sec. B.

29 *The average Wal-Mart customer earns between $40,000 to $45,000...*   Steve Matthews, "The Wal-Mart Effect: Top Retailer Is Widely Seen as Gauge of U.S. Economy," *Seattle Times* (Bloomberg News), October 21, 2003, Sec. A.

This explains why 86 percent of Americans... have shopped Wal-Mart... 29
Sandra Skrovan, *Shopper Update* (Columbus, OH: Retail Forward, November 2005), Fig. 8, p. 8.

Seventy-three percent of families with household incomes over $100,000... 29
Ibid., Fig. 5, p. 6.

...Wal-Mart executives note that the company has only a 3 percent share... 30
Numbers from company reports and Lee Scott, speech to Executive Club luncheon, Chicago, May 17, 2005.

Its U.S. real-estate committee already has approved 1,500... John Menzer, 30
"WMT—Wal-Mart Stores, Inc., at Citigroup 2006 Retail Conference and Field Trip," presentation transcribed by Thomson StreetEvents, February 7, 2006, p. 2.

Analysts at Retail Forward count Spain, France, and Russia... 30
Alfred Meyers (with Sandra Skrovan), "Wal-Mart 2010," paper presented at 2005 Strategic Outlook Conference, New York, 2005, p. 14.

...by 2010, it will ring up more than $500 billion in sales. Ibid., p. 6. 31

In the Dallas area, it owns over 28.5 percent... Maria Halkias, "Wal-Mart 31
and Kroger Bag Larger Shares of the Market," *Dallas Morning News,* February 27, 2006.

Sam Walton called it "spreading out, then filling in." Sam Walton and 31
John Huey, *Sam Walton: Made in America* (New York: Doubleday, 1992), p. 140.

Wal-Mart's Oklahoma City expansion... Bob Walter, "Local Oklahoma 31
City Grocer Survives, Thrives Under Wal-Mart Onslaught," *Sacramento Bee*, November 30, 2003.

The folks who come after me are eventually going to... Walton and Huey, 32
Sam Walton: Made in America, p. 297.

Wal-Mart's employees meanwhile have turned the screws... Information 32
on lawsuits comes from Wal-Mart Stores, Inc., 2006 Annual Report, pp. 42–43.

33   *Retail marketing maven Leo Shapiro notes...*   Leo Shapiro, interview with author, March 2, 2006.

33   *...in Turlock, California, where the city council passed an ordinance...* Marianne Lavelle, "Wal-Mart's Most Wanted," *U.S. News & World Report,* June 27, 2005, p. 36.

34   *Even* Advertising Age *opined...*   Editorial, "What's Good for Wal-Mart," *Advertising Age* 75(16):22, April 19, 2004.

34   *A recent American Demographics Perception Study showed...*   Bradley Johnson, "Wal-Mart Is the Best! No, Wait, It's the Worst!" *Advertising Age* 76 (24):14, June 13, 2005.

37   *...Ford embarked on a 2/2/3 program...*   Derived from the author's experience advising an auto supplier that was part of the program.

38   *Wal-Mart is now synchronizing product data such as packaging...*   Laurie Sullivan, "Wal-Mart to Suppliers: Clean Up Your Data," *Information Week* 1041:24, May 30, 2005, p. 24.

39   *Conservative columnist Pat Buchanan may be right...*   Pat Buchanan, "Europe Pays Price for Welfare," *Pittsburgh Tribune-Review,* April 1, 2006.

40   *...the San Diego Community and Economic Development Department complained...*   City of San Diego Community and Economic Development Department, "Fiscal and Economic Impacts of Large Retail Establishments," August 2004, p. 14.

41   *...Novartis has produced...20 million Coartem brand treatment courses.* Novartis International, 2005 Annual Report, p. 58.

CHAPTER 2

46   *For almost three decades, Jack Kahl was the chief executive...*   The story of Manco and its successor company, Henkel Consumer Adhesives, comes from Jack Kahl, interview with author, November 11, 2005, and Jack Kahl, interview with author and plant tour, November 25, 2005; and sources cited below.

48   *...Walton once decided to make MoonPie-brand snacks...*   Sam Walton and John Huey, *Sam Walton: Made in America* (New York: Doubleday, 1992), p. 77.

To make the loop easier to understand... The description of the produc- 48
tivity loop and the hypothetical example in this chapter are based on the
author's personal experience with the productivity loop while consulting
to Wal-Mart.

In its pure form, EDLP is a strategy... The descriptions and observations 51
related to EDLP and hi-lo pricing in this chapter are based on the
author's years of experience as an executive and as a consultant working
with retailers that employed both these methods.

To Walton, duct tape was the "bailing wire of the twentieth century." Jack 51
Kahl, interview with author, November 11, 2005.

...in a survey by market research firm Retail Forward, shoppers choose 52
EDLP... Debbie Howell, "Supermarkets Take New Tack in Battle
Against EDLP," *DSN Retailing Today,* May 23, 2005, p. 7.

"Shoppers at Trader Joe's are educated about EDLP..." Based on the 52
author's store visits, and Trader Joe's Web site at www.traderjoes.com.

More than two-thirds of people look at flyers... Hung LeHong, "Both 53
EDLP and Hi-Lo Pricing Can Work if Executed Properly," *Report by
GartnerG2,* June 2004, Fig. 3, p. 4.

Safeway chief executive Steven Burd noted... Anonymous, "Safeway 53
Refocuses on EDLP," *DSN Retailing Today,* September 22, 2003, p. 28.

Studies show that customers drawn to promotions... Judith Garretson and 53
Scot Burton, "Highly Coupon and Sale Prone Customers: Benefits Beyond
Price Savings," *Journal of Advertising Research* 43:162, June 2003.

In the GartnerG2 study, 78 percent of consumers claimed... LeHong, 54
"Both EDLP and Hi-Lo Pricing Can Work," p. 1.

It has to generate over $250,000 of additional weekly sales... Based on the 54
author's personal experience.

In Canada, Wal-Mart's entry prompted customers... Stephen J. Arnold, 54
Jay Handelman, and Douglas J. Tigert, "The Impact of a Market Spoiler on
Consumer Preference Structures (or, What Happens When Wal-Mart Comes
to Town)," *Journal of Retailing and Consumer Services* 5 (1):1–13, 1998.

In the United Kingdom, where low prices... John Fernie, Barbara 55
Hahn, Ulrike Gerhard, Elke Pioch, and Stephen J. Arnold, "The Impact

of Wal-Mart's Entry into the German and UK Grocery Markets,"
Agribusiness 22 (2):247, 2006.

56 *Adamson joked with his team that if they kept up that practice...*   Jim
Adamson, interview with the author, February 28, 2006.

56 *One Wal-Mart apparel executive responsible for a $35 billion...*   Nancy
Cleeland, Evelyn Iritani, and Tyler Marshall, "Scouring the Globe to Give
Shoppers an $8.63 Polo Shirt," *Los Angeles Times*, November 24, 2003.

58 *A study to analyze out-of-stock merchandise at 12 Wal-Mart stores...*
"Wal-Mart Improves On-Shelf Availability Through the Use of Electronic
Product Codes," PR Newswire, October 14, 2005, p. 1.

58 *...Wal-Mart is synchronizing product data worldwide.*   Laurie Sullivan,
"Wal-Mart to Suppliers: Clean Up Your Data," *Information Week* 1041:24,
May 30, 2005, p. 24.

60 *For Jack Kahl, the simple choice of the productivity loop...*   Jack Kahl, interview with the author, November 11, 2005.

CHAPTER 3

62 *As Bulls guard B.J. Armstrong observed...*   Phil Jackson, *Sacred Hoops*
(New York: Hyperion, 1995), p. 126.

62 *"The secret is not thinking..."*   Ibid., p. 115.

63 *As business leaders...we have to grasp an important distinction—the difference between what I call* strong-process organizations *(SPOs) and* weak-
process organizations *(WPOs).* The contrast between strong-process
organizations and weak-process organizations was first suggested to the
author by Mark Hansen. The framework presented in this chapter was
developed by the author from observations of company operations and
related results both for Wal-Mart and for numerous other organizations
the author has led, advised, and/or studied.

65 *Perhaps 10 percent of all companies...*   Author estimate from consulting
experience.

66 *Other well-known strong-process firms systematically embed leaders...*
Based on the author's experience consulting with McDonald's and
Walt Disney World.

The study found an inverse *correlation between inventory levels and in-stock* 69
conditions... Thomas W. Gruen, Daniel S. Corsten, and Sundar
Bharadwaj, "Retail Out of Stocks: A Worldwide Examination of Extent,
Causes, and Consumer Responses," paper developed jointly at the
University of Colorado, the University of St. Gallen (Switzerland), and
Emory University, April 18, 2002, p. 45.

...when Wal-Mart executives talk about performance measures... Wal-Mart 73
Stores, Inc., 2006 Annual Report, p. 22.

Every time one opens, managers measure costs... Jimmy Wright (former 73
vice president of distribution for Wal-Mart Stores), interview with
Bill Birchard, November 22, 2005.

Executives such as John Menzer weren't happy a few weeks into January... 75
John Menzer, "WMT—Wal-Mart Stores, Inc., at Citigroup 2006 Retail
Conference and Field Trip," presentation transcribed by Thomson
StreetEvents, February 7, 2006, p. 9.

Author and management professor Oren Harari... Oren Harari, speech 76
at Fleming Companies customer conference, 2000.

The company's record tells the story of a vast... From Wal-Mart Annual 76
Reports, 1979, 1989, 1995, and 2006. Historical annual reports are
available on Wal-Mart Stores Web site: www.walmartstores.com/
GlobalWMStoresWeb/navigate.do?catg=453&contId=5700.

...Jim Collins's advice described in Good to Great... Jim Collins, *Good to* 77
Great: Why Some Companies Make the Leap ... and Others Don't (New York:
HarperCollins, 2001), p. 13.

Take the recent changes in Wal-Mart distribution processes... Mike Troy, 78
"High-Tech DC Streamlines Supply Chain," *DSN Retailing Today,* May 9,
2005, p. 42.

As one Wal-Mart distribution executive says... Ibid. 78

...then-CFO Menzer launched a campaign to drive up asset returns... 78
Details from the author's consulting experience.

As Mark Hansen, the former chief executive of SAM'S CLUBS, says... 79
Mark Hansen, interview with Bill Birchard, October 31, 2005.

79   *In 1995, Wal-Mart productivity, as measured by sales per employee...*
     Bradford Johnson, "Retail: The Wal-Mart Effect," *McKinsey Quarterly*
     1:40, 2002.

82   *McDonald's added an average of over 1,600 new restaurants a year...*
     Calculated from data in McDonald's Corporation, 2005 Financial Report,
     p. 3. Remaining insights from the author's consulting experience and
     discussion with John Miologos, McDonald's Corp. Corporate Vice
     President, Worldwide Architecture, Design & Construction.

CHAPTER 4

88   *As retired vice chairman Don Soderquist writes...*   Don Soderquist, *The
     Wal-Mart Way: The Inside Story of the Success of the World's Largest
     Company* (Nashville: Nelson Publishing, 2005), p. 90.

91   *...partly explaining why SAM'S CLUBS generate just over half...*   Based
     on information from the most recent U.S. Securities and Exchange
     Commission Annual Report (Form 10-K) filings for Wal-Mart (fiscal year
     ended January 31, 2006), Costco (fiscal year ended August 29, 2005),
     and BJ's Wholesale Club (fiscal year ended January 28, 2006); revenue
     per club (U.S. only) was calculated as $122 million for Costco, $70 million
     for SAM'S CLUB, and $47 million for BJ's Wholesale Club.

92   *...Sam Walton read the works of twentieth-century quality guru W. Edwards
     Deming...*   Sam Walton and John Huey, *Sam Walton: Made in America*
     (New York: Doubleday, 1992), p. 289.

92   *Among Deming's best known...*   W. Edwards Deming, *Out of the Crisis*
     (Cambridge, MA: MIT Press, 1982), Chap. 2.

94   *One change was the reduction in packaging for 16 private-label toys...*
     Robert Berner, "Can Wal-Mart Fit into a White Hat?" (interview with
     Wal-Mart CEO Lee Scott), *BusinessWeek,* October 3, 2005, pp. 94–96.

96   *One competitor who quickly caught onto Wal-Mart's...approach is Fred
     Meijer...*   Based on Fred Meijer's recounting this story to the author,
     2003.

97   *Born in Oklahoma during the run-up to the Great Depression...*   Walton
     and Huey, *Sam Walton: Made in America,* pp. 4–6.

"When it comes to Wal-Mart," Walton wrote... Ibid., p. 12.   98

In one story of thrift, a distribution center employee in Brookhaven...   99
Jimmy Wright, interview with Bill Birchard, November 22, 2005.

Retired vice chairman and chief operating officer Soderquist tells the story...   99
Soderquist, *The Wal-Mart Way*, p. 111.

As the story goes, Walton and then-executive vice president Soderquist...   100
Ibid., p. 20.

Armstrong has a larger heart...   Information on Lance Armstrong comes   102
from two sources: Michael Specter, "The Long Ride," *New Yorker*, July 15,
2002; and Sam Walker, "On Sports," *Wall Street Journal*, July 22, 2005,
Sec. W.

CHAPTER 5

When Mark Schwartz took over as president of Kmart in March 2001...   106
Kmart Corporation, 2001 Proxy Statement (Form DEF 14A), April 4,
2001, p. 15.

In an effort to level the playing field with Wal-Mart...   U.S. Securities   106
and Exchange Commission, Litigation Release No. 19344, August 23,
2005.

...the inventory didn't fly. Sales actually fell.   Kmart Corporation, 2002   106
Annual Report (Form 10-K), May 15, 2002, p. 8; and Andrew
Dietderich, "Chronicle of Failed Strategies: Kmart's Long Road to
Bankruptcy," *Crain's Detroit Business* 18 (4):35, January 28, 2002.

As one analyst joked, Kmart operated...   Management Ventures, Inc.,   107
"Kmart Decreasing In-Store Labor," *Selling National Accounts* 8 (4):14,
April 2004.

...Kmart had to retrench radically...   Kmart Corporation, press releases   107
dated March 8, 2002 and January 14, 2003.

As Adamson commented later, "When we got into bankruptcy..."   Jim   107
Adamson, interview with the author, February 28, 2006.

...Roberto Goizueta noted that the average human drinks...   The Coca-Cola   108
Company, 1995 Annual Report, February 26, 1996.

109   *In Canada, the venerable Saan chain was driven into bankruptcy...*
      Marina Strauss, "Saan Chain Gets Creditor Protection, 'Significant'
      Number of Stores Must Close," *Globe and Mail,* January 7, 2005, Sec. B;
      and Marina Strauss, "Bargain Shop Sees Sale as Path to Growth," *Globe
      and Mail,* May 8, 2006, Sec. B.

109   *...scooped up 20 percent of the U.S. market for all CDs.*   Warren Cohen,
      "Wal-Mart Wants $10 CD's," *Rolling Stone,* October 12, 2004.

109   *...Toys "R" Us chain's share of the toy market has dropped...*   Anne
      D'Innocenzio, "Toys 'R' Us Names Storch Chairman, CEO," Associated
      Press Newswires, February 7, 2006.

109   *One study by Iowa economics professor Kenneth Stone...*   Kenneth E.
      Stone, "Impact of the Wal-Mart Phenomenon on Rural Communities,"
      in *Proceedings: Increasing Understanding of Public Problems and Policies—
      1997* (Chicago: Farm Foundation, 1998), Charts 5, 8, 9, and 11.

110   *Market research firm Retail Forward predicts that two...*   As cited in
      Jenny McTaggart, "Taking a Bite Out of Baggers," *Brandweek,* June 27,
      2005, pp. 42–45.

110   *...family-owned Spencer's IGA Superthrift found itself hammered...*   Jim
      Spencer, interview with Bill Birchard, December 16, 2005.

110   *In the state of Oklahoma, where Wal-Mart has blanketed the landscape...*
      Lorrie Griffith, "Wal-Mart Saturation Doesn't Dampen Spirits in OK,"
      Shelby Report of the Southwest (Gainesville, GA: Shelby, October, 2005).

110   *Its grocery market share in saturated Dallas...is 28.5 percent...*   Maria
      Halkias, "Wal-Mart and Kroger Bag Larger Shares of the Market," *Dallas
      Morning News,* February 27, 2006.

111   *...its biggest fans remain those in lower- and middle-income...*   Sandra
      Skrovan, *Shopper Update* (Columbus, OH: Retail Forward, November
      2005), Fig. 5, p. 6.

112   *...Jim Spencer expects that his other IGA store...*   Jim Spencer, interview
      with Bill Birchard, December 16, 2005.

112   *A recent study of retail sales in Mississippi...*   Albert Myles, Kenneth
      Stone, and Georgeanne Artz, *The Economic Impact of Wal-Mart
      Supercenters on Existing Businesses in Mississippi* (Starkville, MS:
      Mississippi State University Extension Service, 2003), pp. 6–7.

...in a study of 62 small retailers in southwestern Virginia... Christopher F. 113
Achua and Robert N. Lussier, "Small-Town Merchants Are Not Using
the Recommended Strategies to Compete against National Discount
Chains: A Prescriptive vs. Descriptive Study," paper presented at the
United States Association for Small Business and Entrepreneurship/Small
Business Institute (USASBE/SBIDA) Joint Annual National Conference,
Orlando, FL, 2001.

One military historian studied the 280 major military... B.H. Liddell 113
Hart, *Strategy*, 2d ed. (New York: Meridian, 1991), p. 144.

"I don't care how many Wal-Marts come to town..." Sam Walton and John 115
Huey, *Sam Walton: Made in America* (New York: Doubleday, 1992), p. 230.

Several authors including Stephen Covey have described the contrast... 117
Stephen R. Covey, *The Seven Habits of Highly Effective People* (New York:
Fireside, 1989), p. 219.

Darin Marra, the third-generation pharmacist... Darin Marra, interview 118
with Bill Birchard, January 4, 2006.

Abt Electronics' president Mike Abt... Mike Abt, interview with the author 121
and store tour, June 2, 2006. Additional material for this section comes
from the Abt Electronics Web site, www.abtelectronics.com.

The store's showroom is so remarkable that Newsweek... Karen Springen 122
and Daniel McGinn, "Beta-Testing Paradise," *Newsweek,* February 21,
2005, p. E9.

Trader Joe's is one supermarket chain... Details on Trader Joe's come 123
from the author's industry experience, store visits, the company Web site,
www.traderjoes.com, and sources listed below.

...Sales of "Two-Buck Chuck" have exceeded... Steve Powers, "Tricks of 124
the Trader," *Business 2.0*, September 1, 2005.

An even larger scale success story in the Wal-Mart economy is Costco 125
Wholesale. Details on Costco come from the author's industry experience, store visits, the company Web site, www.costco.com, and sources
listed below.

Cardinal rule number one at Costco... Steven Greenhouse, "How Costco 125
Became the Anti-Wal-Mart," *New York Times,* July 17, 2005, Sec. 3.

126 *Sinegal takes a salary of only $350,000...* Costco Wholesale, 2006 Proxy Statement (Form DEF 14A), January 25, 2006, pp. 6–7.

126 *The average household income of customers is $66,000...* Kate Delhagen, "BJ's, Costco, and Sam's Club Win Loyalty with Price," *Forrester Research Trends*, March 22, 2004.

126 *In search of surprises, shoppers come back to Costco...* Anonymous, "IRI Panel Data Shopper Insights," Management Ventures, Inc., August 28, 2005.

127 *...Costco dominates warehouse-style discounting...* Sandra Skrovan, *Industry Outlook: Warehouse Clubs* (Columbus, OH: Retail Forward, October 2005).

127 *Costco's annual member renewal rate is 86 percent...* "Event Brief of Q2 2006 Costco Wholesale Corporation Earnings Conference Call," Final Voxant FD (Fair Disclosure) Wire, March 2, 2006; and Management Ventures, Inc., *Retail Insight*, June 16, 2006.

127 *It sells $909 per square foot...* Sales per square foot were calculated based on information from the most recent U.S. Securities and Exchange Commission Annual Report (Form 10-K) filings for Wal-Mart (fiscal year ended January 31, 2006), Costco (fiscal year ended August 29, 2005), and BJ's Wholesale Club (fiscal year ended January 28, 2006). For comparability, figures were calculated for U.S. stores only.

127 *Another example of a major retailer giving Wal-Mart a run for its money is Tesco...* Details on Tesco come from the author's industry experience, company Web site, www.tesco.com, and sources listed below.

127 *...ASDA...trails Tesco in total U.K. retail grocery market share...* Cecillie Rohwedder, "No. 1 Retailer in Britain Uses 'Clubcard' to Thwart Wal-Mart," *Wall Street Journal*, June 6, 2006, Sec. A.

127 *Tesco is so powerful that 60 percent of U.K. shoppers...* Caroline Foulkes, "Store Wars," *Birmingham Post*, October 5, 2005 (survey conducted by ICM for *Retail Week* in 2005).

129 *As Adamson, the turnaround CEO remarked...* Jim Adamson, interview with the author, February 28, 2006.

130 *On January 14, 2003, as part of Kmart's bankruptcy...* Kmart Corporation, press release, January 14, 2003.

CHAPTER 6

Not long after he took over as chief executive... Details of the Levi Strauss 132
story come from company annual reports and U.S. Securities and
Exchange Commission filings as specified below.

They stressed efforts to improve innovation... Levi Strauss & Co., 2002 132
Annual Report, pp. 8–10; Levi Strauss & Co., 2003 Annual Report, p. 2;
Levi Strauss & Co., 2004 Annual Report, front flap; and Levi Strauss & Co.,
2005 Annual Report, p. 1.

The company was absent from the other 50 percent... Levi Strauss & Co., 132
2002 Annual Report, p. 10.

...missing the chance to put itself in front of the 160 million people... Ibid. 132

Levi Strauss executives had reasons... Levi Strauss & Co. 2003 Annual 133
Report (Form 10-K), March 1, 2004, p. 71.

Surveys at the time showed that sales at such traditional... RoxAnna Sway, 133
"The Department Store: Headed for the Dustbin or Ready to Re-energize?"
Display & Design Ideas 15(6):20, June 1, 2003.

...Levi executives admitted that the decision might 'adversely...' Levi Strauss 133
& Co. 2003 Annual Report (Form 10-K), p. 71.

Harvard Business School Professor Michael Porter developed... Michael 134
Porter, *Competitive Advantage: Creating and Sustaining Superior
Performance* (New York: Free Press, 1985), p. 9.

Bain & Company research, for example, studied 38 publicly traded... 135
Amy Balchin, "Winning with Wal-Mart Home Office: Is it Possible to
Supply to Wal-Mart and Still Keep Hold of Decent Profit Margins?" *The
Grocer,* August 7, 2004.

Wal-Mart holds 36 percent of the market for dog food... Jerry Useem, 135
Julie Schlosser, and Helen Kim, "One Nation Under Wal-Mart," *Fortune,*
March 3, 2003, pp. 64–78.

Wal-Mart is the place where consumers buy... "Wal-Mart and RadioShack 135
Secure 60 Percent of the Major Retailer Market Share for Recent Mobile
Device Purchases, According to Telephia: Major Retailers Boast Strong
Showing in Pre-Paid Wireless Market," *Business Wire,* December 7, 2005;
Michael Learmouth, "Store Wars," *Daily Variety,* November 13, 2005;

and Michael Rudnick, "Best Buy Pushes Service in Race Against Mass," *HFN*, August 22, 2005, p. 22.

136 *Wal-Mart is growing organic cotton...* Kelly Nolan, "Organic Clothes Grow Past Woodstock Crew," *DSN Retailing Today* 45 (9):5, 48, May 8, 2006.

136 *...Wal-Mart's direct sourcing of bed and bath products...* "Wal-Mart Pushes Sourcing," *Home Textiles Today* 27 (8):1, October 31, 2005.

136 *When Faultless Starch discovered...* Christopher Leonard, "Stiff Competition," *The Arkansas Democrat Gazette*, February 22, 2004.

139 *When Ocean Spray began supplying...* Anne D'Innocenzio, "Wal-Mart Suppliers Flocking to Arkansas," *The Associated Press*, September 21, 2003.

140 *During NASA's Apollo missions to the moon...* Andrew Chaikin, *A Man on the Moon* (New York: Penguin, 1994), p. 69–70, 298.

141 *...McKinsey & Company found that winning consumer goods suppliers...* McKinsey & Company, "Winning with Customers to Drive Real Results: The 2005 Customer and Channel Management Survey," for Grocery Manufacturers Association, 2005, p. 2.

142 *McKinsey also found that winning vendors...* *Ibid.*, p. 18.

142 *A multi year study of supplier relationships by Bain & Co....* Gib Carey (Bain project leader), interview with Bill Birchard, January 18, 2006.

143 *Today it markets just 200, names such as Dove...* Matthew Boyle, "Brand Killers," *Fortune*, August 11, 2003, pp. 89–100.

145 *Cott is one of them, with 41 percent of its production...* "Wal-Mart Stores, Inc., Bentonville, AR, is Cott's Biggest Customer Generating 41% of Revenues," *Food Institute Report*, November 7, 2005, p. 6.

146 *If Hasbro were to lose its sales to Wal-Mart...* Hasbro, Inc., 2005 Annual Report (Form 10-K), February 2, 2006, p. 6. Hasbro reported that sales to Wal-Mart in 2005 represented 24 percent of Hasbro's consolidated net revenue, and sales to Toys "R" Us and Target each amounted to 12 percent of consolidated net revenue.

146 *Todd Michael manages Michael Farms in Urbana...* Todd Michael, interview with Bill Birchard, January 12, 2006. Additional information

for this section comes from Richard Jones, "A Family Affair," *American Vegetable Grower,* June 2004.

Jack Kahl received his first order from Wal-Mart... Details on Manco 149 and its successor company, Henkel Consumer Adhesives, come from two primary sources: Jack Kahl, interview with the author, November 11, 2005; and Jack Kahl, interview with the author and plant tour, November 25, 2005. Additional information for this section comes from sources listed below.

The company sponsors a duct tape festival.... See www.duckproducts.com/. 150

It runs an annual duct tape prom-dress competition... See www. 150 ducktapeclub.com/contests/prom/.

Procter & Gamble (P&G) is probably the most written... Details on 151 Procter & Gamble come from the author's industry experience, the company Web site, and sources listed below.

...P&G works together with customers... The Procter & Gamble 151 Company, 2005 Annual Report (Form 10-K), August 26, 2005, p. 4.

It is creating a select group of superbrands... The Procter & Gamble 152 Company, presentation at 2005 annual meeting, October 11, 2005.

With its remaining brands, the company invests in constant... Procter & 152 Gamble, 2005 Annual Report (Form 10-K), p. 4.

Wal-Mart subsequently bought the trademark and relaunched White 152 *Cloud...* "Former P&G Brand White Cloud Now Name on Wal-Mart House Brand," *Cincinnati Post,* November 5, 1999.

P&G now competes with... Sarah Ellison, Ann Zimmerman, and Charles 152 Forelle, "Sales Team—P&G's Gillette Edge: The Playbook It Honed at Wal-Mart," *Wall Street Journal,* January 31, 2005, Sec. A.

Vlasic, the maker of pickles, ended up producing... Charles Fishman, 154 "The Wal-Mart You Don't Know," *Fast Company* 77:68, December 2003.

...Signature brand jeans generated $336 million in their first full year... 154 Levi Strauss & Co., 2004 Annual Report (Form 10-K), February 17, 2005, p. 138.

154 *The next year, the Signature line brought in $361 million…* Levi Strauss & Co., 2005 Annual Report (Form 10-K), February 14, 2006, p. 31.

CHAPTER 7

156 *Robbin Franklin worked at the Wal-Mart…* Robbin Franklin, interview with Bill Birchard, February 7, 2006. Franklin's story also appears on the AFL-CIO Web site, www.aflcio.org/corporatewatch/walmart/ walmart_2_profiles.cfm#liberty_serna.

157 *…it now hires over 700,000 employees annually…* Based on 44 percent annual employee turnover per "Wal-Mart: How Big Can it Grow?" *The Economist*, April 15, 2004, multiplied by 1.8 million employees worldwide.

157 *In October 2005, chief executive Lee Scott gave a seminal speech to employees…* Lee Scott, "Twenty First Century Leadership," presentation to employees, October 24, 2005.

159 *Current and former workers complain…* For example, see comments at Wal-Mart Workers Association Web site, www.walmartwork.org/ index.php?id=68.

160 *Franklin, who makes her case on the AFL-CIO's own Web site…* www. aflcio.org/corporatewatch/walmart/walmart_2_profiles.cfm#liberty_serna.

160 *In late 2005, a jury awarded $172 million…* Wal-Mart Stores, Inc., 2006 Annual Report, p. 43; see also "Wal-Mart Workers Denied Lunch Breaks Awarded $172 Million," *Los Angeles Times*, December 22, 2005.

160 *In April 2004, a number of academics held a conference in California…* Ellen Israel Rosen, "How to Squeeze More Out of a Penny," in *Wal-Mart: The Face of Twenty-First-Century Capitalism*, edited by Nelson Lichtenstein (New York: The New Press, 2006), p. 255.

160 *University of California professor Marlon G. Boarnet and three others…* Marlon G. Boarnet, Randall Crane, Daniel G. Ghatman, and Michael Manville, "Emerging Planning Challenges in Retail: The Case of Wal-Mart," *Journal of the American Planning Association* 71(4):442, Autumn 2005, Table 4.

160 *Its average full-time hourly wage in 2006…* Wal-Mart Stores, "Wal-Mart Statement Regarding Quinnipiac Poll," press release, February 3, 2006;

see also http://walmartstores.com/GlobalWMStoresWeb/navigate.do?
catg=512&contId=6046.

...it found that Wal-Mart paid modestly higher... Global Insight 161
Advisory Services Division, "The Economic Impact of Wal-Mart,"
November 2, 2005, pp. 14–16.

...wage rates in the retail sector share... Derived from Bureau of Labor 161
Statistics calculator, www.bls.gov/ces/home.htm.

Many other big companies, such as McDonalds... In Ohio, for example, 161
Wal-Mart is number one, followed by McDonald's, Yum Brands
(e.g., KFC), Wendy's, and Kroger. See Carrie Spencer Ghose, "Wal-Mart
Biggest Employer of Medicaid Recipients," Associated Press, February 24,
2006; see also http://jfs.ohio.gov/RELEASES/EmployerReport.pdf.

Hicks found that the presence of Wal-Mart drives up... Michael J. Hicks, 162
"The Impact of Wal-Mart on Local Fiscal Health: Evidence from a Panel
of Ohio Counties," paper presented at Economic Impact Research Conference: An In-Depth Look at Wal-Mart and Society, Washington, DC,
November 4, 2005, p. 22.

Another study, this one by Arindrajit Dube and Ken Jacobs... Arindrajit 162
Dube and Ken Jacobs, "Hidden Cost of Wal-Mart Jobs: Use of Safety Net
Programs by Wal-Mart Workers in California" (Berkeley, CA: Center for
Labor Research and Education, Briefing Paper Series, August 2, 2004), p. 1.

...when Wal-Mart opened a store in Evergreen Park... Jo Napolitano, 163
"Store Savors Hiring Success: New Evergreen Park Wal-Mart Draws
Many Applicants, as well as Some Critics, at Its Preview Event," *Chicago
Tribune*, January 27, 2006.

Wal-Mart CEO Scott, addressing these issues in a speech in Los Angeles... 164
Lee Scott, "Wal-Mart and California: A Key Moment in Time for American
Capitalism," speech delivered in Los Angeles, February 23, 2005.

...testing new compensation plans that trade off... Pallavi Gogoi, "Wal- 164
Mart's About Face," BusinessWeek Online, August 9, 2006.

A Towers Perrin study showed that health care costs... Towers Perrin, 164
"2006 Health Care Cost Survey, 2006," www.towersperrin.com.

In a highly critical report on Wal-Mart... Democratic staff of the 164
Committee on Education and the Workforce, U.S. House of Representatives,

"Everyday Low Wages: The Hidden Price We All Pay for Wal-Mart," report for Congressman George Miller, February 16, 2004, p. 21.

165 *In a worldwide survey of 86,000 workers, Towers Perrin ...* Towers Perrin HR Services, "Winning Strategies for a Global Workforce: Executive Report," February 2006, www.towersperrin.com.

165 *Studies by research firm Walker Information confirm...* Walker Information, "The Walker Loyalty Report," Executive Summary, November 2005, www.walkerinformation.com.

166 *Although the law was later overturned...* Pallavi Gogoi, "Rollback Ruling Favors Wal-Mart," BusinessWeek Online, July 20, 2006.

168 *Red Lobster restaurants pay employees in the top-quartile...* Kim Lopdrup, president of Red Lobster, interview with the author, June 1, 2006.

168 *Abt electronics...pays salespeople double...* Mike Abt, interview with author, June 2, 2006.

169 *Workers told Towers Perrin that companies were "failing..."* Towers Perrin, "2005 Global Workforce Study," January 2006, www.towersperrin.com.

170 *According to Manny Elkind of Mindtech, Inc...* Much of the material on values was based on Manny Elkind, interview with the author, August 9, August 15, and August 18, 2006. Elkind is president and founder of Mindtech, Inc., www.mindtech3.com.

172 *Cathy made it clear that he valued...* From the Chick-fil-A company Web site, www.chick-fil-a.com/Company.asp; see also Chuck Salter, "Customer-Centered Leader: Chick-fil-A," *Fast Company*, October 2004, p. 83.

172 *Management turnover is less than 5 percent per year...* Carolyn Walkup, "Cathy Emphasizes Values, Ethics at SPIRIT Awards Breakfast," *Nations Restaurant News*, June 12, 2006.

175 *...corresponds with the research of psychologist Abraham Maslow.* Abraham Maslow, "A Theory of Human Motivation," in Abraham Maslow, *The Maslow Business Reader*, edited by Deborah Stephens (New York: Wiley, 2000), pp. 251–275 (originally published in *Psychological Review* 50:370–396, July 1943).

176 *Trish Karter runs the Dancing Deer Baking Company...* Trish Karter, interview with Bill Birchard, April 11, 2006.

Wegmans Food Markets, based in Rochester, New York... Details on 178
Wegmans Food Markets from the author's industry experience, the company Web site, www.wegmans.com, and sources listed below, including "What Makes Wegmans Different," *Washington Post*, February 26, 2004.

Reminiscent of a high-tech executive... Michael A. Prospero, "Moving 179 the Cheese: Wegmans Relies on Smart, Deeply Trained Employees to Create a 'Theater of Food,'" *Fast Company* 87:8, October 1, 2004.

Its operating margins are roughly 7.5 percent... Matthew Kratz Boyle and 179 Ellen Florian, "The Wegmans Way," *Fortune*, January 24, 2005, pp. 62–68.

The higher per-person costs are offset by far lower turnover... Ibid. 180

"Let's take caring," says Wegman... Tony Bingham and Pat Galagan, 180 "A Higher Level of Learning," *Training & Development*, September 2005, pp. 32–36.

In recent years, Wegman has focused on... Ibid. 180

Wegman has specifically made a choice... Christianna McCausland, 180 "If You Build It . . . Will They Shop?" *Baltimore Magazine*, October 2005.

Given that training a new employee costs roughly $4,000... Danny 181 Wegman, "Workforce Development Oversight," testimony delivered to House Education and Workforce Committee, FDCH Congressional Testimony, September 12, 2002.

Few Wal-Mart suppliers offer a more explicit employment compact than 181 *120-year-old S.C. Johnson...* Details on S.C. Johnson from the company Web site, www.scjohnson.com and sources listed below.

It has repeatedly won top grades... Barbara Parus, "Pump Up Your 182 Flexibility Quotient," *Workspan* 47 (8):48, August 2004.

...CEO, H. Fisk Johnson, offers a statement... S.C. Johnson, "Sustaining 182 Values: 2005 S.C. Johnson Public Report," 2005, p. 42.

S.C. Johnson also runs an online learning program... "Springfield 183 Manufacturing, Behlen, and S.C. Johnson Deliver Outstanding 'Return on Individuals,'" *Manufacturing Business Technology* 24 (4):46, April 2006.

"The goodwill of the people is the only enduring thing..." S.C. Johnson, 183 "Sustaining Values," p. 42.

184 *It was even ranked among the top 100 places to work...* www. greatplacetowork.com/best/list-bestusa-2002.htm.

CHAPTER 8

186 *On the evening of January 12, 2006, Wal-Mart looked...* Bill Birchard, onsite reporting at the Nashua, New Hampshire, Planning Board meetings, December 8, 2005, December 15, 2005, January 5, 2006, January 12, 2006, and January 18, 2006. The Nashua story also was reported in detail in local papers. For example, see Tom West, "Planning Board Votes 4-3 Against Wal-Mart Proposal," *Nashua Telegraph,* January 20, 2006, www.nashuatelegraph.com.

189 *A recent McKinsey & Company study commissioned by Wal-Mart and leaked...* Amy Joyce and Ben White, "Wal-Mart Pushes to Soften Its Image: Social, Environmental Initiatives Seen as Part of Larger Effort to Counter Critics," *Washington Post,* October 29, 2005.

189 *Studying Wal-Mart's effect on communities, Emek Basker...* Emek Basker, "Job Creation or Destruction? Labor Market Effects of Wal-Mart Expansion," *Review of Economics and Statistics* 87 (1):178–180, February 2005.

189 *David Neumark, Junfu Zhang, and Stephen Ciccarella...* David Neumark, Junfu Zhang, and Stephen Ciccarella, "The Effects of Wal-Mart on Local Labor Markets," *National Bureau of Economic Research Working Paper No. 11782,* November 2005, www.nber.org/papers/ w11782.

190 *Global Insight, in its study funded by Wal-Mart...* Global Insight Advisory Services Divison, "The Economic Impact of Wal-Mart," November 2, 2005, p. 2.

190 *William Beaver of Bentley College examined...* William Beaver, "Battling Wal-Mart: How Communities Can Respond," *Business and Society Review* 110:2:161, Summer 2005.

190 *Activist group Good Jobs First tallied the value...* Philip Mattera and Anna Purinton, *Shopping for Subsidies: How Wal-Mart Uses Taxpayer Money to Finance Its Never-Ending Growth* (Washington: Good Jobs First, May 2004), p. 7.

In Oklahoma, Wal-Mart received significant tax subsidies... Based on   191
the author's experience as an executive at the Fleming Companies, head-
quartered in Oklahoma.

...aid group Oxfam International has blasted the company... Kate   191
Raworth, *Trading Away Our Rights: Women Working in Global Supply
Chains* (Oxford, England: Oxfam International, 2004), p. 55.

"We find the effects of supercenter entry and expansion to be sufficiently large..."   191
Jerry Hausman and Ephraim Leibtag, "Consumer Benefits from Increased
Competition in Shopping Outlets: Measuring the Effect of Wal-Mart,"
Bureau of Economic Research Working Paper No. 11809, December 2005, p. 2.

...Wal-Mart lowered overall consumer prices by a cumulative 3.1 percent...   192
Global Insight "The Economic Impact of Wal-Mart," p. 1.

Wal-Mart gave $200 million to more than 100,000... Wal-Mart Web site,   192
www.walmartfacts.com/community/walmart-foundation.aspx#a1708.

In 2006, it gave Sesame Workshop $1 million... Wal-Mart Web site,   192
www.walmartfacts.com/community/article.aspx?id=1593.

The company's Volunteerism Always Pays program donates... Wal-Mart   192
Stores, Inc., "Charitable Giving Fact Sheet," 2006, www.walmartfacts .com/
FactSheets/Charitable_Giving_Fact_Sheet_FINAL-WM.pdf.

The Amherst selectmen praised Wal-Mart... Amherst Board of   192
Selectmen, Wal-Mart Commendation, May 24, 2004.

...Basker of the University of Missouri underscores perhaps the key point...   192
Basker, "Job Creation Or Destruction?" p. 174.

Even Head Start, a program for underprivileged toddlers... Macarena   193
Hernandez, "Aren't We Smart Enough to Give Poor Kids a Head Start?"
Dallas Morning News, November 25, 2005, and National Head Start
Association, "The Bush Administration's Fiscal Year 2007 Budget
Proposal Would Slash Head Start and Early Head Start Enrollment,"
Special Report, February 7, 2006, www.nhsa.org/download/advocacy/
PresidentFY2007Budget.pdf.

In McKinsey & Company's global survey of executives... McKinsey &   194
Company, "Global Survey of Business Executives," *McKinsey Quarterly*,
January 2006, p. 10.

194 *A Cone corporate citizenship study showed that 86 percent...* Cone, Inc. "Multi-Year Study Finds 21% Increase in Americans Who Say Corporate Support of Social Issues Is Important in Building Trust," press release, December 8, 2004.

195 *As Ian Davis, head of McKinsey & Company, wrote...* Ian Davis, "The Biggest Contract," *The Economist,* May 26, 2005.

195 *When asked by McKinsey how well their companies anticipate...* McKinsey & Company, "Global Survey," p. 6.

195 *"Most executives view their engagement with..."* Ibid., p. 5.

195 *Recalling the minority-relations—and public-relations—nightmare...* Jim Adamson, interview with author, February 28, 2006.

197 *It has chosen to create connections with onetime antagonists...* Robert Berner (interview with Wal-Mart CEO Lee Scott), "Can Wal-Mart Fit into a White Hat?" *BusinessWeek,* October 3, 2005, pp. 94–96.

199 *Last year, Tyson Foods, Luxottica Group..., and Ty Inc...* Based on author's experience with the Lift Up America program.

202 *As McKinsey's Davis wrote in* The Economist... Davis, "The Biggest Contract," 2005.

202 *Roberto Goizueta, the late chairman of The Coca-Cola Company, echoed these sentiments...* William J. Holstein. "Drink Coke, and Be Nice," *U.S. News & World Report,* June 9, 1997, p. 50–51.

203 *Hillary Clinton, a former Wal-Mart board member...* Beth Fouhy, "Wal-Mart Controversy Pits Clinton's Political Ambition Against Her Past," Associated Press, March 11, 2006.

203 *It submitted a plan for mandatory global-warming controls...* John J. Fialka, "Big Business Joins Global-Warming Debate," *Wall Street Journal,* March 28, 2006, Sec. A.

204 *Danny Wegman, CEO of Wegmans Food Markets...* Danny Wegman, "Workforce Development Oversight," testimony delivered to House Education and Workforce Committee, FDCH Congressional Testimony, September 12, 2002.

205 *Scott has sought to convince others that they are national problems...* Kris Hudson, "Wal-Mart CEO Urges Broader Health-Care Cure," *Wall Street Journal,* February 27, 2006, Sec. A.

David Reiling runs University Bank in St. Paul, Minnesota. Details on 205
University Bank come from David Reiling, interview with Bill Birchard,
April 27, 2006; the bank's Web site, www.universitybank.com; and the
sources listed below.

Reiling also publicly advocates socially minded investing... David Reiling, 207
"Making Profits with the Saints," *Minneapolis Star Tribune,* July 16,
2005, Sec. D.

Clif Bar is another example of a business riding a wave... Details on 208
Clif Bar come from the company's Web site, www.clifbar.com; Gary
Erickson (with Lois Lorentzen), *Raising the Bar: Integrity and Passion
in Life and Business* (San Francisco: Jossey-Bass, 2004); and the sources
listed below.

Erickson has repeatedly emphasized that supporting environmental... 208
Maggie Overfelt, "The Activist," *Fortune Small Business* 13(8):41,
October 1, 2003.

Each tag will save the planet 300 pounds of carbon dioxide... Each gallon 209
of gas produces 20 pounds of carbon dioxide; see www.fueleconomy.gov/
feg/co2.shtml.

Starbucks is one of the icons of social strategy... Details on Starbucks 210
come from the author's industry experience; the company's Web site,
www.starbucks.com; Starbucks Coffee Company, Inc., Corporate Social
Responsibility Fiscal 2005 Annual Report, 2006; and the sources listed
below.

"One reason we're a successful company is..." Howard Schultz, as quoted 211
in Cindy Krischer Goodman, "Starbucks' International Recipe for Satisfied
Workers," *Miami Herald,* December 8, 2004.

Starbucks gave Oxfam International thousands of dollars... Alison 212
Maitland, "Starbucks Tastes Oxfam's Brew: Corporate Social
Responsibility," *Financial Times London,* October 14, 2004.

Leo Shapiro, senior statesman of retail marketing... Leo Shapiro, inter- 213
view with the author, March 2, 2006.

One board member, city Alderman Richard LaRose... Bill Birchard, onsite 214
reporting at the Nashua, New Hampshire, Planning Board meeting,
January 12, 2006.

EPILOGUE

219   *Lopdrup took the helm of Red Lobster in 2004...*   Details on Red Lobster come from Kim Lopdrup, interview with the author, June 1, 2006; the company's Web site, www.dardenrestaurants.com; the company's employee booklet, "Our Compass"; and the source listed below.

220   *It has been the top-rated restaurant...*   "Consumers' Choice in Chains: Seafood," *Restaurants & Institutions,* September 1, 2006, p. 76.

Index

About the Author

"The best guy I've ever known at fuzzy logic" is how one CEO described Bill Marquard. Marquard's penchant for fuzzy logic helps leaders across many industries to connect the dots in this new economy defined by dominant global players such as Wal-Mart.

As a consultant, Marquard has advised some of the world's most influential and forward-thinking companies. As a former Fortune 200 leader himself, he has walked the executive's path. In both capacities, he has won praise for his work to craft compelling new business strategies. He specializes in serving as a thinking partner for senior executives, where he provides a valuable "unbiased opinion"—frank feedback, insightful questions, and bold challenges.

Marquard designed Wal-Mart's first-ever strategic planning process and ran it for three and one-half years. He has advised over 100 companies in 25 industries, including McDonald's, Walt Disney World, Meijer, Citibank, CompUSA, Denny's, Tyson Foods, the Brick Industry Association, and the U.S. Department of Homeland Security.

Marquard spent 17 years at Ernst & Young—8 as a partner—before becoming the executive vice-president and chief knowledge officer of Fleming, a major consumer goods wholesaler and retailer. Most recently, he cofounded Marble Leadership Partners, Inc. with his wife, Leslie, a certified executive coach and corporate transformation specialist. Marble Leadership Partners provides strategic planning, business transformation, and executive coaching services across a broad range of industries. Its mission is to make executives wildly successful.

For eight years, Marquard served as an adjunct professor of finance at Northwestern's Kellogg School of Management. His strategy expertise has been featured on CNN, and he has lectured at DePaul University, Northwestern University Law School, and Duke University's Fuqua School of Business.

He earned a BA at the University of Notre Dame and an MBA at Case Western Reserve University's Weatherhead School of Management.

Contact Marquard by e-mail via bill@wal-smart.com, or at:

Marble Leadership Partners, Inc.
200 South Wacker Drive
31st Floor
Chicago, IL 60606
marbleleadership.com

See the next page for ways you can work with Bill Marquard and Marble Leadership Partners to become Wal-Smart.

Here are some powerful ways Marble Leadership Partners' outside insight can help your organization become Wal-Smart:

- As a *speaker:* Book Bill Marquard for audiences that need transformation–not just motivation.
- As a *Thinking Partner:* Retain Bill Marquard to provide frank feedback, insightful questions, and bold challanges to your senior executives.
- As a *collaborative advisor:* Find the *and* in your business by
  - Crafting and implementing *specific Wal-Smart strategies,* or
  - Transforming your company into a *strong-process organization.*
- As a *catalyst:* Embed Wal-Smart principles into your company strategies at one of Marble Leadership Partners' collaborative *Strategic Actioning Sessions^{sm}.*
- As an *executive coach:* Experience the success of private, personal transformation.

Please visit **www.wal-smart.com** for more details.